Nineteenth-Century Women's Writing in Wales

CW00606414

Gender Studies in Wales
Astudiaethau Rhywedd yng Nghymru

The aim of this series is to fill a current gap in knowledge. As a number of historians, sociologists and literary critics have for some time been pointing out, there is a dearth of published research on the characteristics and effects of gender difference in Wales, both as it affected lives in the past and as it continues to shape present-day experience. Socially constructed concepts of masculine and feminine difference influence every aspect of individuals' lives; experiences in employment, in education, in culture and politics, as well as in personal relationships, are all shaped by them. Ethnic identities are also gendered; a country's history affects its concepts of gender difference so that what is seen as appropriately 'masculine' or 'feminine' varies within different cultures. What is needed in the Welsh context is more detailed research on the ways in which gender difference has operated and continues to operate within Welsh societies. Accordingly, this interdisciplinary series of volumes on Gender Studies in Wales, authored by academics who are currently leaders in their particular fields of study, is designed to explore the diverse aspects of male and female identities in Wales, past and present. The series is bilingual, in the sense that some of its intended volumes will be in Welsh and some in English.

The first titles in this series include: Katie Gramich, *Twentieth-Century Women's Writing in Wales: Land, Gender, Belonging*; Jane Aaron, *Nineteenth-Century Women's Writing in Wales: Nation, Gender and Identity*; Paul Chaney, *Equality and Public Policy: Wales in Comparative Focus*; Ursula Masson, *'For Women, for Wales and for Liberalism'?: Women and Liberal Politics in Wales c.1880–1914*; Nickie Charles and Charlotte Aull Davies (eds), *Gender and Social Justice in Wales*; and Henrice Altink, Chris Weedon and Jane Aaron (eds), *Gendering Borders*. Further volumes currently in the planning stage include an essay collection on the suffrage movement in Wales edited by Sian Rhiannon Williams and Ursula Masson; a monograph by Sarah Prescott on pre-nineteenth century anglophone writing by women in Wales; another edited essay collection by Moira Vincentelli on Welsh women artists; and a Welsh-language volume by Cathryn Charnell-White on gender in eighteenth-century Welsh literature by men and women.

Nineteenth-Century Women's Writing in Wales:
Nation, Gender and Identity

Jane Aaron

UNIVERSITY OF WALES PRESS
CARDIFF
2007

British Library Cataloguing-in-Publication Data
A catalogue record for this book is available from the British Library.

ISBN 978-0-7083-2060-0

Typeset by Columns Design Ltd, Reading
Printed in Great Britain by Antony Rowe Ltd, Wiltshire

Acknowledgements

I am indebted to a number of individuals and institutions for their help with this book. The two main debts I have incurred are to John Koch and Diana Wallace, who read through the whole manuscript with meticulous care and made a great many useful suggestions for amendments; I am very grateful to them both. I should also like to thank the many friends and colleagues who discussed aspects of the book with me and spurred me on, in particular Deirdre Beddoe, Catherine Brennan, Cathryn Charnell-White, Claire Flay, Katie Gramich, E. Wyn James, Ursula Masson, Sarah Prescott, Rosanne Reeves, and my two Gender Studies in Wales co-editors, Brec'hed Piette and Sian Rhiannon Williams.

As for institutions, the book could not have been completed without the aid of an Arts and Humanities Research Council grant, which bought a respite from teaching duties. I should also like to thank the University of Glamorgan for providing sabbatical relief. Without the help of the staff of the National Library of Wales, in particular Huw Walters, the volume would not have been what it is; the opportunity they afforded me of browsing in the Library's stacks led to the inclusion within these pages of many authors whom I would not otherwise have discovered. My debt is great also to the staff of the University of Wales Press, particularly Sarah Lewis, for their enthusiastic support not only of this book but also of the series of which it forms a part.

The book owes its origins to my earlier Welsh-language volume on the image of the Welsh woman in nineteenth-century women's writing, *Pur fel y Dur: Y Gymraes yn Llên Menywod y Bedwaredd Ganrif ar Bymtheg*, but it is not a translation of it.

This present study covers the century with greater thoroughness, and includes twice the number of authors discussed in the previous work. In the struggle to encompass all the material, and because of the difficulties of introducing to an English-language audience texts not available in translation, I have in some cases limited the discussion of the Welsh-language writers included here; readers interested in the hymn writers, for example, will find more extensive analyses of their work in *Pur fel y Dur*.

Though they have since been much revised, parts of this book have also appeared in the following publications: *Women's Writing*, 1 (1994); *Re-Visioning Romanticism: British Women Writers, 1776–1837*, edited by Carol Shiner Wilson and Joel Hafner (Philadelphia: University of Pennsylvania Press, 1994); *Welsh Writing in English: A Yearbook of Critical Essays*, 1 (1995); *Feminisms on Edge: Politics, Discourses and National Identities* edited by Karen Atkinson, Sarah Oerton and Gill Plain (Cardiff: Cardiff Academic Press, 2000); and *A Tolerant Nation? Exploring Ethnic Diversity in Wales* edited by Charlotte Williams, Neil Evans and Paul O'Leary (Cardiff: University of Wales Press, 2003). All of this material is used here by permission of the publishers.

Contents

I JTK

Prologue

In 1804 Catherine Davies (1773–1841) of Beaumaris in Anglesey took up a post in Paris as nurse to the children of Caroline Murat, sister of Napoleon Bonaparte. Her nationality soon became a problem; the children grew attached to her but their uncle requested that she be dismissed: he apparently told his sister, 'women could correspond as well as men', that is, the new nurse might act as a spy.[1] Instructed to hide herself during his visits, her continuing presence in the household was on one occasion inadvertently disclosed to him:

> It happened one morning, as the emperor was walking in the gardens with his sister, the children espied them from one of the windows of the palace, and called out to the emperor, 'Oh, uncle!' He looked up, and saw me; upon which he said, 'Ah, you English there!' I replied, 'Yes, Sire.' . . .
> [P]resently they both entered the apartment where we were. The emperor said to me, 'You English are not good.' I replied, 'Sire, there are some of the English good, and some bad, as well as the French.' 'Do you', he asked, 'like the French as well as the English?' 'Sire', I replied, 'if I were to say I liked the French as well as the English, I should think myself a hypocrite; but I like those of all nations who are kind to me.' His majesty tapped me on the shoulder, and said, 'Bravo! Bravo! I like you, because you are so candid.'[2]

For all her candour it clearly did not occur to Catherine Davies in 1804 to reassure Napoleon by telling him that she was not in fact English. And yet a later passage from her memoir *Eleven Years' Residence in the Family of Murat, King of Naples* (1841) makes it apparent that she felt no lack of attachment to her actual native country. After Napoleon had crowned his sister and her husband, Joachim Murat, king and queen of Naples in 1808, and Davies had moved with their household to that city, she was invited along with the family to visit a British naval vessel which had entered the Bay during a temporary cessation of hostilities. While exploring the 'English man-of-war', as she terms it, she noticed a young midshipman,

> who followed us closely, and who from time to time looked at me with fixed attention. At length he approached me, and asked if I were not a native of Wales. Surprised at the question, I replied in the affirmative. Pleasure beamed in his countenance. 'I too,' said he, 'was born in Wales;' and he proceeded to say that his father was a clergyman living in Caermarthen [*sic*]. We became from this moment intimate friends.[3]

Catherine Davies identifies herself as 'a native of Wales' and feels an immediate intimacy with a fellow countryman; she must also, presumably, have retained a Welsh accent, for the sailor to discover their shared Welshness so quickly. Nevertheless, she would appear to have no sense of herself as having a national identity other than that of the nation-state under whose rule she was reared, and to which she gives the title 'England'. After undergoing with the Murats the downfall of their reign in Naples, including a sustained bombardment by the British fleet and her own arrest by the British on suspicion of being a spy for the ex-queen, Catherine Davies returned to Beaumaris: 'Here, in my native spot,' she says, 'I have remained ever since.'[4] But even after twenty years back home in Wales she could not, when she came to write her memoirs, identify herself in national terms as anything other than 'English', though her intimate bonds and sense of belonging are with the Welsh. The lack of connection in her account between her natal and her national identity is indicative of that confusion to which Raymond Williams once drew attention in his essay 'The Culture of Nations':

> 'Nation', as a term, is radically connected with 'native'. We are born into relationships, which are typically settled in a place. This form of primary and 'placeable' bonding is of quite fundamental human and natural importance. Yet the jump from that to anything like the modern nation-state is entirely artificial.[5]

Artificially imposed 'jumps' between native and national identities were common in Welsh writing of the Romantic period: Wales was frequently represented as a region of western England, sometimes by authors with Welsh connections as well as by their English neighbours. Mary Robinson (1756–1800), apparently herself of

Welsh extraction, in her 1797 novel *Walsingham; or, the Pupil of Nature*, includes an old soldier, Griffith Blagden, who describes himself as born and bred 'a native of Wales, . . . of Glamorganshire', and yet as 'English' when he is fighting the French. Though he had not volunteered to join the army but been captured by a press gang, Griffith makes the best of it and identifies himself with the national cause, saying of one encounter, 'we dealt the foe such an example of English bravery, that the victory was ours before sunset'.[6] To represent oneself as both 'a native of Wales' and English by nationality was not paradoxical for Griffith Blagden, or rather his creator, Mary Robinson, any more than it was for Catherine Davies. Both are echoing the terms of the 1536 Act in which Wales was 'incorporated, united and annexed to and with this realm of England . . . as a very member and joint of the same'.[7] After 1707, when Scotland joined the Union, the official title of that realm was the 'Kingdom of Great Britain', but the new terminology did not quickly prevail, either internally or on the Continent: the 'English', not the 'British', were the people Napoleon perceived as his enemy in Catherine Davies' narrative.

By the end of the nineteenth century, however, the concept of Welsh nationality features much more strongly in the literature of the period. 'I do not remember the time when I was unconscious of my nationality, boasting myself emphatically Welsh and not English' recalls Mabel Holland Grave (née Thomas, born 1861), in her anonymously published collection of autobiographical essays, *Some Welsh Children* (1898). Of Wales she declares: 'How can I choose but love her? What am I myself but a tiny throbbing pulse of her, my Country? . . . I love every stone on her mountains. I love every blade of Welsh grass.' Mabel Holland Grave's mother was half-Manx, and English was the family's language, but her lack of Welsh was not allowed to cloud what she presents as the more essential issue of ethnic identity. 'I think in English; I speak and write in English', she acknowledges, but 'though the words be English, the voice is the voice of Wales. And I can but utter her meaning in whatever language I speak.'[8] Such national zeal is by no means uncommon in *fin-de-siècle* Welsh women's writing: Mallt Williams (1867–1950) entitles her second novel *A Maid of Cymru: A Patriotic Romance* (1901), and concludes it with a scene in which its heroine Tangwystl, still clad in the bardic regalia in which she has been officiating at a pan-Celtic eisteddfod, is trapped in a cave by a herd of overwrought wild ponies, but manages to inscribe a last message to her lover before being trampled to death:

> she undid the tri-coloured bardic ribband at her throat, drew the pin of the broach which fastened it smartly across her bared left arm. The blood started; then very slowly and illegibly she traced on the white of the ribband three words, with lips that quivered and blue eyes dim and strained – '*Gwasanaetha Gymru, Hoel.*' ['Serve Wales, Hoel.']⁹

The trauma and strain accompanying this assertion of Welshness may well be symbolically related to the failure, a few years earlier, of the Welsh Home Rule movement, *Cymru Fydd*, for which Mallt Williams had campaigned. One of her fellow activists in that cause, the Welsh-language novelist Gwyneth Vaughan (Annie Harriet Hughes, 1852–1910), in her allegorical short stories 'Gweledigaeth y Babell Wag' (Vision of the Empty Tent, 1902) and 'Breuddwyd Nos Nadolig' (A Christmas Night's Dream, 1905), gives expression to similar tensions.¹⁰ In Vaughan's tales, the spirit of Wales, personified as female, dies of neglect on a bleak mountainside in the darkest hour before dawn, as representatives of various Welsh institutions turn away to bicker enviously amongst themselves and quarrel over pennies, while their rich neighbours comment – in English in the Welsh-language original – 'these Welsh people are a deuced queer lot. By Jove! they have a sort of notion that they are a separate nation, old man! Queer people!'¹¹ For all their fears as to the future, however, Vaughan's stories, like the writings of Mallt Williams and Mabel Holland Grave, suggest that by the end of the nineteenth century, on the evidence of its women's writing at least, Wales did have a 'notion' of itself as a 'separate nation'. However, that does not appear uniformly to have been the case a century earlier.

The growth of a sense of Welsh national identity within nineteenth-century literature is one of the themes of this book. Its primary concern, however, is to trace the history of women's writing in Wales during that century. Today a rapidly developing branch of nation studies focuses on the manner in which aspects of gender difference are interrelated with ideas of national difference.¹² The specificities of women's experience in Victorian Wales add interestingly to such investigations, for during that period the reputation of Welsh women underwent an unexpected revolution. In 1847 an English government report officially labelled them ignorant and immoral, and responsible, because of their delinquency, for what the report found to be the generally barbaric state of the Welsh: but by the 1890s they were being fêted, both at home and abroad, as better educated and more self-disciplined than women elsewhere, and the moral force behind Wales's renown as a particularly godfearing nation. In the 1840s their accusers were men, and few were the women with the confidence and skills necessary to engage in the public debate; by the 1890s, however, a substantial number of well-known and well-respected Welsh women writers were effectively broadcasting the manifest virtues of their countrywomen. They were the leaders and, to a large extent, the progenitors of a dedicated female army of missionaries, school-teachers, Sunday-school teachers, temperance reformers and Home Rule campaigners motivated by the desire to shed renewed lustre on the good name of their nation and their faith. In their lives as well as their works they sought to promote a new inspiring ideal of Welsh womanhood. This book follows the emergence of that new female ideal as she evolved within the pages of nineteenth-century Welsh-language women writers.

Many of the distinctive characteristics attributed to the Welsh woman originated in the successive waves of Methodist revivals which reconfigured Welsh culture in the eighteenth century. Accordingly, the book begins by tracing the contribution to Welsh culture of the devotional writing of the female Dissenters. Methodism, however, was the *bête noire* of many women writing about Wales in the English language during the Romantic era; the first chapter also follows the complex response of a new wave of anglophone novelists to Wales as a fictional location. One of the most significant developments of the Romantic Movement from the Welsh point of view was the growing interest in antiquarianism, to which, by the 1820s, women as well as men were contributing: the second chapter explores the construction of Welsh national identity in such antiquarian writing. An important aspect of the Welsh response to the 1847 government report on education in Wales, which branded the Welsh woman as unchaste, was that members of the antiquarian movement, some of them Anglicans, joined forces with the Dissenters in resisting the report's findings: chapter 3 assesses the significance of this new alliance in the development of Welsh nation-building, and explores the outcome of its particular focus on women. Indeed, mid nineteenth-century anglophone women writers vary more in their representation of Wales than has hitherto been supposed, or so the fourth chapter argues. Some popular novelists were more openly prejudiced against the Welsh than the 1847 Report itself; at the same time other authors, many of them writing historical fictions and indebted to the antiquarians for their material, glorify the image of the rebellious Welsh who fought for their nation. Within Welsh-language literature, however, the need to confound the iniquity of the 1847 Report continued to function as a moral imperative throughout the rest of the nineteenth century. A Victorian Welsh woman seems to have been presented with three possibilities in terms of choosing an identity: she abandoned her Welsh allegiances, and adopted the English middle-class model of refined femininity, however inappropriate it may have been to her cultural roots and her social position; she defensively asserted her Welshness in the face of insult, and, to prove its virtues, clad herself in an armour of strict propriety which necessarily entailed self-suppression on a larger scale than mere sexual self-control; or she accepted the English definition of herself as the libidinous hoyden of primitive Wild Wales. Welsh-language women writers generally represented their heroines as opting for the second of these identities, and so did many of their authors in real life, too: the fifth chapter of this volume traces their growing self-confidence in that heroic role. Finally, the book's last chapter examines women's contribution to the Welsh Home Rule movement of the last two decades of the nineteenth century, Cymru Fydd.

At that time, Welsh women writers in both languages were numerous and well-known, enjoying a degree of influence on Welsh culture easily commensurate with that of modern women writers today. But their influence was short-lived; very little of their work is in print today, and their names have been forgotten, within both of Wales's linguistic cultures. In 1999, a study of the Victorian poet Emily Pfeiffer, entitled 'Why is this woman still missing?', concluded that this 'excellent poet' was neglected because her Welshness was 'a drawback in London literary circles'.[13] The suggestion is that from an English critic's point of view a writer's Welshness is a disincentive for further investigation of his or her work; the onus, then, is very much on Welsh critics to research their national authors. Currently, feminist scholars in Wales are responding to this demand. In 2003, Pfeiffer's claim to critical attention, along with that of six other female poets of the era, was revisited in Catherine Brennan's volume *Angers, Fantasies and Ghostly Fears: Nineteenth-Century Women from Wales and English-language Poetry*, a study which goes far to restore the reputations of the writers with whom it is concerned.[14] And poems by those writers and others have been included in Katie Gramich and Catherine Brennan's recent anthology, *Welsh Women's Poetry 1460–2001*.[15] This present volume aims to contribute to such studies by introducing the reader to over a hundred Welsh women who published poems, novels, essays, antiquarian and travel writings during the nineteenth century. In order to convey in one volume some sense of the development and diversity of their productions, much compression and omission has of course been involved, and few of the writers have been afforded the space for a fair hearing. But the hope is that at least the book will provide future researchers with points of entry into the world of nineteenth-century Welsh women's writing and what it can teach us about nation, gender and identity.

1 Romantic Wales

In the 1790s the adolescent Jane Austen entertained her family with satires and parodies of the literary fashions of the day in which she makes frequent reference to Wales as a clichéd location of the romantic. Her novella 'Love and Freindship'[*sic*] opens 'in one of the most romantic parts of the Vale of Uske', with a heroine raised to all natural loveliness under the roof of her parents' 'rustic Cot'.[1] In 'Jack and Alice', Lucy, the interesting stranger who is initially discovered caught in a man-trap and subsequently poisoned to death by a female rival, has cause to repent her journey into dangerous English territory from her native heath in wild north Wales.[2] And the brief fragment 'A Tour through Wales – in a Letter from a young Lady' burlesques the vogue for travel writing and amateur landscape-sketching, as the letter-writer scampers through 'a principality contiguous to England . . . which gives the title to the Prince of Wales':

> My Mother rode upon our little poney [*sic*] and Fanny and I walked by her side or rather ran, for my Mother is so fond of riding fast that She galloped all the way . . . Fanny has taken a great many Drawings of the Country, which are very beautiful, tho' perhaps not such exact resemblances as might be wished, from their being taken as she ran along.[3]

The travel writings and novels located in Wales which Austen here satirizes issued in substantial numbers from the London presses during the Romantic period. The works of the Merthyr-born Anna Maria Bennett (*c*.1750–1808), *Anna: or Memoirs of a Welch Heiress* (1785) and *Ellen, Countess of Castle Howel* (1794), were phenomenally successful, and led to the publication of a number of copycat Welsh romances, many of them published by Bennett's publisher, William Lane of the Minerva Press, who specialized in popular fiction. Indeed, the last two decades of the eighteenth century saw the publication of so much English-language popular fiction located in the Celtic countries of Britain that it would be easy to believe that publishers like Lane were issuing instructions much like today's Mills and Boon formulas to their would-be authors, advising them to produce picaresque, sentimental, and mildly Gothic novels, located in the so-called 'Celtic fringe'. Celtic scenery provided such novelists with a fashionably 'sublime' backdrop, against which the 'uncorrupted' native inhabitants of the wild 'fringes' could feature in travellers' tales as embodiments of that still very influential Rousseauesque ideal of the 'Noble Savage'. The vogue also reflected an increase of tourist activity in Britain's hitherto more isolated counties. From the early 1790s on, the war with France closed off the Continent to British travellers, depriving the upper ranks of English society of the previously fashionable European 'Grand Tour', and increasing the lure of the less explored areas of the Isles to those searching for new sights closer to home.

Such travellers necessarily participated in the Anglicization of the Celtic countries, and it has been argued that the Celtic Romantic novel as a genre was also part of a more or less deliberate and conscious Anglicizing process. According to Linda Colley, in her influential study *Britons: Forging the Nation 1707–1837*, the increased interest in Celtic culture which characterized British Romanticism reflected the English government's desire to incorporate more fully into its establishment the landed gentry of Ireland, Scotland and Wales. Faced with the humiliating loss of America in the War of Independence and the very real threat from revolutionary France, England sought to strengthen itself by drawing upon its Celtic resources, through emphasizing the shared Protestantism of England, Scotland and Wales. What remained of a Celtic elite, who had in the past been excluded from the political centre as well as being 'temperamentally aloof and geographically distant' from it, was now being wooed into closer social, political and economic integration with the English power-base.[4] The new enthusiasm to embrace all things Celtic reflected in the travel books, poetry, drama and fiction of the era was part of the construction of 'the imagined community' of 'Britain', which, after 1800 and the Irish Act of Union, included Ireland as well as Wales and Scotland.[5]

But while the canonization of Sir Walter Scott and the increasing critical interest in such Irish writers as Maria Edgeworth (1768–

1849) have meant that few students of Romanticism are today likely to be ignorant of the significance of Scotland and Ireland in the literary geography of the period, the texts with Welsh locations are unfamiliar to most modern readers. Recently, the final chapters of Moira Dearnley's *Distant Fields: Eighteenth-Century Fictions of Wales* (2001), and articles by Francesca Rhydderch and Andrew Davies on the representations of Wales in Romantic fiction, have begun to open up the field,[6] but still comparatively little is known, in Wales as in England, of the literature published during the revolutionary years which deployed Welsh contexts. At least insofar as it involves women's writing, this neglect may have to do with the fact that, from the contemporary, twenty-first century point of view, these texts, paradoxically, are not Celtic enough. Few of them were written by women from Wales, and the few that were came from the pens of writers who had chosen to leave the country and language of their birth behind them, and who were struggling to make a name and a living for themselves within English culture. Consequently, few wrote of Wales in ways which could be construed as supportive of its difference, but today, in post-devolution Britain and Ireland, critical interest in the Celtic literature of the period rests largely on its perceived significance as contributing to the construction of Celtic, rather than British, national and historical identities. Linda Colley's emphasis on a shared Protestantism as successfully unifying Britain during the period of the French wars has been queried by literary critics, who suggest that Colley sidelined Ireland in order to present a portrayal of a Britain much more easily and seamlessly unified after the Scottish Act of Union in 1707 than would appear from the cultural evidence actually to have been the case.[7]

For Katie Trumpener, for example, in her *Bardic Nationalism: The Romantic Novel and the British Empire*, nationalistic preoccupations within Romantic fiction reflect Scottish, Irish and Welsh interest in establishing their specific Celtic identities as much as they mark a concern for the making of Britain. During the second half of the eighteenth century, she argues, Celtic writers conceived 'a new national literary history under the sign of the bard'. The popularity of the material they produced, such as the various editions of early and medieval Celtic poetry, in particular the outpourings of Ossian, affected mainstream fashions to such an extent that, according to Trumpener, 'English literature, so-called, constitutes itself in the late eighteenth and early nineteenth centuries through the systematic imitation, appropriation, and political neutralization of antiquarian and nationalist literary developments in Scotland, Ireland and Wales'.[8] But, in fact, after an opening discussion of 'A Paraphrase of the 137th Psalm, alluding to the Captivity and Treatment of the Welsh Bards by King Edward I' by Evan Evans (Ieuan Fardd, Ieuan Brydydd Hir, 1731–88), Trumpener makes little further reference to writings either by Welsh authors or located in Wales, confining her attention to Scottish and Irish materials. Clearly, she did not find Welsh fictions which suited her argument. She would have had no trouble finding novels located in Wales, but it is certainly more difficult to find ones focusing on the type of aspiring nationhood that she ascribes to the Scottish and Irish fictions of the period.

It is one of the arguments of this present study that women writers' contribution to nation-building in a Welsh context cannot really be said to begin until the 1820s, with women's increased involvement in the Welsh antiquarian and early eisteddfod movements. Earlier nineteenth-century anglophone women novelists who made use of Welsh settings were, for the most part, more estranged from the core values and perspectives of the culture they were writing about than were their Scottish or Irish equivalents: for one thing, they were not writing in the language of the majority of its population. Throughout the century Wales was primarily Welsh-speaking: half a million people, about one-third of the population, were still monoglot Welsh-speakers at the time of the 1891 Census, the first census to collect data on language use in Wales.[9] As travellers to Wales, or as Welsh women who had turned away from their culture, the Romantic novelists were writing for predominantly English audiences, and reflecting their views. The interest of their work lies in part in the fact that it demonstrates how wide the gulf was at the time between internal and external views of Wales.

This chapter examines that divide, firstly by focusing on that body of Welsh-language literature to which women contributed most fully during the Romantic period, namely, religious verse. For all their rootedness within Welsh culture, or rather, perhaps, because of that rootedness, the female hymn-writers were not nation-builders, any more than their novel-writing contemporaries. According to Benedict Anderson in his seminal study of nationalism, *Imagined Communities*, communities resort to nation-building when former influences binding them together, such as powerful dynasties or unifying religions embodied in a 'sacred language', have lost their cohesive force.[10] His argument helps in part to account for the sporadic pattern of nation-building during the first half of the nineteenth century in Wales, when the energies of the Welsh-speaking community were for the most part absorbed in the business of developing a popular unifying religion, with Welsh as its 'sacred language'. The Religious Census of 1851 confirmed statistically that Wales was 'the most religious area of Great Britain', a long-held boast of the Welsh, and one which historians have argued may well have been true from the mid 1830s on.[11] Eighty per cent of those attending places of worship in Wales in 1851 were Nonconformists, with the Calvinist Methodist sect accounting for the largest number. Old Dissent – Baptists, Congregationalists, Unitarians and Quakers – had been a significant force in Wales since the Civil War period; during the eighteenth century successive waves of Methodist religious revivals added the enthusiasm of new Dissent to their numbers. Ostensibly, the energies of the chapel-goers were dedicated to the building and maintaining of a religion, not a nation;[12] the nation-builders of the era – the antiquarians, historians and patriotic poets – in the main remained within the Established Church. Nevertheless, what later came to be accepted by late nineteenth-century nationalists as defining features of Welsh national identity were based on the distinctive way of life developed by the Dissenting communities, so much so that it is difficult fully to appreciate the aims and ambitions of the *fin-de-siècle* nation-builders without an understanding of the values and lifestyles of Welsh Nonconformity. Women hymn-writers contributed to the development of that culture more extensively than has hitherto been recognized, and the first section of this chapter accordingly details their characteristic concerns.

But in the late eighteenth and early nineteenth centuries, Methodist converts were still being persecuted as potentially socially disruptive, and the Methodist way of life was much derided by anglophone commentators. The chapter's second section focuses on women novelists' disparagement of Methodism, and examines also their portrayal of other specifically Welsh characteristics, such as the Welsh language and its culture, often represented as barbaric. On the other hand, in a Romantic epoch which valorized the Noble Savage, that which was deemed to be primitive could at times be judged far more positively. For some women writers of the period, wild Wales was a Romantic zone in which women could enjoy a more natural lifestyle and a greater freedom than was permitted to them in an England represented as more hidebound by artificial social proprieties. The evolution of the class system, with its restrictive role for the middle- and upper-class gentlewoman in particular, was seen by some of these novelists as a distortion of human potential from which Wales was still relatively free. Interestingly, some of the few anglophone writers who, unusually, were sympathetic towards Methodism commend as one of that sect's virtues its power to ignore, break down or transcend social hierarchies. The Welsh-language supporters of Methodism, in their efforts to secure acceptance for it, are more likely to stress the sect's loyalty to the Establishment than its radicalism, but its English-language defenders often express approval of the way the converts paid no heed to social distinctions. The last section of this chapter examines representative examples of those anglophone women novelists and poets who can be said to further a view of Wales as a land of comparative liberty from socially constructed restraints, a view which also later, as we will see, had its part to play in the development of notions of Welsh identity, particularly of Welsh women's identity.

i. Singing of Zion

When the hymn-writer William Williams, Pantycelyn, sought to embody in prose the spirit of the Welsh Methodist Revival, he gave it a female voice: in his fictional *Llythyr Martha Philophur* of 1762, Martha Philophur tells the story of her conversion in a letter to her religious mentor Philo-Evangelius. What women had to gain from the experience is made abundantly clear in Martha's narrative. Before her conversion, she tells Evangelius, she was a confused and conflicted creature, timid in company, fearful and ashamed, and yet full of frustrated pride and aimless passions. After it, convinced according to Calvinist theology of the pre-election of her individual soul through grace, she is transformed: 'I have a share,' she says, 'yes, an eternal share in the living God' ('Mae i mi ran, oes, rhan dragwyddol yn y Duw byw'). No longer timid, she fearlessly shouts out his praises 'before the large congregation' and blesses his name 'under the gaze of the multitudes' ('yr wyf yn eofn i ddweud yn dda am Dduw . . . o flaen y gynulleidfa fawr . . . a bendithio ei enw ef lle bo myrdd yn edrych arnaf'). No longer conflicted, her mind and body now know their place and purpose, and unite in a demonstrative ecstasy of worship, leaping, jumping, dancing and singing, in the face of the derision and persecution of the non-elect.[13]

Williams's choice of a woman to represent the early Methodists fits the historical facts; from the first, the number of female converts was greater than of male. But unlike John Wesley's Arminian Methodists, Welsh Calvinism never named women as preachers or formal leaders of meetings, though its historians have shown that without the contribution of female converts, as assistants and hostesses to peripatetic preachers, and as enthusiasts who walked hundreds of miles to secure the services of preachers for their local gatherings and who were often the first to invite them into new parishes, the revival could hardly have succeeded as it did.[14] It is impossible to overemphasize the significance of religious conversion in these women's lives: Christ, as opposed to any mortal, was the Prince for whom they waited, and the central passion of their lives. The influence of their religion was not compartmentalized away but governed every aspect of their existence, including, of course, their views on gender difference and gender relations. The twenty-fifth rule in the 1802 *Rules and the Design of the Religious Societies among the Welsh Methodists* reads: 'Husbands to love their wives, to honour them as weaker vessels, and not to be bitter against them. Wives to love their own husbands, to submit themselves to them in the Lord, and to obey them.'[15] To 'honour them as weaker vessels' could be said to constitute a contradiction in terms, and the assumption that husbands will have cause for bitterness against such supposedly submissive spouses suggests mistrust of women's capacity to adhere to the rules. In secular terms, then, Methodism would not appear to lead to greater equality between the sexes: indeed, it has been argued that it promoted in Wales a more stringent patriarchal ethos than had previously prevailed.[16]

The living conditions of the majority of the female converts would also have been stringent: many of the English visitors who came to Wales during the last decades of the eighteenth century were shocked by the rigours of the rural Welsh woman's life, compared to that of an English woman of the same class. The fact that in Wales women were still expected to labour in the fields, performing the same tasks as the men, seemed to them particularly deplorable. According to E. D. Clarke, for example, in his *Tour through the South of England, Wales and part of Ireland*, only by her clothes was it possible to distinguish a Welsh woman from the males of the species. 'As for the difference of sex, it would hardly be perceived ... if it was not for the criterion of breeches,' he comments, 'for labour seems equally divided between men and women, and it's as common to meet a female driving the plough, as it is to see Taffy seated at the milk pail.'[17] Similarly, in his *Journey into South Wales in the Year 1799* George Lipscomb expresses concern that female farm labourers should be obliged in Wales to carry out 'the most arduous exertions and business of husbandry'.[18] From the testimony of some of the contributors to Ieuan Gwynedd's *Gymraes*, it would appear that little changed during the next half-century. The 1851 Census shows that nearly one in three women who worked for a wage in Wales were farm labourers, and no doubt many more wives, sisters and daughters of small farmers or crofters also worked on the land as unpaid help. According to the *Gymraes*, such women were expected to labour in the farmhouse and dairy as well the fields, with the result that they put in far longer hours than their male counterparts.[19] Forty years later a letter published in the newspaper *Y Werin* indicated that such practices continued until the end of the nineteenth century in rural Wales: '*Morwyn Ffarm*' (Farm Maid) complains in 1890 that women were still expected to work alongside men in the fields, and to spend long hours on household duties as well.[20] The material conditions which governed the daily lives of the female converts were, then, for the most part, oppressive and onerous, and their new-found religious belief did little to correct the injustices inherent in the patterns of sex discrimination characteristic of nineteenth-century society.

But in other ways Calvinist beliefs and practices did much to alleviate the psychological effects of female subordination. Great stress was laid in the sect's doctrines on the necessity for conversion to be an experience of the 'heart', rather than the 'head'.[21] Humanity being in all its parts essentially sinful, and saved only by virtue of Christ's sacrifice, such human attributes as knowledge, rationality or the performance of good works could have no share in its redemption. Conversion entailed, rather, a shattering of the human ego, a passivity in the face of the divine will, and an opening-up of the 'heart' to receive lightning-flashes of grace. The whole apparatus of logical and conceptual thinking, including language itself, was overthrown in the process; the experience was more likely to find expression through groans, cries and physical demonstrations than through conceptual utterance. According to the conventional division of experience into gendered categories, the capacities to reason, to act and to maintain a strong and assertive will are attributes more associated with the male of the species than with the female, whereas feeling, the body, passivity and a more permeable ego are seen as more essentially female. It would appear, therefore, given this polarization, that conversion requires and values stereotypically feminine modes of response. Christ is the bridegroom and the convert the bride, whatever the sex of the sinner.[22]

Records of the early nineteenth-century Methodist *seiat*, meetings in which members testified to one another as to their religious condition, indicate that the contributions of female members were frequently considered to be of particular value: when reporting that the meeting at Tan-yr-Allt, Cardiganshire, for example, 'continues in its warmth, its zeal, and its love' ('parhau yn ei gwres, ei sel, a'i chariad'), William Williams adds, 'the women are more zealous than the men' ('Mae y gwragedd yn fwy eu sel na'r gwŷr').[23] According to their own testimonies, the female converts particularly appreciated the guidance offered in these meetings by members of their own sex: an 1808 obituary on Barbara Vaughan of Caerphilly by her fellow convert Catherine Jones, for example, expresses gratitude for her 'kind, lively' discourse which during *seiat* meetings was 'beneficial' to other members ('Ac hefyd ei chyfeillach / Garedig, fywiog hi / Yn ein cyfarfod prifat / Oedd fuddiol i nyni').[24] Fanny Jones, the wife of the renowned Methodist preacher John Jones of Talsarn, similarly attributed her spiritual strength to the fact that she was reared under the influence of the 'jumpers and enthusiasts of Llanllyfni, on fire worshipping God' ('bobl dduwiol yn neidio ac yn gorfoleddu yn Llanllyfni, pan y byddent ar dân yn moli Duw'), amongst whom she particularly remembered Ann Parry, known as 'the Deaconess', the main prop of the sect in the parish.[25] It was Ann Parry who, through her reputation for godliness, persuaded effective preachers to visit Llanllyfni, and her prayers for fruitful meetings were said to have a particularly inspiring influence upon their sermons.

From the early years of the nineteenth century on, however, one woman more than any other can be said to have influenced the spiritual lives of generation after generation of Welsh women, and men also, of course. Ann Griffiths, née Thomas, a Montgomeryshire farmer's daughter, is today considered one of the foremost poets, not only of Calvinist Methodism, but of Welsh literature generally. Composed between 1796, when she converted to Methodism in her twentieth year, and 1805 when she died in childbirth, her verses cannot be dated more exactly because she rarely wrote them down; they have survived only by virtue of the fact that she recited them to her maid, Ruth Evans, who, though

herself illiterate, remembered them and repeated them to her husband, the Methodist preacher John Hughes, who finally transcribed
them.[26] For Ann Griffiths herself, the poems served but as a private
oral record which gave the relief of expressive form to the pressure
of intense inward experience. From their first publication, in
Thomas Charles's collection *Casgliad o Hymnau* (1806), they won
favour with Dissenting congregations, but when she composed
them she had no such audience in mind, and was therefore free to
take considerable risks with her mode of self-expression. In an essay
on 'Romanticism in Wales', the historian Gwyn Alf Williams
disagrees with Saunders Lewis's argument that William Williams
should be termed a Romantic poet, but suggests that 'a better case
can be made, perhaps, for Ann Griffiths . . . whose hymns are an
extraordinarily powerful evocation of intensely personal experience'.[27] Through its use of the simplest of ballad forms, typical of
Welsh hymnology, to express a spiritual transcendence of the
material world, Griffiths's verse had an immediate and lasting
appeal; the imagery of her best-known stanza exemplifies that
fusion of the natural and supernatural which led to her canonization as a major Welsh poet:

> Gwna fi fel pren planedig, O fy Nuw,
> Yn ir ar lan afonydd dyfroedd byw,
> Yn gwreiddio ar led, a'i ddail heb wywo mwy,
> Ond ffrwytho dan gawodydd dwyfol glwy.[28]

> [Make me like a planted tree, O God,
> sappy on the bank of the rivers of the waters of life,
> rooting widely, its leaves never more to wither,
> but fructifying under the showers of a divine wound.]

The physicality of this stanza is striking: the image of the showers
of God's blessing fructifying trees in the landscape of the elect has its
biblical source in the Book of Ezekiel, but it can also carry other
associations – Zeus impregnated Danae by means of showers of
gold. Not that Ann Griffiths would have had any such pagan
images in mind, of course; that the language she commonly used to
express spiritual devotion to modern ears sounds so sensual is in
part the consequence of the popularity amongst the early
Methodists of the Song of Solomon, read as a metaphor for the
relationship between the believer and Christ as the Rose of
Sharon.[29] In Griffiths's hymns, the hands of the living God are upon

the believer like a lover's: quoting directly from the Song, she describes how 'his left hand supports my head while the blessings of his right hand embrace my soul'; she lives 'in expectation of him, ready when he comes to open to him promptly and enjoy his image fully'; once in Heaven she will 'kiss the Son to eternity, without turning my back on him again' ('Ei law aswy sy'n fy nghynal, / Dan fy mhen yngwres y dydd, / A bendithion ei ddeheulaw / Yn cofleidio'm henaid sydd'; 'Byw dan ddisgwyl am fy Arglwydd, / Bod, pan ddel, yn effro iawn, / I agoryd iddo'n ebrwydd / A mwynhau ei ddelw'n llawn'; 'Cusanu'r Mab i dragwyddoldeb, / Heb im gefnu arno mwy').[30] 'Remember, Lord, thy betrothed,' she cries, 'leap towards her like the stag' ('Cofia, Arglwydd, dy ddyweddi, / Llama ati fel yr hydd').[31] The 'Rose of Sharon', 'white and blushing, fair of face' becomes the nearly feminized object of her ardent pursuit.

But Ann Griffiths was by no means the only female Methodist convert to give vent to her experience in verse, and many of her contemporaries also echoed the Song in their own hymns. Another of its admirers, for example, was Pegi Shenkin or Margaret Jenkins, one of the early nineteenth-century originators of the Methodist connexion at Laleston in Glamorganshire, who sent to the Reverend Hopkin Bevan of Llangyfelach verses, later published by Bevan's biographer, which similarly glory in Christ as the rose and lily:

> Rhosyn hardd, lili'r ardd, 'does a dardd o'r ddaear ddu,
> A'i olrhain Ef i'r gwreiddyn, Flaguryn sydd mor gu;
> Dyma ngwledd, nefol hedd, gweled gwedd ei wyneb gwiw,
> Mwy hyfryd yw F'anwylyd, na golud pell Peru.[32]

> [Beautiful rose, lily of the garden, nothing from the dark earth,
> is dearer than this Shoot, tracing Him to the root;
> this is my feast, heavenly peace, to see his bright face,
> lovelier is my Darling than the far treasure of Peru.]

The 'Rose of Sharon', 'more beautiful than the sons of men', is 'the apple tree in blossom', and the 'true vine' for Mary Owen of Cwmafan (1796–1875) also ('Rhosyn Saron ... / Tecach yw na meibion dynion ... / Pren afalau hardd ei flodau ... Gwir winwyd-den').[33] To modern Welsh audiences, more familiar with Ann Griffiths's hymns than with the Song of Solomon, such stanzas can read like plagiarisms of her work, though in fact they but follow their biblical origin in the Song.

The struggles and hardship characteristic of her daily life no doubt intensified the female convert's yearning for spiritual gratification. In an 1816 volume currently believed to be the first Welsh-language book (as opposed to pamphlet) published by a woman, Jane Edward, or Jane Ellis as she had become by the time she published further editions of her collection, also relished the sweetness of the Lord's vines ('Grawnsypiau'r wlad sydd felus iawn').[34] One of Edward's most poignant hymns speaks of the effort to continue to believe in God as a God of love and goodness after suffering the loss of a child. 'You took a child from my bosom, give me grace in his place', she pleads ('Cym'raist blentyn o fy mynwes, / Rho im' fendith yn ei le').[35] Given the figures for infant mortalities at this time, her hymn must have been pertinent to many women's lives, but it did not find a place in the denominational hymn-books: it was the publishers and anthologizers of each sect who decided which hymns to reprint, and they tended to be male.

The two hymn collections published by Jane Roberts, of Llanllyfni, Caernarfonshire, *Hymnau Newyddion, ar Destunau Efengylaidd* (New Hymns, on Evangelical Subjects, *c*.1820?) and *Porth y Deml* (The Porch of the Temple, 1834) were similarly soon forgotten: they also feature characteristically female themes, focusing on the spiritual 'marriage' with Christ. Though 'the wrath of the dragon / wants to blacken the wife of the Lamb' ('llid y ddraig / Am dduo gwraig yr Oen'), yet the Lamb insists on having her 'clean as white snow' for the marriage.[36] Roberts uses very feminine dress metaphors to describe her conversion:

> Mae fy nghyfiawnderau'n fyrion,
> Gwisgoedd carpiog, bratiau budron;
> Am fy nghael 'rwyf, heb y rhei'ny,
> Yn y wisg a drefnodd Iesu.
> [. . .]
> Arglwydd gwna fi ynddi'n addas, –
> Gemwaith euraidd wisg briodas.[37]

> [My justifications are scant,
> ragged clothes, dirty aprons,
> I want to be found, without those,
> in the garb ordained by Jesus.
> [. . .]
> Lord, make me fit for it, –
> the golden bejewelled wedding dress.]

19

The contrast drawn here between the filthy rags of daily life and the golden apparel of the saved bride tellingly conveys the appeal of the Christian conversion experience for a Welsh woman of the early nineteenth century: her social position may not have been high, and the daily circumstances of her life effortful and impoverished, but she was promised through her faith a glorious destiny.

Roberts's lines also convey wonder at the paradoxes of the conversion experience, in a manner characteristic of Welsh Methodist hymnology: one of the features of Ann Griffiths's work most frequently remarked upon by her commentators is her use of paradoxes. Her verses become battlefields in which language is pummelled and twisted in the attempt to force it to express experiences which go beyond and shatter the linguistic system itself. In the formation of linguistic concepts, meaning is predicated upon binary opposition: black is black because it is not white; good is good because it is not bad; that which is mortal is transitory and sinful, while that which is divine is eternal and pure. But Griffiths's central preoccupation is with the wonder of Christ as at once God and man; to express her amazement at this mystery, she constructs lines riddled with conundrums. The Crucifixion 'puts the author of life to death, and buries the great resurrection' ('Rhoi awdwr bywyd i farwolaeth, / A chladdu'r adgyfodiad mawr'); the believer is 'living to see the Unseeable' ('Byw i weld yr Anweledig'); the Christian's path to salvation is a 'road' which is 'age-old and never ageing, a road without a beginning, which is yet new' ('Ffordd . . . Hen, ac heb heneiddio, yw; / Ffordd heb ddechreu, eto'n newydd').[38]

The emphasis on exploring paradox in Ann Griffiths's verse led the most influential of her critics, Saunders Lewis, to call her work a poetry of 'the mind and understanding', as opposed to feeling, and accordingly to categorize her poetic voice as 'masculine' ('Canu gwrywaidd, canu'r ymennydd a'r deall yw canu merch Dolwar').[39] R. M. Jones, on the other hand, argues that she shared her preoccupations with the paradoxes of the Christian faith with her fellow Methodist converts generally, all of whom were grappling in *seiat* and prayer-meetings with precisely these conundrums: 'these were matters familiar to little children at the beginning of the nineteenth century', Jones suggests ('dyma faterion a wyddai plant bach yn nechrau'r ganrif ddiwethaf').[40] And indeed it is the case that though they may have lacked Ann Griffiths's sustained intensity and lyricism as a poet, other female converts shared her so-called 'masculine' preoccupations, and gave expression to them. Their work has been largely ignored, in part because often, like Ann Griffiths herself, they worked solely within the oral tradition.

Elizabeth Phylips of Conway in Caernarfonshire, for example, composed a series of verses in 1836 which were not published until 1906, when they were discovered by chance amongst the manuscripts of the poet Alltud Eifion (Robert Isaac Jones), who married her granddaughter. Phylips, too, experienced her redemption as a wonder beyond the grasp of reason, and the word made flesh was to her also a transcendent paradox: 'the father of eternity himself / A child of time in the womb' ('Tad tragwyddoldeb ei hunan / Yn blentyn amserol mewn bru').[41] Repeatedly, she struggles to convey the experience of living in a natural world drenched in the supernatural, so that 'there is nothing in the white heaven encircling me / but the blood of the Man who was on the hill' ('Does yn y nef a'm gylch yn wyn, / Ond gwaed y Gŵr fu ar y bryn').[42] Christ's blood is the air about her; it is the oxygen her soul breathes.

The hymns of Margaret Thomas, born in Llanllechid, Caernarfonshire, in 1779, also survived only by chance: she, too, never published her verses, but wrote them down on the blank pages of her Bible and her copies of Thomas Charles's *Dictionary* and the *Book of Common Prayer*, where they were found by the preacher and editor Thomas Levi, who published some of them in the *Traethodydd* in 1904. Levi believed that Margaret Thomas was the author of the well-known but formerly anonymous hymn 'Dyma Feibl annwyl Iesu' (Here is Jesus' dear Bible), which was inscribed in her books in her handwriting, but the evidence is complicated by the fact that she did occasionally include favourite hymns by others amongst her own verses. At any rate, in the poems that are certainly hers, Margaret Thomas's voice emerges as powerful and by no means conventionally feminine. According to Levi, she was 'masterful in her manner' and made a good disciplinarian: 'preachers who had not received much education or social discipline were sent to her for her to teach them appropriate practices and good behaviour' ('yr oedd . . . yn feistrolgar yn ei ffordd . . . dywedir yr anfonid rhai pregethwyr nad oeddynt wedi cael addysg na disgyblaeth gymdeithasol, ati i ddysgu iddynt arferion gweddus, ac ymddygiad da'). One hymn of hers in particular emphasizes her forcefulness through its mantra-like refrain: 'The righteous order of the Covenant / That's my strength, that's my strength; / It is certain and uncompromising, / That's my strength' ('Trefn gyfiawn y Cyfamod / Dyna 'ngrym, dyna 'ngrym; / Mae yn sicr a digymod, / Dyna 'ngrym').[43]

An equivalent sense of certitude manifests itself in the hymns of Martha Llwyd (née Williams, 1766–1845), the crippled and illiterate wife of a blacksmith in Llanpumsaint, Carmarthenshire. Although her verses do not seem to have been published before Rhuddwawr (John Evan Davies) included some of them in a 1925 memoir to their author, they were popular within the oral tradition: Rhuddwawr tells of one occasion when a visiting preacher to Llanpumsaint gave out a hymn as 'one of the most popular in North Wales at the moment' without knowing that its author was amongst his audience.[44] The hymns Rhuddwawr proceeds to transcribe convey the directness and force of Martha Llwyd's voice, and her confidence that the 'gracious guidance, / of the unchanging God, / is enough for me to die by, / and enough for me to live' ('A goruchwyliaeth rasol, / Y di-gyfnewid Dduw, / Sy'n ddigon i mi farw, / A digon i mi fyw').[45]

Amongst those who did publish their work, a 'masterfulness of manner' is also often evident: the aim of Elizabeth Davies, of Cellan, for example, in writing her '*Cymhorth i hunan-adnabyddiaeth*' (Aid to self-knowledge, 1813), is to 'give everybody clear rules' ('rhoi i bawb reolau clir') as to how to recognize their faults and amend their ways.[46] Scolding her readers and disciplining them was similarly the self-appointed task of Alice Edwards, who, in her *Ychydig bennillion er annogaeth i Sïon i ymddiried yn ei Duw mewn blinfyd a chaledi* (A few verses to encourage Zion to trust in God in troubles and hardship, 1812), warns her readers that they should not ask God for ease; it is more chastisement that the world needs, rather than less:

> Paid a gofyn pam mae'r wialen
> Wedi ei hestyn ar y byd.
> Dywed wrtho'n ostyngedig,
> Pa fodd y bu hi'n cadw c'yd.[47]

> [Do not ask, why has the rod
> been extended over the world.
> Humbly say to him,
> why was it spared for so long.]

But the most vigorous scolder of them all was Jane Hughes of Pontrobert, Montgomeryshire (*c*.1811–80): in her '*Cân ar Niwed Pechodau'r Oes*' (Song on the Harm of the Age's Sins) few of the characteristics of her contemporaries are spared her wrath. Roman

Catholicism was an established enemy of the Methodists, but Jane Hughes believed that there were even worse perils threatening the moral lives of her fellow-countrymen by the middle years of the century: concerts and *eisteddfodau*, 'with their empty foolish laughter' were also 'but hell's ugly devices to hold back souls' ('Dyw'r Eisteddfodau a'r Concerts, a'u gwag chwerthiniad ffôl / Ond dyfais aflan uffern i ddal eneidiau'n nôl').[48] The daughter of Ann Griffiths's maid, Ruth, and John Hughes, who first transcribed Griffiths's poems, Jane Hughes published her first hymn-collection in 1846, and went on regularly producing small books and pamphlets of verse from then until her death in 1880. Well known as a lay evangelist who roamed the villages of north Wales through-out much of the nineteenth century, smoking a pipe as she tramped the hills from one religious gathering to the next, she scolded her audiences on street corners to some effect. According to one member of her impromptu congregations, O. M. Edwards, she 'could speak to young people on the matter of their souls with a sternness and seriousness which they remembered years after she was laid in her grave' ('medrai siarad â phobl ieuainc am fater eu heneidiau gyda grym a difrifwch y cofient am danynt flynyddoedd wedi ei rhoddi hi mewn bedd').[49]

Such dedicated forcefulness was characteristic of many of these early female Methodists. Ann Griffiths frequently addresses Christ with a voice of command: 'Awake, Lord, show your strength', she charges him ('Deffro, Arglwydd, gwna rymusder').[50] Fighting the good fight for her, too, meant becoming a holy terror when necessary; she tells her God,

> Gwna fi'n ddychryn yn dy law,
> I uffern, llygredd, annuwioldeb,
> Wrth edrych arnaf i gael braw.[51]

> [Make me frightening in thy hand,
> so that hell, corruption, ungodliness,
> through looking at me will be afraid.]

These hymn-writers' voices are not feminine, according to the stereotypical ideals of gender difference increasingly enforced within middle-class English culture during the period in which they wrote. They show no inclination to wait passively on God, in obedience to the prescribed code proper to their sex, but use the whole force of their intellect and personality in a traditionally

23

'masculine' manner in the attempt to understand and to evangelize their faith. It cannot be assumed that the manner in which the female is defined within one culture will concur with her construction within another. For all their lack of femininity according to the English pattern, it was women such as these who served as the proper model for Nonconformist Welsh women for the rest of the nineteenth century; this was how a Welsh woman of the right type, a pillar of her religious community, was meant to think, feel and express herself. For many of their contemporaries, however, including more typical female contributors to English Romanticism, such enthusiasts were but figures of scorn, as the next section of this chapter indicates.

ii. Fictionalizing the principality

As the Methodist movement gathered momentum, the new Dissenters became an object of satirical attack in popular and high culture, and in Welsh- as well as English-language literature. In 1746 the satirist William Roberts, in his popular interlude *Ffrewyll y Methodistiaid* (Scourge of the Methodists) accused the sect of promoting licentious sexual behaviour through the arousing atmosphere of its mixed-sex evening gatherings, an accusation frequently to be repeated.[52] Similarly, the mock sermons of the antiquarian and poet Lewis Morris of Anglesey (1701–65) castigated the Methodists as hypocritical: Morris's Methodist preacher advocates his flock to 'Dance and Skip about, for I will absolve you from your Sins, But whatever you do, Do in the dark, that our enemies may not triumph over us for the eyes of the wicked Peep into every corner'.[53] Later the most influential of Welsh Romanticists, Iolo Morganwg (Edward Williams, 1747–1826), also derided the sect, and accused it of fooling the 'silly crowd' with 'mad fanatic jumping, / With folly bawled aloud, / Wild rant and pulpit thumping'.[54] Within Welsh-language culture, however, such critiques grew scarcer as the sects increased their hold upon the population during the first decades of the nineteenth century.

In England, on the other hand, leading literary figures continued to disparage Dissenters throughout the Romantic and Victorian periods.[55] In a series of journal essays, entitled *An Attempt to Shew the Folly and Danger of Methodism* (1809), the poet and influential literary editor and critic Leigh Hunt, for example, suggested that Methodists, and in particular female converts to the sect, never learned to divorce spiritual from physical sensation, but crudely forced the two together. Of testifiers quoted in the Methodist magazines of the period, he says,

> The language of these women is so entirely earthly, that in general if you change the name of the object, you might think their devotion addressed to a mere lover. The Deity is personified in the grossest of images; the soul talks just as the body might be supposed to talk.[56]

Hunt appears to have been unfamiliar with, or not to have accepted, the argument that such language was based on a metaphorical reading of the Song of Solomon. No doubt he would have dismissed as gross the work of some of the Welsh-language women hymn-writers of the period, were he able to understand them. But his aim, Jon Mee argues in his recent study *Romanticism, Enthusiasm and Regulation* (2003), is to distinguish between the vulgarity of religious enthusiasm and the proper exercise of the organs of appreciation in literary taste. According to Hunt, 'the vulgar admire Methodism just as they do violent colours, violent noise, and violent swearing', but the well-bred must be guided by more temperate and self-controlled admirations, as a mark of their rank, and in a manner which adds to the authority of upper-class English culture.[57]

Within the novel genre, attacks on Methodists were also frequent; for the novelists, too, the movement represented a rival attraction against which their largely female audience had to be warned. The Irish novelist Maria Edgeworth includes a pointed assault on the sect, and its unfortunate effects on women in particular, in *Belinda* (1801). In that novel Lady Delacour is in grave danger of losing her sanity under the influence of 'methodistical' reading-matter, so much so that her maid Marriott tells Belinda,

> those books will quite turn her poor head, and I wish they were burnt. I know the mischief that the same sort of things did to a poor cousin of my own, who was driven melancholy mad by a methodist preacher, and came to an untimely end.[58]

Lady Delacour is perusing Wesleyan writing, but other female novelists whose knowledge of Methodism appears to have been garnered during Welsh tours deemed Calvinist Dissent to be equally pernicious, particularly, once again, in its effects on women. After touring Wales, the Scottish novelist Elizabeth Isabella Spence

(1768–1832) included in her collection *Old Stories* (1822) a tale in which a male narrator, visiting north Wales, becomes acquainted with a local woman, Mrs Williams, but is shocked at what he sees and hears when he attends her customary place of worship, a Methodist meeting-house: 'Curiosity tempted me to accompany her to witness a scene at once extraordinary and humiliating. Their worship bordered more on paganism than on that of a civilized and piously inclined people.'[59] Two further visitors to Wales, who stayed for forty years, Lady Eleanor Butler (1739–1829) and Sarah Ponsonby (1755–1831), the Ladies of Llangollen, had little but warm words for their Welsh neighbours generally, except for the Methodists. Dismissing a gardener in 1784, Eleanor Butler notes in her pocket-book that he is discharged 'for his *Sins* and Baseness and Ingratitude. *Mem* (a Methodist)', and Sarah Ponsonby in 1826, listing to a helpful friend their requirements for a new housemaid, asks 'that she May be a Merry Creature Given to talking and Singing – provided they are neither *Raw* Songs nor Methodist Hymns'.[60]

Methodism often fared no better under the pen of writers who professed closer blood-ties with Wales. Admittedly, Mary Robinson (1756–1800) could be said to have justifiable personal reasons for her dislike: she had looked for succour during the early years of her marriage to her affluent Welsh Methodist in-laws, but in the event they did nothing to save her and her child from a debtor's prison.[61] Born Mary Darby in Bristol, in 1758 according to her *Memoir* and her gravestone but two years earlier according to the baptismal register recently researched by Moira Dearnley,[62] Robinson was the daughter of an Irishman born in America and a mother who hailed from the landed Welsh gentry, from the Seys family of Castle Boverton in the Vale of Glamorgan, or so Mary was to claim. In 1773 she married Thomas Robinson, under the mistaken belief that he was the heir of Thomas Harris, brother of Howel Harris, the Welsh Methodist leader, and owner of the estates of Trefeca and Tregunter. But Robinson was only an illegitimate offspring of Thomas Harris's, and not his oldest child at that. In October 1774, the young couple visited Trefeca, with the aim of raising money to pay off their debts, but Harris would not spare his errant son a penny: consequently, from May 1775 to August 1776 the Robinson family was imprisoned for debt in the Fleet prison in London. Soon after their release, Mary ventured on to the London stage as a professional actress, and as Perdita in *The Winter's Tale* made so deep an impression on the then Prince of Wales, later George IV, that a brief but very public love affair flourished between them. At its close her financial situation was temporarily eased by the five thousand pounds secured from the Prince as payment for the return of his love letters. In later life, she successfully developed a new career as a fashionable poet, novelist and self-apologist, presenting herself as more sinned against than sinning, with some success, or so it would appear from Charlotte Dacre's elegy to her as '*most* perfect amongst erring mortals': 'Still, still in the grave thou dost triumph victorious, / Thy fame sounding loud in thine *enemies*' ears!'[63]

Amongst those enemies, Robinson counted her husband's Welsh relatives and their Methodist connections. In *Memoirs of the late Mrs Robinson, written by herself* (1801), she attacks her father-in-law as a hypocrite of the highest order, who 'would frequently fine the rustics (for he was a justice of the peace, and had been Sheriff of the county) when he heard them swear, though every third sentence he uttered was attended by an oath that made his hearers shudder'. Similarly, the countenance of his daughter, Elizabeth Robinson, was 'peculiarly formed for the expression of sarcastic vulgarity'. Mary Edwards, the family's maid and also a Methodist, did not please either: 'a more overbearing, vindictive spirit never inhabited the heart of mortal than that which pervaded the soul of ill-natured Mrs Molly'. To be associated with so uncouth a family lacerated Mary's sensitivities during her stay at Trefeca:

> I had formed an union with a family who had neither sentiment nor sensibility: I was doomed to bear the society of ignorance and pride: I was treated as though I had been the most abject of beings, even at a time when my conscious spirit soared as far above their powers to wound it, as the mountain towered over the white battlements of my then . . . habitation.[64]

In the fictions Robinson published in the 1790s, Methodist characters are included as objects of satire: in *Walsingham, or, The Pupil of Nature* (1797), the hero discovers that a neighbour of his, a promising but penurious poet, is being tormented by his landlord, a Methodist, to whom he owes money. Because he is 'inordinately addicted' to alcohol,[65] the landlord is himself in debt and insists impatiently on payment. When the poet pleads, 'Consider my infants; if you drive them into the street they must perish!', his 'sanctified persecutor' assures him that 'The Lord will protect *them*

... But *I* must be *paid!*'[66] His Methodist wife also denounces literary writers generally, saying of the poet that,

> 'Such vagrants as these only turn our labours in the field of salvation into ridicule, sow the weeds of controversy among the upright, and teach the lambs of our pasture to think for themselves instead of listening to us, who walk in the true path of religion.'[67]

The battle between Methodism and Romanticism, as to who should wield most power over a vulnerable public, the preacher or the man of letters, was clearly being waged in the popular literature of the day years before it came to a head in Hunt's 1809 diatribe.

Methodists are similarly derided for mouthing meaningless absurdities, and for their hypocrisy when it comes to money matters, in Anna Maria Bennett's Welsh novels. In *Anna, or, Memoirs of a Welch Heiress*, the Reverend John Dalton, 'the son of a journeyman carpenter, in a large town in South Wales' and one of the book's worst villains, exploits the orphan Anna in a manner which the text represents as characteristic of Methodist preachers. After an encounter in his youth with 'a late celebrated methodist teacher' who was 'fond of procuring men, for his mission, who were in orders', Dalton had 'pleaded a call of the spirit': 'To a strong voice, a primitive look, a lank thin person, and a large wig, he added the cunning and cant of an itinerant preacher'.[68] In the novel which is generally held to be Bennett's best work, *The Beggar Girl and Her Benefactors* (1797), it is the stupidity rather than the cunning of the Methodist which is emphasized: he is described as '[o]ne who talks about what he does not understand'.[69] Like Mary Robinson, Anna Maria Bennett may also owe to a Welsh past her knowledge of Methodism, such as it was. According to what is considered to be the most reliable biographical account, she was born in Merthyr Tydfil to David Evans, a grocer, and his wife, married a Brecon tanner named Bennett, and moved with him to London, where she kept a slop-shop, only to be rescued from behind the counter by Admiral Sir Thomas Pye, who made her his 'housekeeper' and the mother of two of his children, to whom she was permitted to give his name.[70] The notoriety of their liaison was such that *Anna* sold out on its first day of issue; Bennett's fame, which was apparently commensurate at its height with that of Walter Scott, peaked in 1806 with the novel *Vicissitudes Abroad*, which sold 2,000 copies on its publication day.[71] The marked contrast between the actual lives lived by some of the more colourful London-Welsh novelists and those of the Methodist women back home is another indicator, along with their disparate literatures, of the gulf between the two linguistic cultures at the beginning of the nineteenth century.

In order to increase the exotic appeal of their fictions, Romantic novelists who made use of Welsh locations tended to overemphasize and exaggerate aspects of Welsh difference. In their works, Welsh characters not afflicted by Methodist enthusiasm are still prey to primitive superstitions: indeed, many of them, it would appear, have remained Druid worshippers. As the Cambrian mountains 'rise with bold magnificence' into view at the opening of *The Abbey of Saint Asaph* (1795) by the Anglo-Scottish writer Isabella Kelly (1758–1857), for example, Lady Douglas informs her children that these are the 'regions of inspiration' in former times dominated by Druids, and assures them that 'the people still retain a large portion of their ancient superstition, attributing to certain springs very miraculous influence'.[72] Similarly, the Irish poet and novelist Eliza Ryves (1750–97) begins her 1789 novel *The Hermit of Snowden* (*sic*) with a passage describing two antiquarians making 'an excursion into Wales',

> not merely to view the country and those monuments of Druidical superstition which have been so frequently examined and described, but to visit the villages . . . where they thought it probable the peasants might retain many traditions and customs which would throw light upon the imperfect account transmitted to us of their religious rites.[73]

Stressing the backwardness of Wales of course pandered to the English readers' desire to see themselves as sophisticated by comparison; at the same time it also allowed Wales to feature as a suitable site for an array of Gothic extravaganzas likely to prove popular, for all the supposedly superior good sense of the audience. Anglophone writers from Wales sometimes seem to be trying to unpick the stereotype of Welsh superstitiousness, only to fall back on it again when it serves usefully to introduce exciting ghost stories. In Mary Nicholl of Cowbridge's novel *The Family of George Briton* (1822), for example, the English Amy Briton teases her cousin, Agnes Owen from Swansea, with the slur that, 'You are very superstitious in Wales . . . It is a shame for you, ancient Britons, to be so frightened at nothing.' When Agnes replies, 'I am a Welsh girl, born and bred, yet I can smile at all that folly with the wisest of you English girls', her cousin responds, 'Yes, thanks to your *English* mother.' Agnes will have none of this, and insists that it is, on the contrary, from her father that she has inherited her courage: 'I have a Welsh father who would walk over any of the churchyards in Wales when all the spirits are said to be on the ramble', she says.[74] But at this point in the narrative Amy begs for stories about those spirits said to be abroad in Welsh graveyards, and Agnes complies: Mary Nicholls is colluding with her readers' expectations that a novel with Welsh characters will provide entertaining tales of pre-Christian horror, even as she at the same time tries to stress the modernity and good sense of her Welsh characters.

An earlier text had strongly underlined the stereotype of superstitiousness, insofar as it applied to the Welsh peasantry: in *Delve; A Welch Tale* (1796) by Susannah Gunning (*c.*1740–1800), one central character, Mother Jenkings, is full of entertaining tales of neighbourhood witches, their spells and curses, and how to outwit them. Mother Jenkings becomes the self-appointed carer of the thirteen-year-old orphan Delves, after he has escaped from his guardian into the Welsh countryside. She shelters him in her rude hut, until he is forcibly abducted by an English nobleman and his Welsh wife, eventually revealed to be Delves's aunt. Initially, Delves resists this enforced removal to a higher social class and to England, and so does Mother Jenkings. His abductors offer to pay her off, but she is not interested: 'What, more money,' she says, 'but where is my dear boy?'[75] So appealing a character is Mother Jenkings that, were it not for her extreme superstitiousness, readers might be tempted to believe that Delves would be far happier with her than with his initially intimidating aunt and uncle. At any rate, ten years later, when Delves returns to Wales as the owner of a vast estate, his first concern is to find Mother Jenkings and renew their intimacy: 'I caught her in my arms, and kissing her venerable forehead cried out, "oh my mother".'[76] With this scene, Gunning's text appears effectively to be conveying the pain involved in the Anglicization of the Welsh elite. Delves has gained status and wealth through his enforced incorporation into the English establishment, but he has lost his earlier close relation with the Welsh peasantry, and he laments that loss; the peasantry, in turn, has been bereft by the removal of its nobility. Both classes are, in a sense, orphaned by the historical development they are undergoing.

Perhaps the most interesting of these Romantic fictions from the Welsh point of view also explores the negative effects of Anglicization. Anna Maria Bennett's *Ellen, Countess of Castle Howel* (1794) opens with an idyllic scene from the old Welsh way of

life. In the great hall of Code (*sic*) Gwyn, the north Walian seat of
the Meredith family, servants and masters are at ease together,
complete with family bard: 'there the harper had his seat, and there
. . . the inmates mingled, without a frown on the brow of pride, or
presumption in the bosom of poverty'. But this felicity is soon
interrupted by the return of the soldier son of the house, who brings
with him as a guest an English lord: 'the Lieutenant had no sooner
introduced Lord Claverton by name, than Griffiths [the butler]
hurried the domestics out of the parlour'.[77] The old familial
mingling cannot be maintained in the presence of one who represents the much more strongly polarized English system of rank, and
the impression here is one of loss. But the way of life of the Code
Gwyn household is threatened by material as well as social change.
Because they have neglected to raise the rents of their tenants in
parallel with rising living costs, the Merediths are debt-ridden. In
order to save the estate and its dependants, Ellen, the young
orphaned granddaughter of the house, agrees to marry a wealthy
elderly neighbour, Lord Castle Howel. Lord Castle Howel's establishment is a much more sophisticated one – that is, a much more
Anglicized one – than Code Gwyn; to prepare the rustic Ellen for
the role he has in mind for her, he has earlier paid for her to be
educated at a boarding school in Bath. Her maid, Winifred Griffiths, who, in the primitive Code Gwyn way, is Ellen's closest
companion and confidante, is allowed to accompany her mistress,
but with one condition:

> Lord Castle Howel . . . obtained, as a great favour, that Winifred
> should be admitted into Mrs. Forrest's [the schoolmistress's] family,
> but all conversation was strictly forbid with their young lady: The
> truth is, that though Ellen approached as near perfection as most
> heroines of her age, yet she certainly had a welch accent, which to the
> refined ears of Mrs. Forrest, and her ladies, sounded a little uncouth;
> and, as Winifred's was a barbarous jargon of neither Welch nor
> English, but a bad mixture of both, which she plainly saw would never
> be got rid of, she prudently conditioned for their entire separation.
> Ellen's cheek crimsoned, and a tear of regret filled her eye, at this
> sentence, but a moment's recollection, when Miss Forrest explained
> the reason, changed her regret to gratitude, for such early attention to
> a defect her own ear reproached her with, whenever she spoke, or was
> spoken to, by her polished school-fellows.[78]

Ellen is made to feel ashamed of her Welshness, while at the same
time she does grieve over the estrangement from her servant which

the espousal of English values entails. Saving Code Gwyn materially seems to mean, in that contemporary climate, betraying it culturally.

Bennett's Welsh romances fictionalize the Anglicization process in a manner which accords very closely with some of the case histories described by Linda Colley in *Britons*: Colley's account of the shifting loyalties of the Williams Wynns of Denbigh, for example, could have been the model for Bennett's depiction of the Trevanion family in *Anna, or, Memoirs of a Welch Heiress*.[79] The old Earl of Trevanion is as 'strictly attached to his country' as the early eighteenth-century Watkin Williams Wynn, and takes great pride in the fact that he is 'descended in a regular line from Llewellin, Prince of South Wales'. At the opening of the tale, his daughter, Lady Edwin, eventually revealed to be Anna's aunt, is also single-mindedly Welsh in her loyalties:

> her servants, her tradesmen, even her cattle must be Welch; nay, so attached was she to the Cambrian stream in her veins, she would, as she often declared, rather have chosen to marry her children to the peasant of her own wild hills, than to the nobles of any other country.[80]

But once the orphaned Anna has been recognized as her niece, and she and the Welsh cousin whom she marries have inherited the Trevanion estate, they reconcile Lady Edwin and her – initially – equally Anglophobic spouse to the British establishment and its monarchy: Anna's husband 'by degrees, divested Sir William Edwin of his prejudices, and changed his opposition . . . into a patriotic zeal for the good of his country, and the honour of his prince, which he at length convinced him were synonymous terms'.[81] 'His prince' here refers, of course, to the English Prince of Wales, rather than to the Welsh princes to whom Lady Edwin had previously delighted in tracing back her ancestry. Anna's husband has apparently succeeded in persuading his uncle that English rule is both rightful and beneficial for Wales.[82] In *Britons*, Colley presented the Anglicizing process as one of gain for all concerned, arguing that the sense of a common British identity was not enforced from the centre, but came about in consequence of the need for the various components of Protestant Britain to work more closely together in opposition to the threat from Catholic France. Though admitting that 'this could savour of a selling-out to English values', she argues that 'the

behaviour of these onetime Celtic outsiders can just as appropriately be interpreted as purchasing into what were then the substantial profits of being British'.[83] Yet, while accepting that individual
members of the gentry undoubtedly gained power and international
prestige as a result of this process, one may still query to what
extent any of its 'substantial profits' filtered back to the people of
Scotland, Ireland and Wales, and ask whether it was not for them a
matter of loss as much as – if not more than – gain.

Overall, however, the Anglicization of Wales is generally presented in the Welsh romances of the period not only as inevitable, a
process which no protest can halt, but also as desirable. That, at any
rate, is certainly the moral of *The Clergyman's Tale* (1799), one of
the novels through which Sophia Lee (1750–1824), with her sister
Harriet, strove to augment the fortunes of their aspiring family of
London actors and actresses.[84] On a tour of north Wales, the
Reverend Pembroke hits upon the idea of adopting a Welsh peasant
child and presenting it to his wife as his own illegitimate offspring,
in order to check his wife's pride in their daughter, whom she has
alienated from her father. Spotting a likely lad, he approaches his
mother, only to be 'confounded' by the fact that she and her
children are monoglot Welsh-speakers. He attempts to ingratiate
himself with them by allowing the children to examine his watch,
but such was their surprise at the 'ticking wonder', 'which they all
united to express in the same unintelligible manner' – that is, in
Welsh – that Mr Pembroke 'saw with astonishment that his own
country could afford beings as wholly unversed in the improvements of polished life as the savages of America'.[85] At this point in
the narrative the 'savage' Welsh mother has not realized that her
'polished' visitor's aim is to buy one of her children; when Mr
Pembroke finally puts money in her lap and takes the chosen child
in his arms, she throws back the purse in a transport of fury,
snatches back the child, and appears 'ready to second her incompre-
hensible oration with blows'.[86]

The text's reference to colonized 'savages' might well suggest to
the reader a comparison between Mr Pembroke's behaviour and
that of the British slave-traders still operating in 1799, and held in
abhorrence by a growing number of the more radical and evangelical leading figures of the day. But it would appear that no such
connection was intended by Sophia Lee: Mr Pembroke learns
nothing from the encounter, but continues with his search along the
river valley, where he is rewarded by the discovery of a beautiful boy

struggling in the water. Rescuing the child, and marvelling at the unfairness with which 'Heaven, that denies me a son of my own, has given to these peasants a Grecian Cupid', Mr Pembroke decides to abduct the young god without more ado; he is encouraged to do so by his supposition that because the child speaks Welsh he must belong to the peasant class. On being rescued, the boy

> stared confusedly at Mr Pembroke, and, bursting into tears, demanded vehemently some unknown person, in the same unintelligible tongue that already embarrassed his protector. That gentleman now seriously reprobated the supineness of the clergy, and the negligence of the schoolmasters, who ought long since to have made English the only language in the King's dominions; yet satisfying himself, from this mark of infantine ignorance, that the boy his heart already adopted was, however eminently endowed by nature, only the son of a herdsman, he no longer made it a question whether he should henceforward call him his own.[87]

Clearly, whatever guide Mr Pembroke had consulted in preparation for his travels had not included the information that Welsh was the only language of large parts of north Wales in 1799: the 1801 estimates of language use, based on parochial returns, suggests that no English was spoken throughout the whole county of Merioneth, and that the percentage of monoglot Welsh-speakers in Caernarfonshire was 84.1 per cent.[88] But in this novel to speak a language other than English denotes ignorance and low class status: Welsh is represented as so primitive a tongue that it brands all who speak it not only as peasants, but as peasants ripe for abduction into a more 'polished' culture. Once in England, Mr Pembroke's stolen child quickly forgets his native tongue, and 'with the Welsh language he seemed to lose all recollection of those to whom he had spoken it'.[89] At the close of the novel, it is revealed that he was in fact no peasant but the heir of a titled and landed Welsh family, but Mr Pembroke does not apologize for his offence, neither does the text or any of its characters condemn him for it. It would appear that to acquire the English language and an English upbringing and identity, even as a half-hidden illegitimate, constitutes sufficient compensation for the loss of family, legitimacy, language and culture in Wales. *The Clergyman's Tale* reads like a fictionalization of the 1536 Act which united Wales with England, extending English citizenship and civil rights to Welshmen as long as 'they use and exercise the speech or language of English' and are careful 'utterly to extirpate all the singular sinister uses and customs' by which they differed from their neighbours.[90]

Some of the more radical anglophone texts of the period, however, though they rarely mourn the erosion of the Welsh language, do appreciate the greater freedom of the traditional Welsh way of life, as they understand it, from the strictures of a classed society. The typical hero or heroine of many of these fictions is an orphan, actually of the gentry class but unaware of it, who is roaming footloose and free through the wild Welsh countryside. That liberty comes to an end, of course, as soon as the orphan is 'rescued' and his or her status is recognized by the English establishment. The image of Wales as offering a more natural, class-free zone could prove attractive to the Romantic radical, disillusioned by the restrictions and artifice of contemporary English culture. For some women writers in particular the opportunity to make one's heroine a child of nature, and to free her from the restraints imposed by the English ideal of the proper lady, increased the appeal of a Welsh location. The final section of this chapter examines instances of such imaginings.

iii. A land of liberty

The freedom of a life of retirement in Wales, as opposed to the worldly sophistications increasingly corrupting English life, is a theme frequently emphasized in Romantic fictions: London life, in particular, is invariably represented as morally imperilled when compared to the innocent tranquillity of life in the Welsh 'rustic Cot' or castle. Like Ianthé in Emily Frederick Clark's novel, *Ianthé, or the Flower of Caernarvon* (1798), heroine after heroine, once embroiled in the London scene, yearns 'to return to Wales . . . impatient to revisit the happy scenes of her youth, for which a knowledge of the world had increased her relish'.[91] Both the beauty of Wales's unspoilt scenery and the equally unspoilt naturalness of its inhabitants give it its healing charms. In Emma Parker's novel *Fitz-Edward; or, the Cambrians* (1811), the heroine Eva Meredith, of Plas Gwynnedd in Denbighshire, as she prepares to return to Wales from a London visit, is accused of relinquishing 'the pleasures of the metropolis with great indifference', to which she responds, 'The pleasures of dissipation . . . have never charmed me. I like the society of a few select friends, and I have some in Wales I shall be most happy to rejoin.'[92] Parker, who published under the pseudonym 'Emma de Lisle' and would herself appear to have been a member of the north Wales gentry, wrote her seven novels in Fairfield House in Denbighshire. The elite of the area are warmly described in *Fitz-Edward* as noted for their kindness and liberality: the Merediths are generous, but 'that "most excellent gift of charity" would not have rendered them *particularly distinguishable* in that part of the country, as there is not a spot in the creation where that most amiable of human propensities is more liberally or universally exercised than in Denbighshire'.[93] But it is the peasantry who exemplify 'that real open-hearted kindness which the Welsh may well claim as one of their distinguishing characteristics' in Louisa Weston's *The Cambrian Excursion* (1841), as they assist Mr Howard to teach his daughter Marianne, corrupted by 'her taste for the amusements and dissipation of a London life', where true virtue and happiness lie.[94]

The uncorrupted virtue of the inhabitants of Wales, whatever their rank, is also extolled in the epistolary novel *The Welsh Mountaineer* (1817) by Catharine Hutton (1756–1846), a Birmingham-born novelist. In its opening pages, Dorothy Penrose leaves Plas Morwynnion, her home in north Wales, on her first visit to London. She is warned by her grandmother to be wary of her new environment, for which her Welsh life has not prepared her: 'Thy numerous family, thy few neighbours, and our faithful servants, are not perverted by an intercourse with the world. Though anger, envy, and hatred may be found among them, art and hypocrisy cannot.'[95] The same cannot be said of Londoners, the grandmother warns. But in fact it is not so much the perversions of London which appal Dorothy, once she is established in that city, but its proprieties. After one incident, in which she is assumed to be a prostitute because she has dared to walk the streets unaccompanied by a chaperone, she turns on her friends who are reprimanding her for her recklessness and tells them,

> 'You keep young women in leading strings! You destroy every spark of independence! You render them a set of helpless beings, that are not to move without you! ... I have breathed the free air of my native mountains, and my actions have been as free as that.'[96]

A love of liberty acquired during a childhood amongst the Welsh mountains also proves resistant to the ideology of the 'proper lady' in Olivia More's *The Welsh Cottage* (1820). In this overtly feminist text, which is pre-eminently concerned with the marriage question, Ellen Owen attributes her resistance to the enslavement of propriety to her early upbringing. She explains that,

> In the wild regions of Wales, I had imbibed a love of liberty with the air I breathed. From my childhood I could remember clambering from rock to rock, or rapidly descending the steepest sides of the mountain, fearless of danger, and unacquainted with fatigue. In the metropolis, I found myself a melancholy prisoner, confined within that stated circle of perambulation which the votaries of fashion had marked out; and to venture beyond which was to incur the danger of reproach and the certainty of insult.[97]

She decides to return to Wales and stay single and independent, 'unfettered by the authority and unbiased by the prejudices of others'. The common lot of 'hapless females groaning beneath the yoke of a ridiculous or a merciless master', and 'still humbly endeavouring to endure everything in silent submission', is not going to be hers, she determines.[98]

But just as the risks she took in walking the London streets unchaperoned imperilled Dorothy Penrose, so too, in these fictions, the freedom of movement enjoyed by Welsh women at home increasingly could endanger them. For their environment was fast being infiltrated by visiting Englishman, 'those pests to society, who, under the name of travellers, pursue their vices more than their improvement', according to the afflicted husband of a seduced cottager in *The Orphans of Snowdon* (1797) by Elizabeth Gunning (1769–1823). He describes the advent of the English tourist to Wales as that of 'a serpent, whose poisonous breath' has destroyed the purity of his Welsh Eden.[99] The libertines and rakes who pepper these novels' pages are usually English noblemen, who appear to regard young Welsh females as their natural prey. In Emily Frederick Clark's *Ianthé*, for example, the heroine comes across a bereaved tenant bewailing the untimely corpse of her grand-daughter, and hears the girl's mournful history. Seduced and made pregnant by an Anglicized nobleman's son, the deserted girl expired of grief after the death of her child: 'Winifred Morgan, her grand-mother, was continually blaming herself for not having taken her away from the grandeur she lived in, to her original humble state.'[100] Another unscrupulous English nobleman, Lord Claverton, is the villain of Anna Maria Bennett's *Ellen*, and the vicissitudes of its heroine are largely the consequence of his machinations. 'I'll have that girl!' he announces as soon as he glimpses Ellen, and he sets about planning his future establishment, 'in which, however, he considered it as *too* great an honour for a little country rustic to be included, and therefore intended to keep her for his hours of relaxation, in a small box, near the metropolis'.[101]

Of course, sometimes it is Wales and Welshmen that prove seductive to visiting gentlewomen, rather than vice versa. In Elizabeth Hervey's picaresque and sentimental novel *The History of Ned Evans* (1796), Ned, the son of an impoverished Welsh clergyman, wins the heart of the lovely Lady Cecilia Rivers, only daughter of the Earl of Ravensdale, who appears unexpectedly at the door of his lowly north Walian cot, as the victim of highwaymen. For some weeks she has to convalesce in this rustic abode from a fever produced by the shock of the attack, but in so doing she falls prey to a greater threat to her rank than the highwaymen themselves. Her first encounter with the Welsh harp determines her future; Ned's hands on the strings produce a melody with a transporting effect:

> it warbled for some minutes like the sweet notes of the sky-lark singing at the gates of heaven; then all at once descended in a full stream of the richest melody, that overpowered the soul, and drowned the senses in a rapturous elysium.
>
> Lady Cecilia listened to it with astonishment – her breath seemed to keep pace with the notes through all their variations, and when he came to the close, she was almost exhausted, and . . . had well nigh expired on the strings.[102]

But Ned is far too virtuous a character to take any unfair advantage of her swooning state; in his case, there is nothing contrived or vicious about his seductive appeal, and he is subsequently loyal to a fault in his allegiance to her.

In the case of English seducers of the inhabitants of Wales, however, exploitation is the name of the game. Interestingly, Welsh males as well as females occasionally fall victim to upper-class English predators: in *Cambrian Pictures* (1810) by Ann of Swansea (Ann Julia Hatton, 1764–1838), for example, the young male ward of the Llewellyn family of Dolgelly Castle is kidnapped by the ageing Duchess of Inglesfield and held prisoner in her castle in Cumberland till he should resign himself to her intentions on his person.[103] And in *Eden Vale* (1784) by Catherine Parry (?–1788), the wife of a Welsh clergyman, the innocent and unsuspecting Reverend Mr Wynne, fresh out of Wales and newly betrothed, is lured into a dark corner by an English other, the Honourable Miss Evelyn, and succumbs to her very dishonourable advances.[104] This repeated plot device – of the powerful English seducing and ruining the vulnerable Welsh – can be read as a trope metaphorically representative of the relation between Wales and England generally during these years, though it is unlikely that it was intended as such by many of these authors.

In Ann of Swansea's case, however, the symbolism may have been conscious, for at one point in *Cambrian Pictures* she does draw an explicit connection between the seduction of the Welsh maidens and colonialist exploitation generally. The vicissitudes of her personal career appear to have radicalized Ann of Swansea's view of English society. Born in Worcester to the theatrical family of Roger and Sarah Kemble (Sarah Siddons was her older sister), Ann had spent some of her childhood years in Wales and along the Welsh border, when her parents starred in John Ward's travelling theatrical company.[105] At nineteen, in London, she made an unfortunate marriage to a bigamist, and subsequently was employed for a period as a model in Dr James Graham's notorious Temple of Health and Hymen in Pall Mall, an institution which professed to offer help with sexual potency and fertility problems. After a very public suicide attempt, in which she attempted to take poison in Westminster Abbey, her exasperated family granted her an allowance of ninety pounds per annum on condition that she reside at least 150 miles from London. In later life, in Swansea, after the death of her second husband, William Hatton, she maintained herself by publishing a volume of poetry and fourteen novels, in which Wales, when it features, is frequently presented as the victim of English exploitation.[106]

The chief villain of her *Cambrian Pictures*, Lord Clavering, enters Wales with the manifest purpose of buying it up for his personal gratification. He observes to a resident that 'if any estate within a few miles of Canarvon [*sic*] was to be disposed of he should like to become a purchaser'. Accordingly he is asked, 'has your lordship any notion of residing in Wales?', but replies, 'not absolutely of residing . . . but there is plenty of game in the country, and as I am a sportsman, I should like to have a hunting-lodge'.[107] The buying-up of Welsh property as holiday homes would appear to have become fashionable in England by the beginning of the nineteenth century. However, the game Lord Clavering is hunting seems to be not so much the Welsh hart as the Welsh maiden: he leaves a trail of ruined rustics behind him before finally coming up against a passion for Rosa Percival. Rosa is not as 'come-at-able' (a slang term of the period) as his former victims because she is the legitimate daughter of his friend, Sir Edward Percival. Sir Edward had initially seduced and 'ruined' Rosa's Welsh mother, but had then been persuaded to marry her by the dowry offered by her rich tradesman brother, Gabriel Jenkins. Although Sir Edward abandoned both mother and daughter immediately after the marriage, leaving Rosa to be reared in Wales by her uncle, his interest in her is renewed by Lord Clavering's offer of ten thousand pounds for her hand in marriage. But Rosa resists her titled suitor, much to her uncle's satisfaction: she says,

'Lord Clavering is my aversion.'

'Tol der lol,' sung Gabriel Jenkins, capering about the room, and kicking his wig before him, 'gad, but this is nuts for me to crack; a mountaineer, as your father calls you, to have spirit enough to refuse a lord; but come along, Rosa, I long to let them see a bit of Cambrian blood, pure and honest, neither ashamed nor afraid to refuse the gingerbread gilding of title ... [Y]our father would have sold you without pity, just as if you had been timber on his estate, to this Lord Clavering, and this noble would have bought you: very decent proceedings truly, just as bad to the full as if you had been a negro slave in a West-India plantation.'[108]

In 1810, when this book was published, Britain was preening itself on being the world's foremost opponent to the slave trade, the Abolitionists having finally succeeded in their aims in 1807, after two decades of well-publicized campaigning. To equate the situation of Welsh women, and by implication of Wales generally, with the slave question was therefore strongly to emphasize the moral rightness of saying no to the buying-up of people and of lands by English wealth and influence.

It was not, however, the radicalism of some of its more outré female novelists that aroused the fears of the more conservative elements in the English establishment when they contemplated Wales. In October 1806, Lord Bulkeley wrote to the prime minister of the day, Lord Grenville, warning him that the growth of Methodism in Wales was encouraging amongst the populace an extreme democratic spirit:

I cannot help attempting to draw your attention to the growth and increase of Methodism and Sectarism of every description and denomination in the Principality of Wales. The evil is of great magnitude inasmuch as their principles have a strong republican democratic bias . . . in short they hate all superiority of rank or super eminence.[109]

The Methodists themselves, however, denied any such radical tendencies, and repeatedly stressed their loyal adherence to the established order. The sixteenth rule listed for members to follow in their 1801 *Rules* book reads: 'That they do not speak evil of dignitaries, but that they conscientiously honour and obey the king, and all that are put in authority under him, showing all fidelity in word and deed to the government we happily live under.'[110] Given the severity with which the government was reacting to any incipient social unrest during this period of wars with France and fears of uprisings in Britain influenced by the French Revolution, thus to forswear republicanism was, of course, expedient. But though the Welsh Nonconformists, with the exception of the Unitarians, continued to profess their loyalty to the English throne and establishment long after the revolutionary period, it is unlikely that their belief in the equality of all men and women in the eyes of God, and the importance of democratic election when it came to the organization of each local branch of the sects, did not have their effects on their attitudes towards social hierarchies. The direct political response which Lord Bulkeley foresaw had to be held in check in order to safeguard the survival and growth of the sects, but that does not mean that their religious nonconformity did not under the surface develop a democratic strain in the Welsh.

Or so, at least, it is suggested in the work of a few anglophone women writers who were reared in, or adopted, Welsh Dissenting practices. Unexpectedly, perhaps, English was the language of the first woman to make a name for herself through poeticizing aspects of the Calvinist Methodist experience. An English-language volume on the life and work of the father of Welsh Methodism, Howel Harris, included an elegy which had appeared earlier in a poetry collection published in 1783, *Poems on Various Subjects, Entertaining, Elegiac, and Religious* by Jane Cave (1754–96).[111] In 1783 Cave was living in Winchester, but she was born in Talgarth, Breconshire, the daughter of an English exciseman and glover who had been converted to Calvinist Methodism on hearing Howel Harris preach. In early adulthood she moved to Winchester, probably to find work, and there married another exciseman, Thomas Winscome.[112] Her verse collection was well received; it went into four editions, with new poems being added to each edition. It is clear from many of these poems, the majority of which are religious in theme, that she felt a great respect for her father's religion, and something of a personal nostalgia for it. She attended an Anglican church while living in England, but a poem greeting her father on his eighty-first birthday compares the rituals of the Established Church unfavourably with the enthusiasm of his worship.[113] Again, in the poem 'On hearing the Rev. Mr. R—d read the Morning Service . . .', she criticizes Anglican preachers for the lack of commitment and substance in their sermons; they do not convey the passion of the Christian message, or succeed in awakening their audience from its torpor: 'The giddy hearer enters gay and vain, / And unaffected leaves the Church again'.[114] Her portrayal of Methodist worship in her poem on Howel Harris is considerably more favourable; according to her elegy, Harris's heart glowed 'with pure desire' to save souls, as 'Essential truth he faithfully declar'd' in his impassioned sermons.[115] And yet, for all these connections with the religion of Wales, it is perfectly possible that Jane Cave did not conceive of herself as Welsh. Wales does not even feature as a region of 'Western England' in her writing; she names Welsh places and leaders whose language would primarily have been Welsh, but she does not name the country or the language, let alone draw attention to their difference.

But Jane Cave's poetic voice in other ways sounds much more Welsh than that of many of her Anglicized sisters who did refer specifically to Wales in their fictional writings. Although she persuaded numerous members of the English gentry to subscribe towards the publication of her volume, and lists their names with pride in its opening pages, yet within the book the class hierarchies of English society are strongly criticized. One of her most arresting poems was apparently occasioned by a noblewoman's suspicions that she, Cave, as a woman of low social rank, could not have written the poems to which she signs her name. The 'Lady' is informed that 'there are beauties of the mind / Which are not to the great confin'd':

> Wisdom does not erect her seat
> Always in palaces of state:
> This blessing Heav'n dispenses round;

She's sometimes in a cottage found;
And tho' she is a guest majestic,
May deign to dwell in a domestic . . .[116]

– that is, in a servant, a role which probably Cave herself had filled at an early stage in her career. It is likely that the clarity of her recognition of class prejudice owed much to the democratic influences of her early upbringing within Welsh Nonconformist culture. In the poem to her father on his birthday she stresses that, though he was of low social rank, 'not the most exalted peer' could 'boast superior state':[117] hierarchical social divisions are irrelevant amongst the company of the elected saints. Her upbringing had not been privileged in the material sense: in the poem 'The Author's Plea' she describes the way in which she yearned in childhood for books and for leisure in which to compose, but without the money or time to realize her aspirations: 'The Muses seem'd to court me for their friend / But Fortune would not to their suit attend.'[118] But it had given her repeated experiences of seeing and hearing members of the so-called lower ranks caught up in profound contemplation and expressing themselves with intellectual and emotional intensity. The material circumstances of many of her fellow Nonconformists in Wales during this period were considerably more impoverished than her own, but Cave knew that their insignificance from a worldly point of view did not equate with their intelligence or capacity for self-expression, let alone with their spiritual worth.

It would appear, therefore, that the sect under whose influence Jane Cave was reared had developed in her a critical attitude towards class hierarchies. Another Welsh Nonconformist who expressed similar views with regard to the irrelevance of class divisions was the bilingual poet Elizabeth Crebar (née Morris, 1753?–1832). Crebar appears to have been living in Aberystwyth when she published *Poems, Religious and Moral* (1811), and to have been attending a Baptist chapel; she had been widowed, possibly twice, with children from both marriages,[119] and had been blind for thirteen years. Four of the thirty poems included in the collection are in Welsh, and the fact that one of those four is addressed to her brother suggests that Welsh was Crebar's mother tongue; given her surname, English may well have been the language of her second marriage. She appears to have received a relatively privileged upbringing, which in adulthood she abjured: 'At card-assemblies, balls, and plays, / I spent the blossom of my days', she says, dismissing her earlier pastimes with evident disapproval as 'tinsel'd toys'.[120] Rejoicing in having through the strength of her faith 'overcome the world',[121] like her fellows amongst the Welsh-language hymnists she uses metaphors drawn from mundane domestic spheres to represent her relation with Christ. In 'A humble answer to Revelation iii. 20', for example, she asks,

> And shall my Jesus stand, and knock in vain?
> At my polluted door he knocks again . . .
> Oh! what a black abominable nest
> I have, for to receive my heavenly Guest.[122]

One of her more interesting poems, however, suggests that her family strongly disapproved of her membership of a Nonconformist sect, for reasons to do with the loss in social rank it entailed. Her brother William Morris, a member of the land-owning gentry with an estate in Breconshire, apparently 'wrote to her to contemn her for taking baptism' ('anfonnodd ati i'w diystyru am gymmeryd ei bedyddio'). She responds by pitying him for mocking the 'meeting houses' and their congregations, without knowing that the 'best talents' ('doniau gorau') are to be found there. Were he to deign to attend such a gathering, she tells him, he and his family would 'hear great things from little people in the eyes of men' ('Gan rai bach y'ngolwg dynion, / Cânt hwy glywed pethau mawrion').[123]

One such 'little person' from the worldly point of view was the maidservant Maria James (1793–1868), who in 1801 emigrated with her family from her home in Snowdonia to settle in Clinton, Dutchess County, New York state, where her father found work in the slate mines. The family was Welsh-speaking, and Maria's mother held Welsh-language religious services at their home, attended by other Welsh Nonconformist immigrants to the area. At ten years of age James was sent as a maidservant to the home of her fellow-sectarian, the Reverend Freeborn Garretson, where her talent for poetry-writing, when it early manifested itself, was given every encouragement, particularly as it appeared that the act of composing did not interfere with her household duties: the lines came to her as she performed her domestic tasks. In 1839 her poems were collected by a friend of Garretson's, the Reverend A. Potter, and published under a title which emphasized the nationality of the poet – *Wales, and Other Poems*. For her early years were not forgotten by Maria: in her poem 'Wales' she recollects with loving nostalgia her upbringing in Snowdonia and the part the Welsh language played in it and in her religion:

> I heard Jehovah's praise
> In Cymru's native tongue,
> And hung upon those artless strains, –
> In rapture hung.[124]

In his introduction to the volume, the Reverend Potter draws the reader's attention to the implications of the publication with regard to democratic values. Maria James's talent, he says, corrects the misapprehensions of those who do not accept that creativity belongs equally to every social stratum:

> Men reason as if God dispensed the highest intellectual gifts with a partial hand; as if they must always fall *above* that social line which separates the wealthy and educated few from the poor and laborious multitude; when all experience shows that those gifts are showered often most prodigally among the humble and toil-worn.[125]

After the Wars of American Independence, democratic values constituted the foundation of the culture and constitution of the United States; unlike Jane Cave, Maria James did not need to criticize her society for not accepting that the maid as well as her mistress had the right to be a poet. Indeed, in one poem of hers she draws the reader's attention to her status with some pride. In 'The Broom' she greets her brush as her weapon not only against poverty, but also against physical and mental ill-health; sweeping the floor energetically not only provides her with her keep, but also eliminates cares and fatigues:

> Give me a broom, one neatly made . . .
> With this in hand, small need to care . . .
> What in the banks is said or done –
> [. . .]
> But when I see the young, the gay,
> Untimely droop, and pine away . . .
> Each day less active than before . . .
> With firmer grasp, my broom I hold.[126]

For all that, in the preface to her volume there is evidence to suggest that Maria James herself was not as self-professedly democratic as her master and his family. According to the daughter of the Reverend Freeborn Garretson (whose first name suggests, of course, the wholesale commitment of his family to the republican ideals of their new nation), it was she rather than her maid who was the democrat: 'I well recollect that, in our little disputes as children, she always took the aristocratic, and I the democratic side of the argument', she says.[127] To her co-Americans, then, Maria James's creative success was an example of practical democracy at work, but she herself did not profess to the same degree an allegiance to the values that she nevertheless embodied.

That, too, may arguably be interpreted as an aspect of her Welshness – democratic in practice but, at the beginning of the nineteenth century, not inclined to stress that fact politically, either for fear of reprisals in monarchical and gentry-ruled Britain or because of the degree to which the absorption in religious matters rendered insignificant all secular considerations. Nevertheless, when viewed through the prism of English-language culture, the egalitarianism of Welsh Dissent becomes more apparent. From conservative England's point of view, the picture of Wales afforded by the literature of the Romantic period was disturbing: the Welsh seemed extreme in their new-found enthusiasm, radical in their democratic control of their religious organizations, and prevented from joining the civilized world by their stubborn adherence to a primitive language. These views were to play their part in subsequent nineteenth-century attacks upon Welsh difference by the English establishment. When the most severe of those attacks, the 1847 Report on education, took place, however, the Welsh response was angry and defensive, to such an extent that the backlash to the attack gave rise to an increased, rather than depleted, Welsh patriotism. In the years between the Romantic era and the publication of the education Report a stronger, more protective sense of nationhood would appear to have developed in Wales. Why that was so was due in large part to the nation-building work of Welsh historians, poets and antiquarians. And from the 1820s to 1840s, when the main activity within the Welsh antiquarian movement had moved from the London Welsh societies to the societies of the 'learned clergy' of the Anglican Church in Wales, many prominent and influential women joined in their activities and contributed significantly to the building of the nation. Their work and its political and cultural contexts are the subject of the next chapter of this book.

2 Writing Ancient Britain

The local antiquarian, who takes delight in stupefying passing tourists with an unasked-for flood of historical information, is a familiar comic figure in late eighteenth- and early nineteenth-century novels set in Wales. A female of this species appears in Mary Barker's *A Welsh Story* (1798), 'a Lady Virgilia-ap-Howel, lineally descended from Boedicea on the mother's side, and claiming a very near relationship to *Howel Daw* [*sic*] through her father'. Because she was his only child, her father had prepared Lady Virgilia to take up a custodial role as upholder of the illustrious name of her ancestors; he had 'despotically taken her from the tutelage of her mother', 'notwithstanding she was bringing her forward in confectionary and tent-stitch', and taught her history and Latin in order to equip her as an antiquary. But he is denounced in the novel as 'a very eccentric figure', and his daughter, the unfortunate result of his experiment in female education, is mocked as a comic fool for all her learning. When introduced to Lady Cecilia Margam, 'the sole surviving female of the Ap-Gwergants', Lady Virgilia informs her that 'Nothing has given me half as much pleasure since the discovery of the Roman pavement at Caerwent, as to behold your Ladyship', but Cecilia's only response is a muttered 'Mercy G–d! what Goths!'[1]

As a female antiquary Lady Virgilia-ap-Howel would indeed have been an oddity in late eighteenth-century society. Though antiquarianism had by this time become for many Britons an absorbing pastime, it tended to be a male-only preserve: women were conspicuous by their absence from such learned circles. In her recent study *Antiquities: The Discovery of the Past in Eighteenth-Century Britain*, Rosemary Sweet explains why. Firstly, she says, women were disadvantaged by their usually meagre education, particularly their lack of Latin and Greek; secondly, they would not have acquired that familiarity with legal and historical documents that a gentleman of the period would have gleaned through dealing with his estate; thirdly, given the notions of gender propriety then dominant, they could not have ridden out at will, unaccompanied, to visit ancient sites; and lastly, they would have been forbidden access to public record depositories and the libraries of Oxford and Cambridge. Apparently only one woman, the historian Catherine Macaulay, was permitted the use of the reading room of the British Museum throughout the whole of the eighteenth century.[2]

In fact, if not in fiction, Welsh antiquarian circles at this time were no exception to this pattern of gendered segregation. Patriotic societies such as the Cymmrodorion, established in 1751, and the Gwyneddigion, established in 1770, commissioned and published for the new mass audiences of the printing presses Welsh grammars, dictionaries and histories, and edited bardic 'specimens' whose survival had hitherto depended on manuscript collectors.[3] As students of Welsh 'remains' they participated in what came to be known as the Celtic revival of the second half of the eighteenth century, instrumental in the construction of modern concepts of Scottish, Irish and Welsh nationhood. But the fact that London taverns constituted the most frequent meeting-places of these societies, made up as they initially were largely of London-Welsh members, meant that it was particularly unlikely that educated women would join their ranks.

Nevertheless, one area of the societies' activities did feature female pioneers. The antiquarians' editions and translations of the early Welsh bards offered to an enthusiastic audience new models of poetic style, liberated, in their primitive directness, from the eighteenth-century orthodoxies of verse. The translations which the clergyman poet and antiquary Evan Evans (Ieuan Prydydd Hir, 1731–88) published as *Some Specimens of the Poetry of the Antient Welsh Bards* in 1764, served to inspire many; Thomas Gray, whose 1757 ode 'The Bard' immortalized the historically inaccurate figure of the 'last Welsh bard', slaughtered during Edward I's supposed massacre of the bards during the thirteenth-century conquest of Wales, was not the only poet to be fired by the fruit of such researches.[4] A few female, as well as male, poets responded to the allure of these old texts, one such early enthusiast being Anne Penny (1729–84), née Hughes, the daughter of a north Walian vicar. Penny published in 1780 her own poetic versions of the poems 'An Elegy on Neest' (*sic*) and 'Taliesin's Poem to Prince Elphin'. Her versions are moving, particularly the 'Elegy', in which the poet, lamenting his dead princess, complains that 'Now equal to my eye the light or shade . . . / For she was dearer far to me than light'.[5]

Yet to read Anne Penny's work as that of a Welsh patriot, bent on adding lustre to the national culture of her native country, would be to ignore the thrust of her more original and far better known poem *An Invocation to the Genius of Britain*, published in 1778. In that work she argues strongly for a unified Britain capable of resisting the French and their effeminizing influence. Family ties bound Penny closely to British imperial aspirations: her first husband was a naval sea-captain, Thomas Christian, and her son, Sir Hugh Cloberry Christian, rose to the rank of Rear Admiral in the British navy. In her poem she addresses the 'Genius of Britain' as a force in operation 'from infant Time',[6] begging it to unite 'its jarring sons . . . in Freedom's cause', so that Britain's enemies, in particular the French, should be taught a lesson:

> Shew them that BRITONS were by Heav'n design'd,
> The brightest patterns of their erring kind;
> Worthy the spot to Freedom giv'n and Thee,
> 'This little stone set in the silver sea.'[7]

Nation-building is of the essence of the poem, but the nation in question is not Wales, but Britain. In a manner typical of myth-making nation-builders, Penny here presents that state which came into being with the signing of the 1707 Act of Union with Scotland as one which has existed with all its admirable freedoms and superiorities intact since the beginnings of a divinely ordained creation. She may have admired the aesthetic beauty of early Welsh-language poetry in what may well have been her first language, but her primary political allegiances are to Great Britain, not Wales.

Anne Penny's contribution to the Celtic revival serves as an early example of the dual manner in which it could operate. For some poets and antiquarians what was at stake was the national honour of Wales, reinvigorated now by the growing bulk of published evidence of its glorious past, in terms of both the military and cultural resistance it had offered to the Saxon conqueror and of the beauty and sophistication of its early poetry. For others, the same 'Ancient British' culture represented primarily the past history and antiquity of an English-ruled Britain which had now assimilated into its entity both the Welsh and the Scottish, and was soon in 1801 (in legal terms, at any rate) to incorporate the Irish.

During the early decades of the nineteenth century, when the main focus of the Welsh societies shifted from London to the parlours of the so-called 'learned clergy' in Wales and to the re-established eisteddfodic circles, a number of women joined the antiquarian ranks. These Welsh bluestockings published poems, histories and essays, and edited manuscripts and folk-song collections, with the Welsh past and its traditions as their theme. But the question remains: in so doing, did they see themselves as safeguarding and developing a specifically Welsh national identity, or as contributing the colour and vitality of historical Welsh difference to a new, united Great Britain? This chapter aims to explore that question further through investigating the work of early nineteenth-century female antiquarians and Celtophiles, and begins by focusing on those Georgian and early Victorian poets who, like Penny, incorporated in their writings reference to the Ancient Britons.

i. 'Saxon, think not *all* is won'

The word 'bard', from the Welsh '*bardd*' and Gaelic '*bard*', was originally in English 'a term of contempt, but idealized by Scott', according to the *Shorter Oxford Dictionary*. But Walter Scott was not, of course, the only author to redeem the figure of the Celtic bard in anglophone literature of the Romantic period: from Thomas Gray to William Blake, the bard and his world of prophecy and myth made frequent literary appearances, often annotated with references to contemporary editions of medieval poetry. The Scottish poet Anne Bannerman (1765–1829), for example, makes reference to Evan Evans's *Specimens of the Welsh Bards* in the footnotes to her *Tales of Superstition and Chivalry* (1802). The collection includes a long narrative poem entitled 'The Prophecy of Merlin', in which Arthur is sympathetically presented as a king who will return from the dead to lead his Welsh people to victory over their oppressors.[8] The Roman oppressors of the Ancient Britons also feature in a Welsh imitation of James Macpherson's Ossian forgeries by the Worcestershire-born poet Mary Darwall (née Whateley, 1738–1825). After settling in Newtown, Montgomery-shire, in 1793, Darwall published 'The Moaning of Ella the Daughter of Glendalwin', a presumably unintentionally comic pastiche in which the unfortunate Ella laments with much Ossianic mellifluence the loss of her sister, 'the blooming Elfrida, fearless and light of heart', raped and murdered by a Roman knight 'inflam'd with lawless love', and the death of her betrothed, the 'dauntless' Cadwal, as he sought to avenge her family's dishonour.[9]

The romance of Wales as a place of myth, as well as rebellion, also features in the poetry of Lucy Aikin (1781–1864); in her 'Cambria: an Ode', from *Epistles on Women, exemplifying their Character and Condition in Various Ages and Nations* (1810), Wales is portrayed as 'the poet-land', its vales echoing to the 'votive strains' of the Druids and bards.[10] A more sustained use of Welsh themes characterizes the poetry collection published by Janetta Philipps in 1811: the number of Welsh names among the list of subscribers to this volume would suggest that Philipps was probably Welsh by birth. Her longer narrative poems, often located in Snowdonia's distant past, concern the tragic misadventures of Welsh-named heroes and heroines, while in her sonnets she seeks to reanimate the 'strange songs' of 'Bards and Druids', commanding that 'wild enthusiast', Fancy, to 'awake the strains of ages past' so that heroes will again 'ride sublime' along the ridges of her mountain home.[11] As texts which recreated and idealized Wales's preconquest past, such material played a part, however small, in the resurgence of interest in Celticity, and helped to create a cultural atmosphere in which Welshness could feature as a positive aspect of one's identity, rather than a source of contempt.

The appropriateness of aspects of Welsh myth and history for the Gothic genre also aroused enthusiasm for Welsh locations amongst poets as well as novelists: such writers as Ann of Swansea and Mary Robinson include in their oeuvre Gothic ballads set in medieval Wales and peppered with Welsh-sounding names and doom-laden Druidic prophecies.[12] Robinson achieved some success with the ballad 'Llwhen and Gwyneth' (1782), based, according to her introductory note, on a sixth-century Welsh poem by the bard 'Tateisin' (*sic*).[13] The opening stanzas of the poem are indeed arresting: one dark night in 'Llathryth' the lady Llwhen rushes wildly and bloodily ('Each footstep mark'd with gore') through a thorny and tempestuous landscape ('the vivid lightning's transient rays / Around my temples play'), in the hope of once more meeting her beloved:

> 'When will my troubled soul have rest?'
> The blue-eyed Llwhen cried;

As thro' the murky shade of night
  With frantic step she hied.

'When shall these eyes my GWYNETH's face,
  My GWYNETH's form survey?
When shall these longing eyes again
  Behold the dawn of day?'

The names suggest that Llwhen and Gwyneth shared that type of 'romantic friendship' between women for which the Ladies of Llangollen were famed, but Llwhen's beloved when he eventually appears is in fact male, though disembodied. His first words are, 'I am thy GWYNETH's GHOST, sweet maid', and the poem proceeds to a tragic denouement, 'When, lo! to join the parting shade, / The MAIDEN'S SPIRIT FLEW!'[14] The popularity of the ballad was such that it provoked at least one poem of gratitude from an admirer of Mary Robinson,[15] and its influence, or the influence of poems like it, is apparent in later ballads of the period. In Janetta Philipps's collection, for example, the heroine of 'Enid' comes to the same ghoulish end as Llwhen, following the 'beckoning shade' of her beloved Owen to an untimely grave.[16] Welsh myth and legend also provide Gothic colouring in Philipps's ballad 'Edmund and Bertha': on 'Snowdon's bleak summits', Modred, the son of King Arthur and his betrayer in his last battle of Camlan, according to Philipps's footnote, becomes the fell murderer of Edmund and Bertha.[17] Nonsensical as this material may appear today, at the time its high Romantic flavour at least had the benefit of associating Welshness with exoticism, rather than contemptibility.

From the 1820s on, however, it was not Mary Robinson but a very different poet who most pervasively influenced the representation of Wales in nineteenth-century women's anglophone poetry. Felicia Hemans (née Browne, 1793–1835), the daughter of an Irish merchant and his aristocratic German/Italian wife, was born in Liverpool but her family moved to north Wales, to Abergele, when she was seven, and she lived there for next twenty-seven years, publishing her poetry from the age of fifteen to great acclaim. Cefn yr Ogof Pass, which loomed up immediately behind her childhood home, for centuries featured as a key battle-site between the princes of Gwynedd, in their strongholds in Aberffraw and Dolbadarn to the west, and the invading armies of the Saxon, Norman and Plantagenet kings of England, coming over Offa's Dyke to the east. According to the nineteenth-century Welsh historian Jane Williams, 'no spot in the Principality has been more thoroughly saturated with blood'.[18] At the time of the Browne family's arrival in Abergele, a revival of antiquarian interest in the area promoted a local enthusiasm for the old battle-sites and their histories, in which Felicia, as a young woman, participated. In 1821 she produced a series of lyrics to accompany the volume *A Selection of Welsh Melodies*, for which the airs had been collected and edited by John Parry; her contribution was largely made up of intensely patriotic poems, such as 'Chant of the Bards before their Massacre by Edward I' and 'Owen Glyndwr's War-Song', taking up arms on behalf of the Welsh nation in its struggles against its thirteenth-century conquerors and its later rebellions against English rule. In 'The Dying Bard's Prophecy', for example, a Welsh bard, after Edward I's final defeat of the last native Welsh prince in 1282, proclaims with his last breath, 'Saxon, think not *all* is won':

> 'Dreamer! that numberest with the dead
>   The burning spirit of the mountain-land!
>
> 'Think'st thou, because the song hath ceased,
>   The soul of song is flown?'

The poem is as much of a 'we will survive' anthem as any late twentieth-century Welsh-language protest song, and closes with the early nineteenth-century poet affirming that, though the medieval bard is long dead, 'yet the mountains stand . . . / And this is yet Aneurin's land – / Winds! bear the spoiler one more tone of pride!' Footnotes to the poem identify the 'spoiler' as England's king, and Aneurin as 'the noblest of the Welsh bards', as if to ensure that no reader could be in doubt as to the identity of the nations in conflict here.[19]

Given Hemans's extraordinary popularity throughout most of the Victorian period,[20] these poems probably did as much as Scott's to add allure to the figure of the 'bard'; they also, of course, promoted Welsh patriotism, and were appreciated as such by the Welsh societies of her day. Hemans was hailed as a 'poet for Wales' and made an honorary member of the Royal Cambrian Institution, to her gratification, it would appear. According to her own testimony, she regarded herself as a naturalized Welsh woman, and could at least read, if not speak, Welsh: some of her verses in *Welsh Melodies* are translations from Welsh-language originals.[21] In 1822, she composed and delivered in person a poetical address for a

London Eisteddfod, held under the auspices of the Cymmrodorion, in which she publicly presented herself as working within the Welsh bardic tradition. The poem eulogizes the Welsh bards of old as inspired by their historic freedom-fighters: it was 'the battle-fields of days gone by' and the 'tombs of heroes' which imbued the lines of the early medieval Celtic poets with 'bold freedom's soul'. Nor are their latter-day counterparts, in whose ranks Hemans, through her use of the first-person plural possessive adjective, includes herself, wanting in Welsh 'patriot-feeling':

> Land of the bard! our spirit flies to thee!
> To thee our thoughts, our hopes, our hearts belong,
> Our dreams are haunted by thy voice of song!
> Nor yield our souls one patriot-feeling less
> To the green memory of thy loveliness
> Than theirs, whose harp-notes peal'd from every height,
> *In the sun's face, beneath the eye of light!*[22]

Yet when Tricia Lootens, in her contribution to Angela Leighton's *Victorian Women Poets: A Critical Reader* (1996), suggested that 'Few poetic careers can have been more thoroughly devoted to the construction of national identity than was that of Felicia Hemans',[23] it was not to these poems, or indeed to the Welsh nation, that she referred. For Hemans's subsequent global fame rested primarily not on her *Welsh Melodies*, but on the poems in which she celebrated 'the stately homes of England',[24] and the imperial conquerors who issued forth from them to dominate so much of the nineteenth-century world. In 'England's Dead', for example, which immediately precedes 'The Meeting of the Bards' in nineteenth-century editions of Hemans's poetry, and which was also published in 1822, the poet, whilst ostensibly mourning those who fell in Britain's eighteenth-century imperial wars and its more recent engagements with Napoleon, also by implication glories in the worldwide expansion of English dominion:

> Go stranger! track the deep –
> Free, free the white sail spread!
> Wave may not foam, nor wild wind sweep,
> Where rest not England's dead.[25]

It would appear that Hemans served as the national poet of two nations at once, though the very existence of one of those nations, Wales, could be affirmed only at the cost of deconstructing the 'greatness' of the other, into which the first had by conquest been subsumed. Not-insubstantial numbers of England's military dead, albeit of an earlier date, rested beneath Hemans's own back doorstep in Abergele, but, in the poems in which she evokes the battles in which they died, it is to their opponents that she accords her moral approbation and patriotic fealty.

But though Hemans's position may appear complex and conflicted to modern-day readers, in her times it was not an uncommon response to the unification of Britain then in process. As a review of another poem of hers indicates, to celebrate any aspect of the heroic past of the Isle could be seen as a glorification of the new 'Great Britain', even if those earlier heroes had lost their lives in fighting for freedom from the English. In 1819 Hemans defeated fifty-seven competitors, including James Hogg, to win first prize in a Scottish poetry competition held 'to give popularity to the project of rearing a suitable national monument to the memory of Wallace'. The prize poem is very similar in its rhetoric to that of her *Welsh Melodies*: in it William Wallace persuades Bruce to take up arms against England by forcefully instilling in him the conviction that Scotland 'is no land for chains . . . / The soul to struggle and to dare / Is mingled with our northern air.'[26] The *Edinburgh Monthly Review* welcomed the judgement, rejoicing in the fact that 'a Scottish prize, for a poem on a subject purely, proudly Scottish, has been adjudged to an English candidate', because it 'demonstrates the disappearance of those jealousies which, not a hundred years ago, would have denied such a candidate any thing like a fair chance with a native'. The reviewer asserts that 'We delight in every gleam of high feeling which warms the two nations alike, and ripens yet more that confidence and sympathy which bind them together in one great family'.[27]

Binding together the inhabitants of the Island of Britain in one great family of fighters would appear to be the underlying purpose of Hemans's Welsh as well as Scottish verses. Her own immediate family was steeped in the ethos of British imperial militarism: two of her brothers were officers in the Royal Welch Fusiliers, and her husband, whom she married in 1812, was an infantry officer wounded in the Peninsular War. Her *Welsh Melodies* suggest that the Welsh should not forget their Ancient British courage in combat, but should resurrect and exercise it in the interests of present-day Britannia. In 'The Fair Isle', for example, native Britons are rallied in defeat after the coming of the 'spoiler', the Anglo-Saxon, by a bardic voice which prophesies their final triumph:

> Sons of the Fair Isle! forget not the time
> Ere spoilers had breathed the free air of your clime;
> [. . .]
> Ages may roll ere your children regain
> The land for which heroes have perish'd in vain;
> Yet, in the sound of your names shall be power,
> Around her still gathering in glory's full hour.
> Strong in the fame of the mighty that sleep,
> Your Britain shall sit on the throne of the deep.[28]

That last line presumably refers to Britain's recently established naval supremacy, the primary cause of Napoleon's downfall: adopting the voice of the bardic prophet, Hemans appears to be exhorting the Fair Isle's Celtic tribes to take an active, possessive pride in its nineteenth-century imperial triumphs as won in their name, Britons, to the sound of which now much power accrues. Yet her argument here is belied by her choice of terminology in her more obviously jingoistic poems, in which she consistently refers to Victorian imperial Britain as 'my England': 'the name of England' is the 'victorious word' which will 'Sound on, and on, for evermore', striking 'the fire from every heart / Along the banner'd line'.[29] Her allegiance was to Wales as a distinct, colourful 'member or joint' (to use the terminology of Henry VIII's 1536 Act) of that realm of England now, usefully for incorporative purposes, also known as Britain.[30]

As such, her stance was one that was often adopted by later poets, particularly English-born poets who visited or settled in Wales and developed an enthusiasm for the country. Janet Wilkinson, for example, who was living in Brymbo Hall in Denbighshire when she published her *Sketches and Legends amid the Mountains of North Wales: in verse* in 1840, but who describes herself as a '*Saesones*' (Englishwoman), echoes Hemans throughout her series of cantos in praise of Wales. Beginning by addressing 'most glorious Wales!' as the 'dominion of the free!', Wilkinson seamlessly knits together Ancient and contemporary Britons as if uncomplicatedly they had but one identity. A passage describing the Nant y Bele area in Denbighshire presents it as the natural fortress to which 'Britain's chiefs withdrew' in the face of the Saxon onslaught: 'high o'er the foes they bade Defiance wave'. But it goes on to suggest that such heroic British associations made the spot a particularly suitable setting for the tower monument recently erected by Sir Watkin Williams Wynn in memory of the battle of Waterloo.[31] That slippery word 'Briton' can in one line denote the Ancient and Welsh, and in the next the modern and imperial, as if they were one and the same.

Similarly, Augusta Eliza Marshall (1801–69), another 'Saesones' who settled in Denbighshire, in the introduction to her poetry collection *Odds and Ends* (1853) presents the Welsh as constituting 'the background of the British History, as well in race, as in political constitution and social character'.[32] 'Such were our fathers', she tells her English readers after having described Ancient British resistance to the advance of the Roman legions in her poem 'Snowdon', and goes on to ask 'shall we disown / The claims on us their rugged virtues give?'

> . . . rather trace we here the opening ray
> That, brightening into glorious Liberty,
> Inspired Britannia's sons alone to stay
> The march of universal tyranny.[33]

It would appear to be Great Britain's historical process the reader is invited to 'trace' here, rather than that of Wales. But to that history the 'Aboriginal British spirit' has contributed most nobly, according the appendix attached by Lady Marshall to her longer, book-length poem, *A Prince of Wales Long Ago: A Bardic Legend of the Twelfth Century* (1855), which lists the successes of Welsh battalions in Britain's nineteenth-century imperial wars to prove her point.[34] The poem, which recreates the events that lay behind Prince Madog's legendary leave-taking of Wales to discover America, opens with a paean of praise in favour of Lady's Marshall's adopted country, and of protest at its neglect within English-language literature:

> Land of the torrent, the lake, and the mountain,
> Land of the echo, the harp and the song!
> Why are no voices resistless recounting
> The charms and the triumphs to thee that belong?
>
> Land of true hearts, noble thoughts, and kind feeling,
> Land of the lovely, the brave, and the free!
> Why are not tongues in sweet harmonies pealing
> Their duty, their love, and their homage to thee?[35]

But she closes by reassuring her reader that contemporary Welsh-men pay homage first and foremost to their nation-state: for all their fighting spirit on the battlefields of the Empire, 'at home, the Ancient British are as obedient to the laws of their country, as they are ready abroad to lay down their lives for its honour and renown'.[36] Initially *A Prince of Wales Long Ago* read as an unequivocally patriotic Welsh poem, but within it, too, Welsh valour becomes an aspect of British valour, and the Welsh are presented as fully integrated into imperial Britain. It would appear that '*all*' is indeed 'won' by the Saxon, insofar as his struggle was with Wales; but according to some of the female historians of the era the situation was more complex, as the next section of this chapter explores.

ii. History of the Cambro-Britons

Early in the nineteenth century, before the centre of Welsh antiquarian activity had fully shifted from its original base amongst the London-Welsh to the parsonages of the literary clergy in Wales, a few women started to make their presence felt in the patriotic circles of the Welsh societies. In 1818, the *Cambrian Register*, a periodical established by the lexicographer and prominent member of the Gwyneddigion, William Owen Pughe, 'to investigate the hidden repositories, and to bring to light what may be deemed most rare and valuable' in the manuscripts and oral traditions of Wales,[37] published a poem entitled 'Lines on Bodfel Hall, the birth-place of Mrs. H. L. Piozzi'. Its readers are charged not to forget that they owe to the said Bodfel Hall in Caernarfonshire the fact that 'propp'd with care' the critic Samuel Johnson 'prolonged his course another stage', and was able to produce his *Lives of the Poets*.[38] Hester Lynch Piozzi née Salusbury (1741–1821) was herself the author of the poem, and while her claim to fame in Wales and in the pages of the *Cambrian Register* as the guardian of Johnson may not be self-evident, what is evident is her wish to feature in that patriotic periodical. During the period of her first marriage, to a wealthy London brewer, Henry Thrale, Hester Piozzi enjoyed that friend-ship recorded in her *Anecdotes of the Late Samuel Johnson* (1786), but in later life, with her second husband, she returned to settle in Wales, in Flintshire, and her Welshness seems always to have been of importance to her. Admittedly, she begins one of her autobio-graphical essays by mocking her countrymen for their alleged genealogical fervour: 'I heard it asserted once in a mixt company', she says, 'that few men of ever so good a family could recollect, immediately on being challenged, the maiden names of their four great grandmothers: they were not Welshmen.'[39] But the remark serves to initiate a detailed account of her own ancestors, the Salusburys, and their rich contribution to Welsh and British life. She appears to have associated Welshness with a vitality not encouraged within the English social circles in which she moved: of her own portrait by Joshua Reynolds she wrote,

> In these features so placid, so cool, so serene,
> What trace of the wit or the Welshwoman's seen?
> What trace of the tender, the rough, the refin'd,
> The soul in which such contrarities join'd![40]

The blandness of Reynolds's portrayal of her did not suit her sense of her own self-contradicting sharpness and rough directness, traits which she here appears to connect with her Welsh birth.

Yet for all her avowed Welshness, the degree to which Hester Piozzi consistently furthered a progressive view of Wales is questionable: contradiction seems to have been a feature of her writings generally, as well as of her personality. In her ambitious *Retrospection: or A Review of the most striking and important events, characters and situations, and their consequences, which the last eighteen hundred years have presented to the view of mankind* (1801) she makes no attempt to square her expressed identification with the Welsh in their freedom struggles and her horror of the modern-day Irish for attempting to wrest the same freedom from the same nation. 'Cold-blooded cruelty' denotes the English who killed Llewelyn, but contemporary Ireland is 'restless and turbulent, inflamed by blasts of irregular patriotism' in its farcical attempts to emulate the Americans and break the tie with England.[41] When she considers Europe in 1801, her reactionary abhorrence of the French Revolution is presented in extreme terms: France teaches its three-year-olds '*literally* to suck their fellow-creatures' blood' she says, and it has taught 'our own fools here in England' to sing, 'Plant, plant the tree, the glorious tree, / Midst blood and bones and slaughter', a reference to the 'Tree of Liberty' and its popularity with British radicals of the period.[42] Nevertheless, in the 1780s she had welcomed to her soirées in Streatham some noted radicals, including Helen Maria Williams (1761–1827), who herself was Welsh on her paternal side, though the death of her father in her infancy and her upbringing in England by a Scottish mother left little trace of any Welsh influences on her work. Williams's insistence on going to France in 1792 and the publication of her *Letters from France* (1794), sympathizing with the Revolution, soon alienated Piozzi, however.[43]

Many members of the Welsh societies flourishing in London during the years in which Hester Piozzi resided in that city would have felt greater sympathy for Helen Williams's radicalism: the 'Welsh Tom Paine', Jac Glan-y-Gors (John Jones, 1766–1821), for example, who published Welsh-language poems and pamphlets arguing the cause of republicanism and the rights of man, was first a member of the Gwyneddigion, and then, in 1794, one of the founders of the Cymreigyddion. But in 1818, as the hub of Welsh antiquarian activity moved from the London-Welsh taverns to the parlours of a group of Anglican clergy in Wales, the societies became more conservative in their politics. Walter Davies (Gwallter Mechain), vicar of Manafon, David Rowland (Dewi Brefi), curate of St Peter's, Carmarthen and John Jenkins (Ifor Ceri), vicar of Kerry in Montgomeryshire, under their leader Thomas Burgess, Bishop of St David's, established what came to be known as the Cambrian Society, with the aim of promoting bardism and of reanimating the eisteddfod, and thus, they hoped, improving the image of the Established Church amongst the Welsh.[44] Welsh antiquarianism could no longer be connected primarily with the more radical and progressive factions in society. And yet in one sense the newfangled societies proved more democratic than their forerunners: the Welsh parsonages of these learned clergy were more easily accessible to women than the London taverns of their predecessors, and the contribution of female members to the Cambrian Society's activities seems to have been particularly welcomed.

During the first of the eisteddfodau held under the Society's auspices, at Carmarthen in 1819, a woman was amongst the recipients of bardic orders: Elizabeth Jones, soon to be the bride of Ifor Ceri, was given the bardic name Eos y Bele 'on account of her literary merit', according to the periodical *Seren Gomer*. Eos y Bele tried her hand at English-language poetry, but does not appear to have published her work, and the few English-language verses by her which have survived do not suggest that in this case much was lost by her restraint.[45] Nevertheless, her presence in that first eisteddfod is an indicator of a changing attitude towards women amongst Welsh antiquarian ranks. In 1821, the *Cambro-Britain* announced that six women had been appointed members of the newly revived Honourable Society of Cymmrodorion,[46] now also led by the learned clergy. In their selection of women members, however, the Cymmrodorion could be accused not only of an Anglican bias, but also of outright nepotism: at least four of the six were the daughters or wives of prominent clergymen. Eos y Bele, by now wife of the vicar of Kerry, featured once again; another of the new members was Fanny Luxmore, of whom little is known except that she was the daughter of the Bishop of St Asaph. A third, Mary Richards (Mair Darowen, 1787–1877) of Darowen, near Machynlleth, in Montgomeryshire, was also the daughter of a clergyman, but she was a gifted harpist in her own right as well, and noted, too, for her 'zeal in the cause of Welsh Literature'.[47] The only substantial poet amongst the six was Felicia Hemans, but the two remaining new Cymmrodorion members were of significance as prose writers. Hester Cotton, daughter of Sir Robert Salusbury Cotton of Llewenni in Denbighshire, and a niece of Hester Piozzi, was an antiquarian who taught herself Welsh and apparently translated into English the Welsh-language classic *Drych y Prif Oesoedd*.[48] And lastly Angharad Llwyd (1780–1866), who had earlier in 1821 been made a member of the bardic order by the Cambrian Society, was now also enrolled amongst the Cymmrodorion's ranks.

Angharad Llwyd was that rare thing, an accomplished female antiquarian and historian of the early nineteenth century who was steadfast and uncompromising in her patriotic commitment to Wales: consistently, the English feature but as marauding Saxons or Normans in her histories, and the modern Welsh are exhorted to regain their 'love of freedom' in relation to their own history, not that of Great Britain. Like Mary Barker's fictional Lady Virgilia-ap-Howel, she had been tutored in classical languages and literature by her father, John Lloyd, the vicar of Caerwys until his death in 1793. John Lloyd had won fame as a collector and copier of Welsh manuscripts, and his daughter added substantially to his collection.[49] In 1827, she published an edition of Sir John Wynn's *The History of the Gwydir Family*, drawing attention in her introduction to the fact that the volume included the (historically spurious) account of Edward I's massacre of the Welsh bards, source of Thomas Gray's famous poem: 'this circumstance alone may stamp a most intrinsic value on the MS', she comments.[50] Five years later, her *History of the Island of Mona* won first prize in the Royal

Eisteddfod at Beaumaris, 'royal' because it was attended by the then Princess Victoria,[51] to whom accordingly the *History* was dedicated when it appeared in print. Nevertheless, and for all that Llwyd was also an admirer of Felicia Hemans and at more than one point in her writings approvingly quotes Hemans's Welsh lyrics,[52] her *History* is unambiguously Welsh rather than modern-day British in its loyalties. The term 'Britons' in Llwyd's writings always designates the Ancient Welsh, besieged as they were by the brutish 'Saxons'. In describing Egbert, King of the West Saxons, who invaded Anglesey in the ninth century, for example, she comments, 'There was something in the Saxon character, so little susceptible of those impressions which humanize and polish the rudest nations, that even at this period . . . they retained their native barbarism', thus neatly turning the tables on the more ubiquitous English account of the 'Aboriginal Britons' as primitives.[53]

Throughout her *History* Llwyd is intent upon correcting the misleading and inaccurate coverage of Welsh history given in earlier pro-English records; for example, when the historian Rymer describes Edward I as overcoming Llewelyn's 'rebellion', Llwyd comments, 'Such was the colour he gave to his lawless invasion of another's territory'.[54] The death of Llewelyn is mourned in her text as the end of Britain, and the territory over which he reigned is referred to as the remains of an 'ancient British empire', as if to pre-empt the later claims of English imperialism:

> With him closed the only sovereignty, which had remained of the ancient British empire; – an empire which had withstood the arms of imperial Rome. The fall of this people, as an independent nation, who had been forced into a long and unequal contest, in defence of their rights, with no other resources than valour, and a fond attachment to their mountains and liberties, will be entitled to a tribute of admiration and esteem, as long as manly sentiment and the love of freedom shall remain.[55]

Interestingly, in praising the courage of the Cymry, Llwyd draws particular attention to the valour of Welsh women. Quoting Tacitus, she relates how during the Roman period the women of Anglesey became so aroused against the invaders because of their indiscriminate slaughter that they themselves took up arms against the Romans and attacked them with great cruelty, causing havoc. Llwyd adds, 'This heroic spirit seems inherent in the women of Cambri, who in our own time, and without the aid of husbands or brothers, overcame and made prisoners, some hundreds of French-men, who had landed at Milford Haven.'[56] She is referring, of course, to the abortive attempt of the French to land in Fishguard in 1797, averted by a parade of scarlet-shawled local women from whom the French fled, mistaking them for British troops.

But even Angharad Llwyd is ready to accept that there may be some advantage in Britain once again, as in ancient days, thinking of itself as one nation. What she denies, however, is any place for the Saxon in this new confederation. According to her, Providence has

> formed of the several people inhabiting these Islands, one British nation enjoying unexampled blessings, whose destinies, temporal and eternal, whether under the denomination of Cimbri [that is, Welsh] – Cornish – Celts – Scotch – Irish, &c. are bound up still in the glorious and awful events connected with this Country, – a Country that has witnessed the rise and fall of the oppressive sway of the Roman, Saxon, and Norman Dynasties.[57]

Here the Saxons and the Normans are placed as firmly in the past as the Romans – oppressors all, whose sway fell after it rose. The Acts of Union with Scotland and Ireland have but served to reunite the old tribes, and has left only Britons in charge of the Islands – except, of course, for that '&c.'

The degree to which Angharad Llwyd's *History of Anglesey* is a radical text may be assessed by the discrepancy between its por-trayal of Anglo-Welsh relations and that of other contemporary histories, even those which on the face of it profess nothing but partiality for Wales. At the close of *Stories from the History of Wales* (1833), by 'A Lady of the Principality', a child who has just been regaled with a detailed history of the country asks his father, 'Don't you think, dear Papa, it would have been much better for Wales if it had never been conquered?' But the father replies, no, Wales is at peace now because it was conquered; had it not been it would have continued to fight with England, and would not have enjoyed 'the ease, freedom, or comfort' that it does at present.[58] Eliza Constantia Campbell (née Pryce, 1796–1864) was the 'Lady of the Principality'; though of Welsh parentage, she was the widow of a captain of the Royal Navy, and her loyalties were strongly with the new Great Britain.[59] A further publication of hers, *A Catechism of Welsh History* (1837), closes with another pedagogic father informing his son that, ever since the Act of Union, 'the Welsh have never been found behind their English neighbours in valour, faith and loyalty, when the cause of Old England has required their services', as if no 'Welsh cause' remained after 1536. 'We are all now, on the Island of Great Britain at least, one free, united, and happy people', he adds.[60]

However, 'A Lady of the Principality' does at times contradict herself or confuse her terms when it comes to attaching labels. In *Stories from the History of Wales* the Saxon is referred to throughout as 'the invader', and his opponents, the 'Britons' – not the Ancient Britons – are described as those who 'lost the sovereignty of the island'.[61] No attempt is made to explain the relation between the past 'Britons', who lost the Island to usurpers, and the present 'Great Britons', who inherit it as one happy family. As well as lamenting the fall of Llewelyn and his bards, Campbell also details with great disapprobation the punitive behaviour of Henry IV after the failure of Owain Glyndŵr's rising: 'During his reign', we are told, 'he instituted many very oppressive laws against the Welsh nation.' '[T]he finishing stroke to their independency was given by the statute 27 Henry VIII. chapter 26', she claims, apparently radically rejecting the 'happy family' rhetoric of the Act of Union and presenting it here as constituting the last act in the subordination and colonization of Wales. But at this point the Lady seems to recollect her ultimate goal of emphasizing Wales's current well-being, and she adds,

> Thus were these brave people gradually conquered into the enjoyment of true liberty; being insensibly put on the same footing, and made fellow-citizens with their conquerors; – a generous method of triumph which the Republic of Rome practised with great success till she reduced all Italy to her obedience, by admitting the vanquished states to partake of the Roman privileges.[62]

Yet the concept of being 'conquered into the enjoyment of true liberty' surely cannot be other than self-consciously paradoxical; further, after 1831, when Giuseppe Mazzini founded the Young Italy movement, to compare Wales's treatment under England to that of Italy under imperial rule would appear to invite a national liberation movement in Wales equivalent to the Italian Risorgimento, rather than to persuade the Welsh to be at peace with their 'vanquished state'.

And yet Eliza Campbell is no nationalist, or at least she is no Welsh nationalist: she stirs her audience up to protest against Wales's fate, only to chastise them for so doing. Her modern-day loyalty is unswervingly given to Britain, or rather, as she, like Hemans, persists in calling it, England, an England that includes Wales. To be thus caught between two contending nationalities without apparently experiencing the situation as fraught was, as we have seen, not uncommon at this time. As well as the poets discussed in the last section, another prose writer on Wales who exemplifies a similar ambivalence was the Scottish novelist Catherine Sinclair (1800–64). Sinclair visited Wales a number of times in the early decades of the nineteenth century, and the book in which she recorded her travels, *Hill and Valley, or Wales and the Welsh*, proved popular: it had already sold over three thousand copies by the time the second edition appeared in 1839.[63] Few travel guides have eulogized Wales as consistently as this text: Bangor and its neighbourhood, according to Sinclair, 'may truly be called the Paradise of Wales'; Aberystwyth 'seems peculiarly calculated for the promotion of health and happiness'; and 'travellers could not possibly discover any drive in South Wales otherwise than charming'.[64] Her admiration for Wales owes much to her sense of its history, in which its freedom fighters, particularly Owain Glyndŵr, loom large: from Llangollen to Dolgellau, 'Owen Glendower, long the admiration and the terror of his numerous foes', lurks in her imagination ready to attack round every boulder. As a fellow Celt, her sympathy for the conquered Welsh is on the face of it unambiguous; the Welsh castles feature in her text as straightforwardly the sites of the colonial oppressor. Of Edward I she writes,

> No one ever built castles in the air with more ease and frequency than this monarch did on the earth; for the Welsh were forced like the children of Israel during their bondage, to assist in building for a hard master; and many are the fortresses yet remaining, which they unwillingly erected to confirm the English oppressor in maintaining his tyrannical authority.[65]

And yet Sinclair has few words of praise for the inhabitants of the modern-day country through which she travelled; she likes their music, their history, and their language, too, but she finds them lacking in vitality and intelligence: 'though the Welsh be moral and amiable, they are generally far from clever', she concludes.[66] The intended reader of her book is clearly English, or possibly Scottish, but certainly not Welsh. She values the country largely for the recreational benefits it offers the traveller; its colourful past is of interest purely as history, not as an incitement to present-day national pride.

Nevertheless, the frequent references within such books as hers and Campbell's to the history of the Welsh as long-term freedom-fighters must at least have helped to keep the concept of Wales as a potential nation, and of its inhabitants as a separate people, alive in the consciousness of its early Victorian readers. But the writings and activities of another woman of English birth did far more during this period to establish Welsh nationality, and it is her contribution and that of the circle of like-minded women she influenced that are the subjects of the last section of this chapter.

iii. Lady Llanover and her circle

In the Royal Eisteddfod held at Cardiff in 1834, the prizewinning essay on the topic 'The advantages resulting from the preservation of the Welsh language and national costumes of Wales' began with a fanfare asserting the proud nationality of the Welsh. 'Nationality is a virtuous feeling . . . absolutely essential to public honour, and the security of every social community', declares the essayist, adding, 'there are no people amongst whom this interesting quality is more evidently manifested than the inhabitants of Wales'. It is because its existence 'has in an eminent degree contributed to the maintenance of national feeling' that 'well-wishers' of Wales should do all they can to preserve and promote the Welsh language.[67] At the time and for decades to come, few were more active and zealous in furthering that cause than the writer of the essay, Augusta Waddington Hall, later Lady Llanover (1802–96). Born in Llanover, near Abergavenny, to English parents who had purchased the estate some ten years previously, and married in 1823 to Benjamin Hall, MP for Monmouthshire, she used her own and her husband's not-inconsiderable wealth to enlarge Llanover House and establish it as a centre for the promotion and preservation of Welsh culture. In a border-country locality in which the Welsh language was otherwise rapidly losing ground during this period of intensive Anglicization, she funded Welsh-language schools, made a spectacular success of a series of lavishly celebrated eisteddfodau in Abergavenny, peopled her home and estates with Welsh-speaking servants and tenantry, established a harp factory to save the Welsh triple harp, did her

utmost to support the flagging Welsh flannel industry, and welcomed to Llanover House a coterie of like-minded Welsh and Celtic
aficionados.[68]

In her fervour for all things Welsh, Lady Llanover, or Gwenynen
Gwent (the Bee of Gwent) to give her her bardic name, had
probably been influenced by her godmother, Elizabeth Brown
Greenly (1771–1839), of Titley Court in Herefordshire. Lady
Greenly, whose own bardic name was Llwydlas, had herself done
much to promote the Welsh language and its heritage, most notably,
perhaps, as the patron of Iolo Morganwg, whose antiquarian
activities she helped to fund from 1806 to 1826.[69] Both women
were amongst the founding members of the Abergavenny Cymreigyddion Society when it was established in 1833, and both also
supported the Welsh Manuscript Society, which preserved Iolo
Morganwg's manuscripts: Lady Greenly was the only female member of that Society's committee.[70] Gwenynen Gwent seems to have
been particularly eager to encourage other Welsh women's interest
in patriotic and antiquarian activities: the Llanover circle included a
number of gifted women, such as the antiquarian Angharad Llwyd;
Maria Jane Williams, the collector of Welsh folk music; Charlotte
Guest, the translator of the *Mabinogi*; and the historian and
biographer Jane Williams, Ysgafell. Her generosity to her friends
and protégées was caring and personal; for example, when she was
convalescing from an illness under the care of Lady Llanover, Jane
Williams, addressed her in an unpublished poem as one who comes
'where'er she treads to bless, / And touch the springs of latent
happiness'.[71] The warmth of Gwenynen Gwent's hospitality, as well
as her not-inconsiderable eccentricity, is also evident in her book
The First Principles of Good Cookery (1867), which never misses
an opportunity to praise all things Welsh at the expense of things
English: not merely Welsh lamb, beef, toasted cheese and flannel,
but even Welsh haystacks, are manifestly superior to English ones.[72]
And in that book too she inserts a plea for the proper preservation,
not only of jelly stock and salt beef, but also of the Welsh language,
arguing that 'every *soul* had as absolute a right to the use of his own
language as the beasts and birds'. '[A]ny man', she says,

> would be considered insane *out* of these islands, if he convened
> meetings to propose that all nations should not only agree to learn one
> common language, but that each should abandon its own tongue *for
> the purpose* of the *better* cultivation of the human intellect, the
> preservation and diffusion of literature, and the maintenance of that

nationality which is the mainstay of religion and morality, and the support of the throne![73]

The final clause of that last quotation, however, alerts us to another, more unexpected, aspect of Lady Llanover's enthusiasm for the Welsh language: far from promoting division within the Kingdom, she sees it as actively supportive of the English monarchy. The same theme was also stressed in her 1834 prizewinning essay, in which she argues that the survival of the old language has helped to keep His Majesty's Welsh subjects free of the insidious modern taint of republicanism:

> amongst the various 'advantages' which have resulted to the Principality from the 'preservation of the Welsh language', we must by no means overlook the firm and hitherto impassable barrier it has presented to the progress of sedition and infidelity . . . those infidel principles which have of late been so successfully disseminated through the medium of the English press, which have been still more fatally sown in France, and against which our Breton brethren like ourselves have been defended by their language.[74]

Though revolutions may come and go elsewhere, within Celtic languages and Celtic cultures the old feudal order is preserved, it would appear. But as the Chartist uprising in south Wales at the end of the 1830s and the Rebecca Riots in west Wales in the 1840s were soon to make abundantly clear, the image of Wales which Gwenynen Gwent seeks to promote here has but dubious relation to historical reality. She seems ignorant, for example, of the late eighteenth-century republican tracts of Jac Glan-y-Gors, *Seren tan Gwmmwl* (A Star under a Cloud, 1795) and *Toriad y Dydd* (The Break of Day, 1797), written and distributed with the express purpose of disseminating among Welsh monoglot circles the ideas of the French Revolution.[75] A Welsh-language upbringing does not seem to have prevented Richard Price from supporting the American Revolution, or held back Robert Owen, the founder of the co-operative movement, from developing his socialist principles. But present-day realities seem always to have represented only obstacles to be overcome for Gwenynen Gwent in her pursuit of her own particular version of the Welsh dream.

In the second part of her prizewinning essay she turns her attention to Welsh costume, and here again a deeply conservative ethos underlies her arguments. Welsh folk traditions, if retained in the face of a corrupting modernity, not only save the peasant from republican and socialist sedition; they also save him, and in particular her, from the potentially disruptive dream of achieving upward social mobility. Lady Llanover is probably best remembered today for her creation and very successful popularization of the so-called 'traditional' Welsh costume for women: the high black beaver hat, trademark of the Welsh tourist-trap shop, was, in particular, her own invention.[76] Encased in Welsh flannel and helmeted in her hard hat, the Welsh woman will be armed against any aspiration to emulate the English leisured classes; instead, she will persevere with the traditional role of her mothers and grandmothers. '[T]he Welsh-women of the last generation were taught from their earliest years, as well under the roof of the freeholder, as in the cottage of the labourer, *that* proper pride which is derived from the practical knowledge and exercise of every variety of household occupation', Augusta Hall claims. But

> of late years a false *standard* of *respectability* has been established, which has in a great many instances effected such a change of costume, as is utterly incompatible with a proper discharge of *household* and *agricultural duties* – What woman, dressed in the thin and comfortless materials, now so frequently substituted for the substantial produce of the Cambrian loom, is capable of properly discharging the duties . . . which in every family . . . must entirely depend upon female exertions?[77]

The fact that Lady Llanover on every possible occasion herself wore the 'traditional' costume she had invented, and took great pride in her practical domestic knowledge, should not blind us to the import of this passage, which would keep all Welsh women, of the middling 'freehold' class as well as the wives of tenant holders, artisans and labourers, tied to the kitchen sink. In one sense it is true that the very active female model configured here might be said to constitute an improvement on the passive ideal of English middle-class feminine gentility current at this time, but, in that it places Welsh women firmly within domestic boundaries, it hardly constitutes any substantial amelioration of their position. What it does do is to posit an image of an ideal Wales as freed not only from the potential sedition of the working class, but also from the aspirations of an ascendant middle class, thus eradicating all threat to the supremacy of Lady Llanover's own class, the landed gentry. Both the Welsh language and Welsh costume, then, act to safeguard the happy families of feudal rule, which is represented in this essay as an essentially Welsh way of life. Given that these Welsh tribes, in Lady Llanover's vision of them, pledge heartfelt feudal loyalty to the English monarchy as their 'own' lords and masters, the result is an image of Wales as an atavistic niche of childlike charm, tucked safely away under the protective wing of the world's most powerful empire.

This picture of Wales won favour with many anglophone women writers, and remained of appeal to some well into the twentieth century; it reappeared in the romantic fiction of popular writers like Allen Raine (1836–1908) and Edith Nepean (*c*.1890–1960), for example, for all the former's somewhat sporadic concern with more realistic social issues. After its London publication in 1836, Gwenynen Gwent's essay seems immediately to have spawned a spate of publications on Welsh folk culture, such as Melesina Bowen's *Ystradffin: A Descriptive Poem, with an Appendix containing Historical and Explanatory Notes* (1839), a long book-length poem in which a Wordsworthian Welsh guide introduces an English tourist to the landscape and communities of rural Carmarthenshire, emphasizing in particular the folk customs of the area and their ancient wisdom. According to the guide, little has changed in these communities since the medieval period; their inhabitants live out their innocent existences under the sway of the passing seasons, with their appropriate ritual celebrations, and with little to fear except the possible sighting of a 'Fetch Candle or *Cannwyll Corph* [*sic*]', the portent of death to a family member.[78]

Yet in preserving a record of such customs, which were in fact in the process of being relegated to oblivion by the onward march of Dissent, such texts did future generations some service. In particular, the pioneering work of Lady Llanover's protégée Maria Jane Williams (1795–1873) saved for posterity a body of folk music that might otherwise have been lost.[79] Having gathered a number of old airs and their accompanying Welsh lyrics from the oral memory of local peasantry, Williams not only performed them publicly, accompanying herself on the harp or guitar, but, in 1844, edited and published them, under the title *Ancient National Airs of Gwent and Morganwg*, thus rescuing them from likely oblivion. The published collection provides another telling instance of Lady Llanover's indefatigable persistence when it came to the practical furthering of the Welsh-language cause: without her interference the lyrics accompanying the airs would not have been given in Welsh. An 1840 exchange of letters between Gwenynen Gwent and Iolo Morganwg's son, Taliesin ab Iolo, makes it clear how she fought to get the original Welsh words (or as close to them as propriety allowed) published alongside the music; the fact that she succeeded added significantly, of course, to the antiquarian and historical value of the publication. Yet her reasons for thus persevering, as given to Taliesin at least, are once again unexpected; she tells him that:

> Miss Wms induced me to take a good deal of pains to obtain the Queen's permission to dedicate a Vol. of her MSS. Collection of Welsh melodies. I did so on *express promise* – *Welsh* words should be added, and her majesty gave leave for Miss W. to dedicate Welsh airs *with Welsh words* to her, and sent a gracious message about her recollection of her Welsh subjects. Since this – strange to say – every effort has been made . . . to induce me to be satisfied without any Welsh words . . . I stood to my ground.[80]

It would appear that Williams's *Ancient National Airs* of necessity had to include the songs' Welsh-language lyrics first and foremost because Queen Victoria had been promised Welsh words, and so nothing else would do. Of course, Lady Llanover is here playing on the susceptibilities of her protégée when it came to pleasing the monarch, but her satisfaction with the Queen's 'gracious message' indicates her endorsement of the system of rank and patronage of her day.

Maria Jane Williams's volume was based on her winning entry to an 1837 Abergavenny Eisteddfod competition, sponsored by Lady Greenly, for the 'best collection of original unpublished Welsh airs, with the words as sung by the peasantry of Wales'. That Eisteddfod was also the occasion on which Lady Charlotte Guest (1812–95) first took the opportunity to discuss with the barrister Arthur J. Johnes and Tegid, the Reverend John Jones, her ambitious plans for translating the Welsh myth cycle, the *Mabinogi*.[81] After the publication in 1849 of the three-volume edition of her translation, in which she was aided by Tegid and Carnhuanawc, the Reverend Thomas Price, Guest was hailed as 'one of the most remarkable women of the Victorian age'; her work was received as a 'true description of the Celtic genius', and as such inspired Ernest Renan's *Essai sur la Poésie des Races Celtiques* (1854), Matthew Arnold's *On the Study of Celtic Literature* (1867) and Tennyson's *The Idylls of the King* (1859), the best-known poem of the Victorian era.[82] Critical opinion to this day rates Guest's translation as 'the most powerful Anglo-Welsh work to emerge from Wales in the nineteenth century', for the elegance of its style and its prose rhythm, 'somewhat in the style of the Old Testament'.[83] Yet had it not been for the incitement and encouragement she received from the Abergavenny Cymreigyddion and from her acquaintance with Lady Llanover, it may be doubted whether Charlotte Guest, for all her undeniable brilliance, would have undertaken so prodigious a literary enterprise: during the rest of her life her abilities manifested themselves more practically in philanthropic and business activities, and later in china- and fan-collecting, rather than in writing.

The fact that no adequate English-language translation of the *Mabinogi* at that time existed appears to have operated upon Lady Guest as a challenge, a clear opportunity to exercise her intellectual capacities in a worthy cause. She had started to learn Welsh in 1833, a few days after her first arrival in Wales as the wife of Josiah John Guest, owner of the Dowlais Iron Company, which she was herself later to run for a short period after his death in 1852, at which time it was the largest ironworks in the world. The daughter of the ninth Earl of Uffington – 'my blood is of the noblest and most princely in the kingdom', she wrote in her journal[84] – Lady Guest was an autodidact with a particular interest in philology: before her marriage she had taught herself Arabic, Hebrew and Persian, as well as the Classics. In the journals she kept throughout her life she records that she had 'given myself almost a man's education from the age of twelve when I first began to follow my own devices'. At times she despaired, however, of finding in her role as a Victorian wife and mother a suitable outlet for her energy and intelligence: 'I have learned that there is but one answer to the question I have so often asked myself "What can a woman do?" "Nothing!"', she writes in a journal entry for November 1840.[85] In that year, however, she had not only worked on the translation which was to make her famous, and helped her husband to run the ironworks, but also given birth to her fifth child. For all her own sense of frustration, Lady Guest in fact managed to do more than most to disprove the notion that a woman's role in the reproductive cycle disabled her for any other form of productivity. In January 1838, five days after the birth of her fourth child, she records with evident satisfaction that 'I got permission to set to work with my dictionaries on a fresh sheet of the Mabinogion', and on 11 September 1840, shortly after the birth of her sixth child, she explains that 'I always rally when I have plenty of work, and to-day I had cheques to draw for the Works and other things appertaining to business to attend to, besides correcting a proof sheet for the Mabinogion'.[86] In terms of her involvement with the ironworks also, her contribution was of immediate benefit to the women and children of Dowlais, as well as to the workers themselves: under her care Dowlais became the first place in Wales to offer evening-school education for adult men and women, in addition to excellent schools for girls as well as boys.

Such was the calibre of the women Lady Llanover gathered about her in Abergavenny; not only Charlotte Guest but also Angharad Llwyd, as we saw in the previous section of this book, and Jane Williams, Ysgafell, as we shall see in the next, contributed prodigiously to Welsh learning and culture. Not only through her own work, then, but also through that of other women she inspired, Lady Llanover added new and rich dimensions to her epoch's appreciation and understanding of Welsh difference. Nevertheless, she was what the historian Chris Williams, referring to her Gwent contemporary Sir Thomas Phillips, has termed a 'Unionist Nationalist',[87] whose allegiance was to Wales as a contributory nation to a greater Britain ruled by the English monarchy, rather than as a potentially sovereign nation justified in seeking its independence. At the same time, her contribution, particularly to the survival of the Welsh language, was important, and it was to become yet more so as the 1840s advanced. A singular event at the close of that decade saw the Anglican Lady Llanover working in tandem with some of the cultural leaders of the Welsh Nonconformists in a campaign aimed explicitly at raising the national self-consciousness of Welsh women. In this cause, largely because of Lady Llanover's involvement and that of members of her immediate circle, the forces of Welsh antiquarianism united with those of Dissent to further a new epoch of Welsh nation-building. But this development was of such key significance to the formation of nineteenth-century Welsh identity that it merits a chapter of its own.

3 Becoming National

The 1847 *Report of the Commission of Inquiry into the State of Education in Wales* 'painfully, but very effectively' forced the Welsh to reassess their national identity, according to twentieth-century historians: the experience was painful because of the shameful and debasing nature of the identity the Report attributed to them.[1] Jelinger C. Symons, one of the Commissioners who prepared the Report, gave it as his considered opinion that though 'the Welsh are peculiarly exempt from the guilt of great crimes', yet there are 'few countries where the standard of minor morals is lower'.[2] 'Petty thefts, lying, cozening, every species of chicanery, drunkenness (where the means exist), and idleness' were characteristic failings of the Welsh, a race incapable of greatness, even in crime, except for one large-scale vice: many of the witnesses to the Report informed its Commissioners that 'want of chastity is the giant sin of Wales'.[3] This laxity was said to be encouraged by the Nonconformist religious sects; according to the Report, Welsh women's sexual incontinence was 'much increased by night prayer-meetings, and the intercourse which ensues in returning home'. And it affected not just the lower classes in Wales, but the people as a whole: Welsh 'want of chastity', reported the Commissioners, 'is not confined to the poor. In England farmers' daughters are respectable; in Wales they are in the constant habit of being courted in bed.'[4] Courting in bed referred to the practice of acknowledged lovers getting to know one another better while lying, supposedly fully clothed, in the woman's bed. For lack of any other private space during the winter months, the practice had been common in other parts of rural Europe, too, before the mid century,[5] but the Victorian morality of middle-class England, with its stress upon the sanctity of the marriage-bed, was by now demanding a change in sexual mores.

The original aim of the Report was to collect information which would empower Parliament to take more control of Welsh education, and thereby, it was hoped, allay social unrest: in making his request that 'an Inquiry . . . be made into the state of Education in the Principality of Wales, especially into the means afforded to the labouring classes of acquiring a knowledge of the English language' in March 1846, the Welsh MP for Coventry, William Williams, had referred to the recent activities of the Welsh Chartists and the Rebecca Rioters as evidence of the need to invest in education in Wales in order to civilize a population prone to rebellion.[6] Monoglot English commissioners were duly sent into Wales to inquire into the levels of education attained by a population still in many parts monoglot Welsh. Not surprisingly, their report, when it appeared in December 1847, found that the standard of education in Wales in general was deplorably low, particularly with regard to the teaching of English. The Report connected this lack of educational access to English civilization with what it claimed to be the barbarity and primitive backwardness of the population, and went way beyond its brief in producing a document of unprecedented official condemnation of Welsh morality. No earlier report on Wales had preached on the ethical failings of the inhabitants so extensively, and none had previously focused on extramarital sexuality as a particular Welsh weakness. The Report demonstrated a typically Victorian double standard in its attribution of blame for heterosexual misconduct to the female partner only, and in its assertion that her corruption struck at the moral root of her society generally: according to Symons, 'want of chastity in women . . . is sufficient to account for all other immoralities, for each generation will derive its moral tone in a great degree from the influences imparted by the mothers who reared them'.[7] And not only was the Report misogynistic, it was also racist in its claims that the flaws it condemned belonged to the Welsh per se, as an aspect of their ethnicity, rather than as attributes belonging to any one group or class within the nation. In Wales the three-volume Report became notorious as the 'Treason of the Blue Books', 'blue' because of the colour of the volumes' bindings, and a 'treason' because Nonconformist Wales had hitherto pledged its allegiance and loyalty to the government that now turned on it and vilified it.

From the point of view of Parliament, there was only one way through which the Welsh could shed their debased image and that was through a rapid process of anglicization. In her recent study of the language of the Report, Gwyneth Tyson Roberts compares its underlying policies to those at the time being implemented by the British in India. The Blue Books were documents of cultural colonization, she argues; they labelled the Welsh way of life as degenerative, and emphasized the need to acquire English culture in its place, in a manner comparable to Thomas Macaulay's notorious 'Minute' on British policy in India, and his dismissal of Indian culture as barbaric. His policy, Roberts pointed out,

> depends precisely upon the creation of this sense of their own inferiority in the colonized people, who, in order that the power of the colonizer can be maintained, must be convinced that all legitimate authority (cultural, social and linguistic as well as political, economic and military) comes from the colonizing power, which alone has the ability to judge rightly themselves, their society and the world in general.[8]

The Blue Books, similarly, she argues, sought to erode the self-esteem of the Welsh to such an extent that they would accept anglicization as the only solution to their national shame. But the success of this policy was only partial, for such was the outrage aroused in Wales that it succeeded in drawing together in opposition to it not only the Nonconformists, but also a largely Anglican group of patriotic antiquarians, including Lady Llanover and her circle. Together they sought to reconstruct the Welsh as a homogeneous and virtuous people who deserved to survive as a nation, even on English terms.

The first lengthy critique of the Report was published in 1848 by one of Gwenynen Gwent's protégées, Jane Williams, Ysgafell (1806–85). Her *Artegall; or Remarks on the Reports of the Commissioners of Inquiry into the State of Education in Wales* is a sharp and incisive analysis of the way in which the Report attempts to justify an English governmental takeover of the educational system and curriculum in Wales. She exposes the Commissioners' technique of making much of all the negative evidence they had collected, and little of the more positive material. '[T]hey fictitiously theorize a national character out of the refuse dregs that have filtered through from its higher and better state', she says; 'Every beautiful picture that intrudes is unfavourably hung in the sub-gallery of an appendix . . . Nothing bad is omitted.'[9] Their next step was to attribute the blame for all these alleged national faults to the continuing existence of the Welsh language: with an irony which characterizes her style, Jane Williams says of the Commissioners' Report that,

> After multiplying and magnifying the short comings and mis-doings of the Welsh, the whole aggregate of imputed enormities is traced ... to one origin, their ignorance of the English language; in utter forgetfulness of that sad taint of hereditary sin which 'infects every person born into this world,' and alike the Saxon and the Celt. Gazing too intently upon their scarlet catalogues of Welsh iniquities, the Commissioners never fail to see, floating before their closed eyes, that verdant accidental colour the English language.[10]

She also draws attention to the utilitarian manner in which the Commissioners went about their task of examining Welsh school-children, and objects to their fixation with 'facts, facts, facts', even in contexts where factual knowledge was impossible. For example, one Commissioner reported the fact that a class of Welsh children could not tell him what an angel was as proof of their ignorance. But, says Jane Williams, what pupil in the best English public schools could give a correct answer if he were asked 'in the French language', that is, in a language foreign to him, to describe an angel?[11] Only a fool would rush in with an answer to such a question. But for the Commissioners this was merely another proof of Wales's need of the English language.

Though she mocks the Commissioners, and refers disparagingly to the 'transatlantic inelegance' of their style, Jane Williams closes her diatribe with an earnest plea to the people of England for help to withstand the likely intervention of their government in Welsh freedom. '[T]he direct and unprecedented interference of the Executive Government, in the regular management and inspection of Schools', demands, she says, 'Preventive Opposition from the watchful Friends of BRITISH LIBERTY.'[12] This final appeal is arrived at unexpectedly through a comparison between the Welsh situation under English rule in the nineteenth century and the situation of the Saxons under Norman rule during the early medieval period. When discussing the report of the Commissioner Ralph R. W. Lingen on the counties of Caernarfonshire, Glamorgan and Pembrokeshire, Ysgafell comments,

> 'My district,' says Commissioner Lingen, 'exhibits the phenomenon of a peculiar language isolating the mass from the upper portions of society.' This phenomenon which strikes the Commissioner so much is

not without many parallels in history. One of them, familiarly known, may be appositely mentioned here. Through many centuries Norman French was the language of the English Court, and of the English nobility and judicature, yet the depressed and despised Saxon clung to his native literature ... and at last it absorbed also the dialect of its conquerors. They would *if they could* have forced their language ... upon conquered England. They tried various means to effect it, *and they failed*.

Liberty is better appreciated, and far better understood in these days. England expects a liberal government, free trade, the freedom of the press, and universal religious toleration, yet oh, most strange anomaly! should her rulers deny to their Cambrian fellow-subjects mere freedom of speech, the use of their ancient mother tongue! Can tyranny itself go farther, unless it touch the unuttered and indignant thought?[13]

She is attempting to alert her English readers to the injustice of their government through reminding them that Britishness supposedly glories in the idea that Britons 'never, never, never shall be slaves'. If that is their boast, then they should defend their British neighbours, the Welsh, from the imperial nineteenth-century 'Normans', who once again are threatening the freedom of Britons in the name of an oppressive civilization.

Passages like the above indicate the value Jane Williams placed on history and what it could teach modern-day commentators; in 1869 she was to publish a *History of Wales: Derived from authentic sources*, described by Daniel Lleufer Thomas in the first *Dictionary of National Biography* as remaining 'even to this day the best history of Wales in the English language'.[14] Staunchly patriotic, the *History* focuses on early Wales and its battles against the Saxon and Norman invaders: Llywelyn, the last Prince of Wales, does not die until two-thirds of the way through the text, and much of the rest of the volume is devoted to Owain Glyndŵr's war of independence.[15] As the editor of the literary remains of the Abergavenny Cymreigy-ddion's founder, the Reverend Thomas Price, Carnhuanawc,[16] Williams's contribution to the antiquarian work of the Llanover circle was central, but her patriotism was evident long years before she ever met Carnhuanawc and Gwenynen Gwent. In a volume of poetry she published in 1824, at eighteen years of age, poems like 'A Welsh Bard's Lamentation for the Death of the Last Llewellyn Prince of Wales' mourn the prince's death as the end of Welsh freedom: 'Oh! Cambria mourn, dear hapless country mourn, / Our prince is dead, our liberty is gone.'[17]

Although an Anglican, Ysgafell was also deeply sympathetic to the Puritan and Nonconformist tradition in Wales. The bardic name she chose for herself signified her pride in her own republican ancestors: 'Ysgafell' was the name of the Montgomeryshire farmhouse in which her Roundhead forefather Henry Williams had campaigned with Vavasor Powell in 1654 against Cromwell's attempt to take power from the people during the Interregnum. Her respect for contemporary Nonconformist Welsh culture is indicated in the work by which she is best known today, her edited transcription of the oral autobiography of Elizabeth Davis, or Betsy Cadwaladyr, who travelled the world as a maid on the merchant ships of the British Empire, ending her career as a nurse with Florence Nightingale in the Crimea.[18] In her foreword to the autobiography, Ysgafell connects Betsy's strength of character and moral sturdiness with her upbringing in Bala, where her father, Dafydd Cadwaladyr, was a preacher with the Calvinist Methodists. 'Her character may appear to resemble rather the strength, the sternness, and the varied aspects of the mountains, than the soft sunshine of the Lake of Bala', says Ysgafell, but '[i]n principle, in moral excellence, and in religious orthodoxy, she was always steadfast. The influence of her home-training was manifested amidst a thousand inconsistencies, and many apparent contrarieties.'[19]

Clearly Betsy, at least, though reared amid the 'nightly prayer-meetings' of Welsh Nonconformity, was not easily led astray. In *Artegall*, Jane Williams rubbishes the arguments the Report puts forward on the alleged lack of chastity of Welsh women, first by pointing to the fact that many of the witnesses to the Commissioners found much to praise in the women of Wales, but their testimony was given no prominent place in the report, and secondly by referring to Ieuan Gwynedd's published statistics showing that there was only 0.8 per cent difference between the numbers of illegitimate births in Wales and those in England.[20] Her dismissive tone suggests that it was only to be expected that the Report should leap on any such scandalous complaint, and connect it with Nonconformity, in order to build up its evidence against Welsh-language culture. In her diatribe she effectively combined her knowledge of two worlds, the Welsh past and its present-day realities, to disparage the Blue Books, and in her writing generally she brought Wales into clearer focus, and sought to disseminate amongst an English-language audience greater knowledge and appreciation of the country. In so doing she was continuing her resistance to the 1847 Report, understood as an attempt to annihilate Welsh difference.

Neither was she, of course, the only Welsh writer to be thus animated into productive pro-national activity by the 'Treason of the Blue Books'. In response to the threat of the Report two of the most powerful, but hitherto divided, forces in mid nineteenth-century Wales were drawn closer together, the world of the Welsh Nonconformists on the one hand, previously not generally concerned with issues of national identity, and that of the Anglican Welsh antiquarians and nation-builders on the other. This chapter aims to explore the contribution of women writers to this new mid nineteenth-century 'marriage' of opposites by examining: firstly, Lady Llanover's involvement in the first Welsh-language periodical for women, edited as it was by an Independent minister; secondly, the literary construction of an ideal Welsh woman presented to post-Blue Books Nonconformist women for their emulation; and thirdly, representations of the Welsh in the fiction of some mid-century Anglican and anglophone novelists. The irony of the Welsh situation in mid nineteenth-century Britain, however, is that so overwhelming was the prestige of Great Britain as a modern, progressive and all-conquering imperial nation-state, that even as these embryo nation-builders sought to win appreciation for Welsh difference and create a homogeneous Welsh nation they were, in part, following English value-systems.

i. The sacred marriage bed

The first number of the first Welsh-language periodical for women, *Y Gymraes* (The Welshwoman, 1850–1), opens with an 'Address to the Welsh women of Wales' ('*Anerchiad i Gymruesau Cymru*') in which the author, who signs herself 'Gwenllïan Gwent' makes a capitalised appeal to the Welsh woman to 'APPEAR AS SHE IS' ('*YMDDANGOS YR HYN YDYW*').[21] This is not a liberal invitation to free self-expression; on the contrary, Gwenllïan Gwent has very definite, indeed dogmatic, views as to how Welsh women should by rights appear. As the patron of the new journal was Lady Llanover, and as the 'Address' in many instances echoes the ideas expressed in her earlier prizewinning 1834 Eisteddfod essay, the general critical assumption is that Lady Llanover was its author.[22] Three basic characteristics mark out the Welsh woman, according to the 'Address'. First, and most importantly, she must be virtuous: Gwenllïan Gwent insists that '*honourable* they must be, whether poor or rich, in moral superiority, if they truly deserve to be called Welsh women of Wales' ('*anrhydeddus* y rhaid eu bod pa un bynag ai tlawd a'i cyfoethog, mewn rhagoroldeb moesol, os gwir deilyngant eu galw yn "Gymruesau o Gymru"').[23] Secondly, she must speak Welsh, for 'we know that God has used our language as an instrument which will save us from much of the wretchedness that has corrupted the English' ('Gwyddom fod Duw wedi defnyddio ein haith fel offeryn a'n cadw rhag llawer o drueni a ddygodd llygredigaeth ar y Saeson'). Thirdly, she must wear the Welsh national costume, as devised by Lady Llanover. Only when clad in an armour of Welsh flannel and wearing the 'Welsh HAT' ('*HET* Cymru') will the virtuous Welsh-speaking woman clearly show herself possessed of that '*patriotic* spirit, which is not only the most innocent, but also one of the most beneficial things with which a human mind may be filled' ('ysbryd *cenedlgarol*, yr hwn sydd nid yn unig y mwyaf diniwaid, ond yn un o'r pethau mwyaf llesol y gellir llanw meddwl dyn ag ef').[24]

A dread motivates the 'Address', the fear that Welsh women are succumbing to the temptation of 'wearing *a mask*' ('gwisgo *mwgwd*'), an English mask, and are willing, even eager, to ape the English in dress and speech. Worse still, Gwenllïan Gwent fears that they are about to imperil the next generation by neglecting to speak Welsh to their offspring, and by dressing them, not in sturdy Welsh flannel, but 'in poor-quality cotton . . . which is not suitable except for the inhabitants of India' ('mewn cottwm gwael . . . yr hwn nid yw yn addas ond i drigolion yr India'). She tells her Welsh women readers that '*your* culpable neglect and your heart's betrayal will be the cause if your inarticulate descendants do not sound their first words in the language God gave to our forefathers in the morning of the world' ('Eich esgeulusdod beius *chwi*, a brad eich calon fydd yr achos, os na bydd i'ch hiliogaeth floesg swnio eu geiriau cyntaf yn yr iaith a roddodd Duw i'n henafiaid ym moreu y byd').[25] Her 'Address' is a trumpet-call, summoning Welsh women to the great battle to secure the survival of the race, and its redemption from disgrace: according to the logic of the piece, if the Welsh woman can be persuaded to become actively patriotic, then the future of the race and its language are assured.

For all the similarities between this 'Address' and the essay with which Lady Llanover triumphed at the Cardiff Eisteddfod, in one significant way they differ: here no connection is drawn between Welsh patriotism and loyalty to the English monarchy and government. Whereas in 1834 the Welsh language was (erroneously) praised as free of the taint of republicanism and French sedition, in 1850, after the Blue Books, it is still presented as 'pure' and 'innocent', but now no attempt is made to determine its politics vis-à-vis the English throne. With this omission, Lady Llanover's views were rendered more suitable for the periodical in which they now appeared, which was soon, in its third number, to include one of the most scathing indictments of British imperialism ever penned in Welsh, the essay 'Saisaddoliaeth' (The worship of the English). In this article the Welsh are warned against the fascinations and glamour of imperialism, which in reality is but greed and blood lust. 'We dare to say that the spirit of the nation is such that we would not wish to see the Welsh imitating it', the essayist says of England ('anturiwn ddywedyd fod ysbryd y genedl y fath ac na ewyllysiem weled y Cymry yn ei efelychu'), before proceeding to list England's crimes:

> A ydym yn barnu ein brawd yn galed? Atebed ei hanes o'i diriad yn ynys Thanet, ar oror Caint, hyd ei loddestoedd gwaedlyd yn y Punjaub a Borneo yn 1849. Carn lleidir y greadigaeth ydyw. Ymffrostia yn ei ddysg, ei wareiddiad a'i grefydd. Ei ddysg yw cigydd-dra, ei wareiddiad ydyw ysbail, a'i dduw ydyw ef ei hun. Nid ydym yn darlunio personau, ond ysbryd y genedl, fel y mae yn ymddangos ar ddalenau yr oesoedd.[26]

> [Are we judging our brother harshly? Let his history answer from his landing on the island of Thanet, on the borders of Kent, to his present bloody slaughters in the Punjab and Borneo in 1849. He is the arch thief of creation. He boasts of his learning, his civilization and his religion. His learning is butchery, his civilization is robbery, and his god is himself. We are not describing individuals, but the spirit of the nation, as it manifests itself on the pages of history.]

In drawing so direct a connection between the Anglo-Saxon conquest of post-Roman Britain and nineteenth-century British empire-building, and in characterizing both processes as crimes, the *Gymraes* essayist was making a strong stand: in 1850, in the year in which the Crystal Palace was built and the Great Exhibition organized to dazzle the world with the technology and wealth of Britain and her empire, few commentators condemned British imperialism so wholeheartedly.[27]

'Saisaddoliaeth' is unsigned, but its author is known to be Ieuan Gwynedd (Evan Jones, 1820–52), a Nonconformist minister and the editor of the periodical of which Lady Llanover was the chief patron. Their partnership marks a significant moment of connection and cooperation between Welsh Nonconformity and those Welsh antiquarians and nation-builders who still adhered to the Established Church. From this period on patriotism was to become part of the rhetoric of Welsh chapel culture, to an extent which would previously have been thought of as a secularization and abasement of 'true religion'. But it was a specifically Welsh, as opposed to British, patriotism, and as such could be opposed to the pro-imperial warmongering which, as we saw in the last chapter, marked the writings of some of the antiquarians. In an 1851 *Gymraes* article Ieuan Gwynedd pleads with his readers to adopt pacifism as their cause, and to give their support to the Peace Society and its secretary, the Welshman Henry Richard. 'O mothers and maidens of Wales', he cries, 'what will you do to bring to an end the practice of men selling themselves to kill others, and to get killed themselves?' ('O famau a rhianod Cymru, beth a wneir gennych i roddi pen ar yr arferiad i ddynion werthu eu hunain i ladd ereill, a chymeryd eu lladd eu hunain?'), and proceeds to answer his own question with a number of practical recommendations. 'As you rear your children', he advises Welsh mothers,

> na ddangoswch filwr iddynt i'w fawrygu ond i ymgroesi rhagddo, na adewch gleddyf, na dryll, na bidog ymysg eu teganau, ond megwch hwynt yn llawn casineb enaid at ryfel a'i effeithiau difãol. Na ddeued o'ch genau na chwedl na chân i draethu clod rhyfelwyr, ond dysgwch i'r rhai bychain egwyddorion bendigedig cyfiawnder a heddwch.[28]

> [don't present soldiers to them as admirable but as objects of dread, don't allow them a sword, or a gun, or a bayonet among their toys, but rear them full of soul hatred for war and all its destructive effects. Let not your lips utter a story or a song in praise of fighters, but teach the little ones the glorious principles of justice and peace.]

Y Gymraes is full of such pleas to the Welsh woman to behave according to higher moral principles than those which direct the lives of Englishwomen; Ieuan Gwynedd's hope was to demonstrate that women brought up in Nonconformist Welsh-language culture were more virtuous than their sisters elsewhere, rather than less so.

Like Gwenllïan Gwent in her 'Address', he too calls upon Welsh women to defend the good name of their nation and religion through publicly exemplifying their purity and high-mindedness: Welsh women must 'believe with all their heart and all their soul that "marriage and the *unpolluted bed* is honourable for all"' ('credu a'u holl galon ac a'u holl enaid, mai "anrhydeddus yw priodas yn mhawb a'r *gwely dihalogedig*"').[29] Of course, the virtuous woman had been an important figure in the growth of Nonconformist Wales before 1847, but she was not so often summoned publicly to manifest herself as such before the days of the Blue Books. Like the Old Testament heroines who had helped to rescue Israel from her enemies, Welsh women were now expected to engage in the fight to avenge their nation's wrongs. They too, like Deborah in the Book of the Judges, had to act the role of 'mothers in Israel' and lead their people out of shame and dishonour;[30] the term 'a mother in Israel', used as praise of the good Welsh woman, became a common trope in Welsh-language literature after 1847.

But though Ieuan Gwynedd was eager to defend the Welsh woman as a pillar of chastity, he also expressed his fear that the accusations of the Blue Books had within them an element of truth; courtship on beds was, after all, still being practised in many parts of rural Wales:

> Nid ydym i anghofio ... fod un drwg neillduol yn anurddo nodweddiad anrhydeddus Merched Cymru. Tra y dirmygwn hyd dyfnderoedd ein henaid y tylwyth sydd wedi ymdrechu gosod anniweirdeb Cymru allan fel pla arswydlawn ... etto nis gallwn gelu mawr ofid calon am fod achlysur i'r gelyn gablu. Hoffem weld Cymru yn BUR ... Hoffem glywed pob gwraig yn gallu cymharu dydd ei phriodas a dydd genedigaeth ei chyntafanedig, yn ddi-floesgni.[31]

> [We are not to forget that there is one particular ill which mars the honourable character of Welsh women. While we deplore from the depths of our soul the tribe that has attempted to portray Welsh lack of chastity as a fearful plague ... yet we cannot hide much heart anguish that the enemy should have cause to blaspheme. We would like to see Wales PURE ... We would like to hear every woman able to compare the date of her marriage and the date of the birth of her first-born without stumbling.]

And according to some of the male contributors to *Y Gymraes* there was no doubt about the matter: the unmarried Welsh woman was a shameless wanton, who must be chastised into changing her ways.

A series of articles published in the periodical on the typical behaviour of Welsh women in the country's various counties is nearly as condemnatory as the Blue Books themselves. 'Brodor', for example, in his prizewinning essay on the 'Social and moral condition of the women of Cardiganshire', castigates the women of his county with sweeping certainty and biblical rhetoric:

> Mae anniweirdeb yn clwyfo calon llawer mam, yn dinystrio cymeriad llawer geneth, yn tlodi amgylchiadau llawer teulu, ac yn peri i Seion Duw wylo dagrau o herwydd cwymp eu merched. Dyma eu pechod parod. Dyma y gelyn sydd yn lladd ein rhianod, ac yn ysbeilio gogoniant ein gwyryfon; a diau genym mai prif achlysur y trychineb hwn yw eu trefn garwriaethol . . . Trueni gweled merched glandeg a diwair, yn rhoddi eu cyfeillach i wylliaid y nos, yn ngoblygion y tywyllwch . . . Fel hyn, neidiant i ganol y tân yn wirfoddol, ac ymruthrant i'w dinystr eu hunain yn ewyllysgar . . . Mae effaith y cyfeillachau nosawl yn aml i'w gweled yn y ffeiriau, &c., yn y llygadrythu, y gwamalu, a'r crechwenu a wna llawer o'n merched ynfyd ac halogedig . . . Heidiant ym mreichiau eu gilydd, gan weryru ar eu ffordd i'r lladdfa, ac ynfydu ar eu taith i'r dihenyddle.[32]

> [Want of chastity wounds the heart of many a mother, destroys the character of many girls, impoverishes the circumstances of many families, and causes the God of Zion to weep tears over the fall of the girls. This is their ready sin. This is the enemy that kills our maidens, and steals the glory of our virgins; and we do not doubt that the main reason for this disaster is their system of courtship . . . It is tragic to see fair and innocent girls giving their company to the brigands of the night, in the folds of darkness . . . In this way they leap into the fire voluntarily, and rush willingly to their own destruction . . . The effect of the nightly meetings is often to be seen in the fairs, etc, in the ogling, the joking, and the guffawing of many of our foolish and tarnished girls . . . They flock in one another's arms, neighing on their way to the slaughterhouse, and fooling on their journey to the scaffold.]

It appears that the Welsh woman was no 'mother in Israel' after all, but a dangerous Jezebel – on fair-days at least. The fairs – the old enemies of Methodism – often get the blame for women's fall in *Y Gymraes*'s essays; of course, no mention is made in them of any possible role that Nonconformist evening meetings might play in the less sacred nightly congresses. According to Ieuan Ceredig, for example, 'a row of young women arm in arm' (*'res o ferched ieuainc yn mreichiau eu gilydd'*), eyeing up the local talent as they parade town streets on fair-day, tempt young men into offering them a drink in nearby taverns, thus bringing about their rapid descent down the slippery slope to perdition: 'women are the reason why so many of our young men have broken their Temperance vows, and turned into public and uncontrollable drunkards', he tells his readers ('y merched yw yr achos fod cymaint o fechgyn ein gwlad wedi tori eu hardystiad Dirwestol, a throi yn feddwon cyhoeddus ac afreolus').[33]

For the two years of its circulation, most numbers of Y *Gymraes* contained at least one article by a male correspondent repeating such accusations. It appears that one way in which Welshmen responded to the Blue Books was by scapegoating Welsh women: they and they alone were responsible for the nation's tarnished good name. In a 1952 discussion of the destructive psychological effects of the colonizing process, Frantz Fanon describes the function of scapegoating within colonialism. A colonized people are scapegoated as base and barbarous by the colonizing culture, eager to rid itself of the attribution of primitive traits by projecting them on to an 'other'. Within the colony, however, those educated in the ethos of the dominant mother country can only find a scapegoat for themselves within the lower ranks of their own people. Hence, a self-alienating and disempowering split develops within the national consciousness of the colonized: 'the young Negro, identifying himself with the civilising power, will make the nigger the scapegoat of his moral life', explains Fanon.[34] The Blue Books, in their representation of Welsh women as responsible not only for Wales's professed sexual libidinousness, but for all the nation's moral failings, had offered to Welsh men an obvious scapegoat for their so-called primitiveness. But in using it as they do in some of Y *Gymraes*'s articles, Welshmen are simply repeating the Report's accusations, as if in acceptance of the English judgement that the Welsh were 'backward' and had to change their ways.

According to political scientists, it is a characteristic feature of nations emerging from colonization that, in the attempt to engender pride in the new nation and rid it of the labels 'inferior' or 'primitive', they fall into the trap of valuing themselves according to the colonizers' terms. 'Nationalism', Partha Chatterjee argues in his book *Nationalist Thought and the Colonial World*, 'denies the alleged inferiority of the colonized people', but does so on the grounds 'on which colonial domination was based'.[35] The leaders of Welsh culture after 1847 could have responded by maintaining that Wales had a right to its own language and customs, whether or not they were seen as barbaric by the English: instead, their first concern appears to have been to prove themselves virtuous according to Victorian England's standards. Or rather, ideally, to prove themselves more virtuous than their neighbours, because of their Welshness, not despite it – that is, to beat the English at their own game. Welsh women, in particular, now had to demonstrate unequivocally their superlative virtue, as acquired through the teachings of Welsh Nonconformity. After 1847 the chapels took a heavily punitive and intrusive line on women's sexuality: errant female sexual behaviour was policed and penalized by public excommunication from chapel membership, and the prohibition was extended to pleasure-seeking pursuits generally as frivolous and potentially dangerous, particularly for women.

In the struggle to establish Welsh superiority what was needed were role models for the nation's women that were virtuous and worthy of emulation, but distinctively and unquestionably Welsh. No one was more aware of this necessity than Ieuan Gwynedd; though he did not succeed in attracting promising new women writers to contribute to his journal, he made as much as he could of the few available models. In his first address to his readers, for example, he refers to 'a most entertaining and educational book called MY SISTER'; 'the book as a whole is worthy of the attention of our young women', he says ('llyfr tra difyrus ac addysgiadol o'r enw FY CHWAER . . . y mae y llyfr oll yn deilwng o sylw ein Merched ieuainc'). He was also enthusiastic about an 1850 poetry collection about to be published by Elen Egryn, and expressed the hope that the volume would inaugurate a new wave of Welsh women's writing.[36] The next section of this chapter assesses the contribution that these texts, along with one other influential memoir, made to the image of the ideal Welsh woman constructed in response to the accusations of the Blue Books.

ii. Forging a female ideal

Margaret Jones (1814–41) came to fame after her early death by virtue of the memoir *Fy Chwaer* (My Sister, 1844) written by her brother Thomas Jones, Glan Alun. Her father, a comparatively prosperous merchant in Mold, Flintshire, gave his only daughter an expensive, English-language education in Chester, but after she had returned home, Margaret Jones experienced a religious conversion to Calvinist Methodism, and she dedicated the rest of her short life to the exigencies of her faith. When *Fy Chwaer* appeared it contained not only an analysis of the life and experiences of its subject, but also extracts from Margaret Jones's diaries and fifty-three of her letters. Because of the education she had received, Margaret Jones wrote in English, but her writings were translated into Welsh by her brother for publication in the memoir. As the foreword to the book points out, this was the first time that a volume giving so detailed a picture of a young woman's thoughts and feelings had appeared in Welsh, and it came to be hailed as a milestone in Welsh-language publication. After 1847, in particular, it was frequently referred to in Welsh periodicals as a book which proved without doubt the purity of young unmarried Welsh women, for all the Blue Books' lying reports to the contrary.

The differences between two reviews of the book, both published in the periodical *Y Traethodydd*, the first in 1845 and the second on the publication of the second edition in 1855, illustrate the book's role in the fight against the 1847 Report. In 1845 the anonymous reviewer barely referred to Margaret Jones, apart from applauding in the last paragraph the respect she showed to preachers; most of the review is devoted to promoting the reviewer's not very favourable views of women generally.[37] The tone of the second review is quite different, and makes it clear that by 1855 *Fy Chwaer* was considered a volume of great importance. The reviewer says,

> Byddai yn llawenydd mawr genym glywed fod yr argraffiad hwn wedi ei lwyr werthu: a bod galwad am un arall, ac un arall, ac un arall, nes y byddai lle i ni hyderu ei fod yn llyfr teuluaidd trwy holl Gymru, ac yn nwylaw holl ferched y Dywysogaeth.

> [It would make us very happy to hear that this edition had been sold out, and that there was a call for another, and another, and another, till we could believe it was a family volume throughout Wales, and was in the hands of every young woman in the Principality.]

It is Margaret Jones herself who is of importance now; the reviewer lays emphasis upon her 'purity' as 'refined by the religion of the Lord Jesus' ('wedi ei goethi gan grefydd yr Arglwydd Iesu'), compares her life favourably to that of celebrated Englishwomen, and concludes by suggesting that 'we cannot but think that Miss Jones was closer to *feminine* perfection than any of them' ('nis gallwn lai na meddwl nad oedd Miss Jones yn tynu yn nes at berffeithrwydd *menywaidd* nag un o honynt').[38] After the Blue Books, a purity refined by Nonconformist religion to a higher degree of perfection than that attained by any Englishwoman was precisely what Welsh leaders wanted to see in the nation's women.

Readers familiar with mid nineteenth-century English notions of 'feminine perfection' are likely to be taken aback by the memoir's portrayal of Margaret Jones's character, however. By 1855, a very distinctive model of the ideal female was proving highly influential in England: Coventry Patmore's praise poem to *The Angel in the House* (1854) was gaining much approbation. Patmore's 'Angel' is also 'pure', but not through any hard-won religious refinement; rather than having resolutely disciplined herself, she appears never to have awoken to the idea of sexuality. Her husband, the poem's narrator, says of her, 'she's so simply, subtly sweet, / My deepest rapture does her wrong.' Marriage has made no difference to the profound virginity of his bride:

> . . . her gay and lofty brows,
> When all is won which hope can ask,
> Reflect a light of hopeless snows
> That bright in virgin ether bask.

As she ages within the marriage, through some strange reversal the Angel in the House grows ever more childlike, 'More infantine, auroral, mild, / And still the more she lives and knows / The lovelier she's express'd a child.' 'Compact of gentleness', there is nothing in her world except love and tenderness. She does not act, think or develop, for all she could aspire to be she already is, by virtue of her gender:

> Marr'd less than man by mortal fall,
> Her disposition is devout,
> Her countenance angelical
> [. . .]
> No idle thought her instinct shrouds
> [. . .]
> And therefore in herself she stands
> Adorn'd with undeficient grace.[39]

As the nineteenth century progressed, Englishwomen of all classes were encouraged to take the Angel as their model.[40] But the ethos of the 'Angel' does not easily accord with the orthodoxies of Calvinism, as it was practised by Margaret Jones and other female members of the Welsh Nonconformist sects. Female Calvinists, like male ones, could be pure only by virtue of God's grace, not by virtue of their gender; the notion that through her sex woman was 'marr'd less than man by mortal fall' must have seemed particularly nonsensical to devout Bible readers familiar with the Book of Genesis. Such qualities as dependency, childlikeness and amiability were part and parcel of 'feminine perfection' according to Patmore's model, but there is no mention of such attributes in her brother's account of Margaret Jones.

Rather, it is the sternness of her character, as revealed in her letters and diary entries, that is likely to strike contemporary readers. She scolds herself mercilessly for the least carelessness or frivolity, confessing at one point, for example, that she 'spent an hour this afternoon in a friend's house, and returned home with a guilty conscience. To think that I could spend an hour in empty talk and frivolity! ... I have today sinned against the light, against commitment, and against conscience' ('Treuliais awr y prydnawn heddyw yn nhŷ cyfeilles. . . a dychwelais gartref gyda chydwybod euog. I feddwl fy mod yn gallu . . . treulio awr mewn ofer siarad ac ysgafnder! . . . Yr wyf heddyw wedi pechu yn erbyn goleuni, yn erbyn argyhoeddiad, ac yn erbyn cydwybod').[41] Such an innocent indulgence would have been part of the childlike charm of Patmore's Angel, but for the ideal Welsh women it was a sin. As her brother says, Margaret Jones's writings, particularly her letters, show that hers was a 'determined and resolute character' ('*caracter penderfynol a diysgog i'w weled ynddynt*').[42] There were three children in the family, but in 1834 the second brother, Kenric, died after a long illness. His brother admits that Kenric, before his illness, 'had lost his hold on the privileges of religion and had lived rather thoughtlessly' ('wedi gollwng ei afael yn ei freintiau eglwysig, ac wedi bod yn lled anystyriol ei fywyd').[43] To Margaret, her brother's illness was for him a necessary discipline. In one of her letters she tells a friend,

> Y mae i mi y gorchwyl gofidus o fynegi i chwi fod fy anwyl frawd wedi ei gaethiwo i'w wely . . . ac ofnaf fod pob gobaith o'i wellhâd wedi diflannu. Pa un bynnag ai byw ai marw a wna, y mae genym sail dda i gredu mai 'da yw iddo ei gystuddio'.[44]

> [I have the painful task of telling you that my dear brother has been confined to his bed . . . and I fear that every hope of his improvement has disappeared. Whether he lives or dies, we have good reason to believe that it is 'good for him to be chastised'.]

'Resolute' indeed was the response of Kenric's only sister to his illness; she shows little of that sweet tenderness and sympathy which was supposed to be of the essence of femininity, according to the contemporary English ideal.

For all that, on occasions Margaret Jones was capable of taking pleasure in very tender, 'melting' feelings; indeed, it would appear that the aim of all her tireless efforts to refine and strengthen her character was to arrive at such a state. But it is in a religious context only that the melting is to take place, not as part of her dealings with others, unless, of course, those others were themselves ready to share in the spiritual experience. After her conversion at eighteen years of age, she became a dedicated Sunday-school teacher, who wrote constantly to the girls in her class as well as to her friends, attempting to persuade them of the horror of such crimes as succumbing to the charms of a lover who was not a member of the same sect. She was forced to write sternly to one friend in May 1840:

> Yn awr rhaid i mi ddweyd wrth fy anwyl _____ y newydd wyf wedi ei glywed, ond yr hwn nis gallaf ei gredu; sef eich bod chwi, fy chwaer a'm cyfeilles hoff, ar fedr gwneyd cyfammod priodasol â gwr ieuangc, am yr hwn y rhaid i mi ddweyd ac arfer yr iaith fwyaf tyner am dano, nad ydyw yn byw yn ofn yr Arglwydd.

> [Now I must tell my dear _____ the news I have heard, but which I cannot believe; that is, that you my sister and dear friend, are about to enter into a commitment to marry a young man of whom I have to say, speaking most tenderly of him, that he does not live in the fear of the Lord.]

But she had been misled about the alleged romance, and in her next letter could tell her friend of her relief at hearing that the story had no foundation. In her joy, she becomes more expansive than usual about her own feelings: 'I always feel like a guilty sinner longing to return to favour with her Father', she says. 'Some of the promises are to me very sweet and melting' ('Yr wyf fi yn parhaus deimlo fel pechadures edifeiriol yn dymuno cael dychwelyd i ffafr ei Thad. Y mae rhai o'r addewidion i mi yn dra melus a thoddedig').[45] In another letter, she has relapsed into a cold and stony state, but longs for strong spiritual experience to break and melt the resistant heart: 'The following lines suit me entirely', she tells a sympathetic correspondent.

91

Fy nghalon, caled yw,
O! tyred Ysbryd Duw,
    Chwilfriwia hon!
Dwg fi at Grist a'i groes,
I wel'd ei farwol loes;
Dim arall gwn nid oes
    All ddryllio mron.[46]

[My heart is hard,
O! come Spirit of God
blast it to smithereens!
Lead me to Christ and his cross
to see his mortal pain;
nought else I know
can shatter my breast.]

It is no wonder that the letters of Margaret Jones pleased her contemporary readers so much: in them, a process of compelling interest to nineteenth-century Welsh chapel congregations is described with intensity and passion, that is, the experience of spiritual 'melting', in which the ego and its defences break up and abandon their resistance when confronted with the divine. Women refined in the furnaces of the Lord, to a purity sterner and harder than that prescribed for them in English-language culture, met the needs of the leaders of Welsh Nonconformity after 1847; they hoped the influence of Margaret Jones's memoir would 'lift up again many girls and mothers in Israel of a similar mind' to that of *My Sister* ('cyfodi llawer eto o ferched a mamau yn Israel o gyffelyb feddwl').[47]

Both Margaret Jones and Ann Griffiths are referred to as female ideals worthy of emulation in the foreword to the next important Welsh-language memoir of a woman, *Yr Athrawes o Ddifrif* (The Dedicated Teacher, 1859), but now another name is added to the roll-call of Welsh heroines, that of Mary Anne Edmunds (1813–58). Mary Edmunds's memoir was from the first consciously constructed as an answer to the accusations of the 1847 Report, and to the 'servile feeling of the Welsh . . . that there is nothing virtuous or praise-worthy unless it has come from central England, when in reality nothing makes us less than the English, except our own belief that we are lower' ('deimlad gwasaidd y Cymry . . . nad oes dim yn rhinweddol nac yn glodfawr os na fydd wedi dyfod o ganol Lloegr: pan mewn gwirionedd nad oes dim yn ein gwneyd yn is na'r Saeson, oddieithr ein gwaith ni ein hunain yn credu ein bod yn is').[48] Born in

Carmarthen to a devout Calvinist Methodist family, Mary Anne Jones taught at Rhuthun before being appointed as headmistress of a girls' school at Bangor, where she met and married John Edmunds, the headmaster of the neighbouring boys' school. Together with her brother, J. W. Jones, John Edmunds wrote and edited her memoir after her death.

Apparently, Mary Anne Edmunds was an early feminist, who believed strongly in the equality of the sexes. According to her husband,

> Byddai yn haws ei hargyhoeddi fod goleuni y lleuad yn rhagori ar eiddo yr haul, na pheri iddi gredu fod cyneddfau y rhyw fenywaidd yn wanach mewn un gradd na'r eiddo y rhyw arall. Priodolai y gwahaniaeth sydd mewn rhai amgylchiadau i'w ganfod rhyngddynt i'r dull maswaidd y bydd y rhyw fenywaidd yn cael eu haddysgu. Credai bob amser, pe caent eu harfer o'r dechreu i ymdrechu amgyffred pethau dyrys a dyfnion, y cryfhai eu meddyliau yn gyfatebol, ac y byddent yn ogyfuwch a'r rhyw arall yn mhob peth, ac mewn rhai pethau yn rhagori.[49]

> [It would be easier to persuade her that the moon surpassed the sun than to make her believe that the nature of the female sex was in any degree weaker than that of the other sex. She attributed the differences which in some circumstances are to be seen between them to the servile way in which the female sex is educated. She always believed that if they were encouraged from the start to struggle to grasp difficult and deep matters, their minds would be strengthened accordingly, and they would be equal to the other sex in everything, and in some things would surpass them.]

And in order to prove her point, during the time she taught in Bangor, Edmunds established a competitive examination, to take place every six weeks, between her pupils and the boys of her husband's school. He had to confess that 'the girls stood their ground very successfully, often excelling in many things, and never at any time far below the goal' ('fod y merched yn sefyll eu tir yn hynod o lwyddianus, yn aml yn rhagori mewn llawer o bethau, ac nid un amser ym mhell islaw y nod').[50]

Other fraternization between the schools' students was frowned upon, however; much emphasis is laid in her memoir on the sternness of Mary Edmunds's response to any hint of premarital liaison between the sexes, particularly amongst members of her sect. 'On hearing of people being tolerated as chapel members when they had fallen or were living in sin, she suffered to such an extent that it greatly affected her health', said her husband ('Wrth glywed am bersonau yn cael eu goddef yn aelodau eglwysig, a hwythau wedi syrthio, neu yn byw mewn pechodau; teimlai i'r fath raddau nes effeithio yn drwm ar ei hiechyd').[51] But unlike the Commission- ers of the Blue Books, Mary Edmunds was firmly of the opinion that in such circumstances the erring male was at least as much to be blamed as the female. In an essay on 'Modesty' included in the memoir, she argues that to scold a sexual philanderer publicly was, paradoxically enough, one of the responsibilities of modest women:

> Pe clywem, hyd yn nod un o ddylanwad uchel yn esgusodi beiau y boneddigion, neu yn rhoddi enwau tyner ar bechodau, na fyddwn yn rhy wylaidd i siarad yn hyf o blaid y gwirionedd. Y tafod, medd un awdwr, ydyw cleddyf merch; ac yn mha achos y gellir ei arferyd yn fwy anrhydeddus nag mewn amddiffyn y gwirionedd, ac agor ein genau dros y mud? Ceir clywed bechgyn ieuainc, weithiau, yn ymffrostio o'u hymddygiad gwael ac anfoneddigaidd tuag at un o'r rhyw arall. Y mae gwyleidd-dra yn peri i ni edrych arno gydag andfoddlonrwydd, a gwgu arno, nes gwneyd iddo deimlo ei iselder ei hun a'n purdeb moesol ninau.[52]

> [If we hear even someone of high influence excusing gentlemen's faults, or giving gentle names to sins, let us not be too modest to speak bravely on behalf of truth. The tongue, says one author, is the sword of woman; and in what way could it more honourably be wielded than in defending the truth, and speaking up for the dumb? Sometimes young men may be heard boasting of their poor and ignoble behaviour towards one of the opposite sex. Modesty compels us to look upon him with dissatisfaction, and scowl at him, till we have made him feel his own baseness and our moral purity.]

A militaristic morality is of the essence of Mary Edmunds's character; the tone of most of the extracts from her notebooks and poems included in the memoir is stern and self-critical in the extreme. In 1832 she writes, 'I do not ever remember spending my birthday, even in childhood years, without serious and weighty feeling: the idea of my responsibility to God for the time I'm given on this earth is incorporated with my first memories' ('Nid wyf erioed yn cofio treulio dydd genedigol, hyd yn nod yn mlynyddoedd mebyd, heb deimlad difrifol a thrymaidd; y syniad o'm cyfrifoldeb i Dduw am yr amser a roddwyd i mi ar y ddaear sydd wedi ei blethu a'm hadgofion boreuaf').[53] According to the Angel in the House ideal, women were perpetually childlike, but the 'Dedicated Teacher' seems never to have been a child in her life. The difference between her sternness and the emphasis on melting in the memoir *Fy Chwaer* shows how the Welsh feminine ideal hardened between 1844 and 1859, as part of the response to the Treason of the Blue Books'. The 'Dedicated Teacher' was welcomed as one who had 'reached the good grade of "a mother in Israel"' ('cyrhaeddodd radd dda "mam yn Israel"');[54] she was the answer to *Y Gymraes*'s call for a voice to raise Welsh women 'above shame and hateful mockery' ('*goruwch gwarth a dirmyg cas*').

That last quotation comes from a verse address to the women of Wales composed by Elen Egryn, or Elin Evans of Llanegryn (1807–76). Published in the first number of *Y Gymraes*, it hails that periodical as a new dawn for Welsh women, which will dispel the old stereotypes:

> Haera yr amaethwr weithiau,
> Nad oes eisiau arnom ni;
> Ond dysgu magu lloi yn raenus,
> Pesgi moch, a threfnu'r tŷ . . .
> Ond ca weld ei gamgymeriad,
> Wrth oleuni y GYMRAES.[55]

> [The agriculturist sometimes swears
> that we need to learn nothing
> except how to nurture calves well,
> fatten pigs and keep house. . .
> But he will see his mistake
> by the light of *The Welsh Woman*.]

In his turn, Ieuan Gwynedd greeted the publication of her poetry collection, *Telyn Egryn* (Egryn's Harp) on its appearance in 1850 as an occasion of 'national honour' ('anrhydedd cenedlaethol');[56] he and the book's editor, Gwilym Hiraethog, hoped that numerous Welsh women would be roused to emulate it.[57] In Elen Egryn they felt they had found a Welsh woman who evinced in her verses at least as much intellect and sophistication as any English woman of the period.

It is, however, a very Welsh type of literary sophistication that characterizes Elen Egryn's work. 'Don't linger, come away from the influence of the English / who murmur a strange language' ('Na thariwch, deuwch o duedd – Saeson / Sy'n sisial iaith ryfedd'), she says in her *englyn* 'I wahodd Miss Humphreys . . . adref o Loegr' ('To invite Miss Humphreys . . . home from England'),[58] and certainly there is little of the influence of that 'strange language' on the characteristic themes and style of her poetry. Elen Egryn was born in Llanegryn, Gwynedd, the daughter of the village school-teacher, John Evans, who passed on to her his enthusiasm for the traditional Welsh poetic metres.[59] She must have been well known as a poet before *Telyn Egryn* appeared, as many of the poems it includes are *englynion* or *cathlau* of greeting to other local male poets. Participating in a lively bardic culture, the roots of which stretched back to the pre-medieval period, she engaged in tradi-tional competitions using the intricate consonantal patterning of the old Welsh forms. Many of her poems resemble more closely the work of the eighteenth-century women poets, whose verses were preserved in manuscript collections, than that of the later Victorian poets who came immediately after her.[60]

And yet problems which belong very much to her own period seem to preoccupy Elen Egryn in some of her more startlingly original poems: the poem 'Sigh' ('Ochenaid'), for example, in which she addresses her own sigh directly, seems concerned with the disjunction between the social politeness now increasingly being required of women and genuine feeling. The speaker of the poem strives to present an urbane, gracious face to the world, but her sigh belies the pretence:

> Ochenaid, ai'th ddifyrwch yw
>   Datguddio briw fy mynwes?
> Er ymdrechiadau fwy na rhi',
>   Ti fyni ddweyd fy hanes.
> [. . .]
> Wrth gwrdd â chyfaill yma a thraw,
>   Er estyn llaw yn llawen,
> Dy chwedl yma myni ddweyd,
>   Er llwyr ddadwneud fy llonwên.

> Sigh, is it your pleasure
> to reveal my breast's wound?
> For all my numberless exertions
> you insist on proclaiming my history.
> [. . .]
> Meeting friends here and there,
> though I shake hands cheerfully,
> you your tale will utter,
> to the complete undoing of my smile.

Here, a code of social manners and niceties appears to have alienated the speaker from her own truth, but her sigh insists on making that truth heard. In the second half of the poem, however, the speaker reconciles herself with this voice she has sought to repress; the sigh becomes 'the only ointment for my pain' ('unig eli'm cur') because it exposes to her the hollowness of her self-betrayal. And as it is the only true part of her, it will be her sigh that will eventually, she trusts, take her up to heaven in its embrace (literally 'in thy lap': 'yn dy g'ol').[61] The poem 'Sigh' relates interestingly to the Calvinistic Methodist belief that the heart is stronger than the head, and its instincts truer than rational thought: body language here, as expressed by the sigh, is more genuine than the artifices of social conformity practised by the conscious subject. Elen Egryn appears to be exploring in secular verse that concept of the body as Christ's temple which more commonly found expression in the hymns of Ann Griffiths and some of her followers.

But truth's enemy now is not wantonness or lasciviousness but, on the contrary, a code of manners which demanded the maintenance of a stiff upper lip and the appearance of propriety, whatever the subject's feelings. As such, it can be said to be an Anglicized code: what was being asked of Welsh women by their own leaders was a public show of self-control, as defined by English notions of respectability. Given that in a poem like 'Sigh' Elen Egryn ultimately resists such pressures, her work can be said to be setting its face against Anglicizing influences, as they were increasingly affecting her society. In both her choice of metrical forms and her choice of themes, she is struggling to hold on to behaviour patterns prevalent in Wales before the Blue Books and its inculcation of notions of middle-class morality. As such, her work can interestingly be juxtaposed with a body of English-language fictions of the same era, in which English visitors to Wales respond to Welsh difference.

iii. Welsh livings

Accepting a Welsh living can endanger the mental health of the English clergy, according to one Scottish novelist of the period, Margaret Charlotte Jones (born *c*.1826), the daughter of Sir George Campbell, of Edenwood, Fifeshire, who married David Jones of Pantglas, High Sheriff of the county of Carmarthen, in 1845. The marriage was an unhappy one, or so at least a startling document published by Mrs Jones in 1862 would suggest. In *Glimpses . . . Mr & Mrs Jones of Pantglas* she accuses the High Sheriff not only of numerous affairs with their domestic staff, but of having infected her with a venereal disease: she 'had the disgust and mortification of discovering that he had imparted to her what could only have been self-acquired by intercourse with the lowest of the low'.[62] But the document seems to have been written primarily in defence of her own chastity, after her husband had employed detectives to spy on her relations with an Irish baronet, Sir Richard Levinge, whom she subsequently married in 1870, after David Jones's death.[63] Her novella 'The Welsh Living' (1853) is a much more sober affair than her autobiographical story, however. It recounts the trials and tribulations of Henry Percy, an English gentleman in reduced circumstances through no fault of his own, who is initially delighted to be presented with a Welsh living. Percy and his wife arrive in his Carmarthenshire parish full of good intentions and anticipating no problems:

> he understood Llandovery to be what is called an English parish; viz, that the church service was performed in the English tongue, and that, with the exception of a few aged persons, invariably worshippers at the meeting-houses, the young and general population had discarded the Attic vernacular, anxious to dissipate that cloud which had so long hovered around their social improvement and foreign intercourse, and had adopted the sister language.[64]

On finding that he is mistaken, and that the 'Attic vernacular' is the language of the majority of his parishioners, some of whom have no English, Percy, who is conscientious to a fault, initially rises to the challenge. With 'strict diligence' he applies himself to learn the 'harsh and guttural Cimbrian dialect', fortified by the knowledge that he is 'endowed by nature with an intuitive facility for acquiring languages'.[65] But he has not reckoned with Welsh, which according to Margaret Charlotte Jones is amongst the world's languages 'perhaps the *most* difficult of all to acquire'.[66] To the grave detriment of his health, Percy struggles manfully on, but to no avail. His parishioners commiserate with 'the poor sickly gentleman', but have to confess that 'what with the cough, and the sort of Welsh he has got hold of',[67] he is of little use to them.

Finally Percy is forced to accept the truth of the matter: for all practical purposes, Welsh cannot be acquired as a second language, for 'unless a person is born and bred in Cambrian hills, and acquires the dialect as a child, the natives never understand one'.[68] In 'The Welsh Living' Welsh is presented as a teasing mumbo-jumbo which

can belong only to the primitive Welsh; the vocal apparatus of more
civilized races, particularly that of the English, has evolved to so
much greater a degree of refinement that they are incapable of
uttering its syllables. Such bizarre exaggerations indicate the difficulty Victorian England had with accepting Welsh difference as a
contemporary reality. The struggle ends for Percy when, on
attempting to give a sermon in Welsh, he faints outright in the pulpit
from the stress and fatigue of his task; half-dead, he returns to
England, where he quickly recovers. Margaret Charlotte Jones
closes her text with a direct address to the reader to press home the
moral of her tale. 'The writer is not of opinion – far from it', she
says, 'that the Welsh language is worthy of preservation and
perpetuation.' However, though 'it may be, and doubtless is, advis-
able that English should be taught wherever practicable', yet 'large
masses of the natives are accessible only through the medium of the
Welsh tongue'. If they are not to be 'cut off from the consolations of
an orthodox and educated ministry, and too frequently forced into
the ranks of dissent', they must have native preachers.[69] Here, the
answer to the problems of the Established Church in Wales, then, is
temporarily to provide Welsh-speaking parsons for Welsh-speaking
parishes, while at the same time attempting to phase those parishes
out by busily promoting English-language education for all.

That is precisely what happens in Lilia Ames's *The Welsh Valley:
A Tale* (1859) when a Welsh-speaking clergyman, the Reverend
John Owen, arrives in his new north Walian parish armed with an
English wife. He discovers that one of the main obstacles retarding
the spiritual development of otherwise promising parishioners, like
Gwen Evans, the local miller's daughter, is illiteracy. During her few
years of schooling Gwen has never been taught to read Welsh, but
neither has she gleaned much English: she cannot understand the
Bible when it is read to her in English. Her new rector has the
solution. 'Here is the Book of God in both languages almost sealed
against you, my poor child', he tells her (presumably in Welsh); 'We
must see to this. Mrs Owen intends having a class at the rectory
every Wednesday afternoon at two o'clock; would you like to
come?'[70] That is, Gwen will be taught to read in English: Mrs Owen
has no Welsh, and it does not seem to occur to John Owen that it
would be simpler to teach Gwen to read in her first language than in
her second one. However, Gwen develops a profound admiration
for his wife, is overjoyed at being invited to become one of her
maidservants, and before the close of the tale is not only fully

literate in English but well on the way to becoming a refined young woman, who manages to win her erring father, the miller, back to the Christian fold. That is, of course, to the Church of England's fold: there is barely a reference to the Nonconformist denominations throughout the text, though their members constituted seventy-five per cent of Welsh congregations at this time.

Gwen's story is precisely the type of solution to Welsh cultural difference that Ieuan Gwynedd and Lady Llanover feared and fought against: through ignoring the existence of Welsh Dissent the novel makes Anglicanism and the English language the only route to spiritual as well as social progress in Wales. As much as Margaret Charlotte Jones's more overt protest, Ames's obliteration of Welsh-language religious alternatives is indicative of the manner in which sectarian battles were becoming national as well as doctrinal clashes in mid nineteenth-century Wales. 'In Wales the various religious sects appear . . . as antagonist powers', comments another woman writer, disapprovingly. The narrator of Amy Lane's *Sketches of Wales and the Welsh* (1847) is very much attached to her Welsh cousin Betsy, but disappointed to find in her 'a too exclusive preference of her own received religious doctrines'. Nevertheless, she finds much to admire in the manner in which Betsy's religious practice takes her beyond the conventions of social class. 'When my Cousin attended public worship, which she did most regularly, she would place herself in a corner, and amidst the humblest of her country people, pour out her desires and praises to the Divine Majesty', she says.[71]

Betsy appears to be a Dissenter, but her religious fervour would not, of course, have been out of place within at least one branch of the Church of England. Since its establishment in the late eighteenth century, the evangelical movement within Anglicanism had promoted amongst its congregations a value-system similar in many ways to that of the Dissenting sects. Indeed, when the evangelical Anglican Hannah More, one of the most influential and popular women writers of her day, first published her novel *Coelebs in Search of a Wife* anonymously in 1808, it was mistaken for a Methodist tract by some of the leading reviewers of the day.[72] In 1853 a Welsh woman published another novel which might easily have been similarly misinterpreted: Eleanor Griffiths's *World Worship* seems intent upon deliberately blurring the distinctions between Anglicans and Dissenters. The question of sectarianism, and of church or chapel membership, is dismissed as entirely insignificant in this fiction. Far from leading to dangerous excess, 'enthusiasm is the soul's health' in *World Worship*,[73] while adhering too slavishly to the secular mores of a debased and materialist society endangers mental balance. These maxims are spelt out in the novel's plot: the unfortunate Clara Smedley, a middle-class English visitor to Wales, is at the close carried to a madhouse in a state of 'confirmed and hopeless lunacy',[74] not because she has succumbed to religious enthusiasm but, on the contrary, because she has resisted it. Caught up in the trammels of 'world worship', Clara denied and betrayed the near-conversion she experienced on a wild Welsh hillside, under the guidance of Welsh evangelist Winfred Egerton. At a crucial moment, when Clara is close to succumbing, Egerton, to encourage her, describes his own conversion, which occurred when, after a period in which he had neglected his religion, he suddenly once again found himself, as if by whim, entering through 'the doors of a place of religious worship'. '"Was it a church or a Dissenting chapel?" asked Clara, with abrupt eagerness. "That is of little moment", replied Mr Egerton . . . "It was truth, urged with simple fervour, and with great plainness of speech."'[75]

Nevertheless, the evangelicals in this text are all Anglicans rather than Dissenters, albeit Anglicans of a markedly Low Church bent. Welsh hymns, however, have a peculiar importance for them: Egerton's daughter Margaret is at one point asked to sing 'that wild Welsh hymn that you say you learnt in your childhood'.[76] Egerton by now is dead, and the scene takes place in urban England, where Margaret lives with her guardian. But when she complies and sings the Welsh hymn, she sees again in the mind's eye the wild landscape in which she learned it, and hears 'the piping of the stone-chat' and 'the plashing of the busy rill' which sounded through her childhood. For the hymn 'has a voice which stirs the heart to its depths': 'there are tones that sweep over the heart's inner temple, and bring to light names and effigies that have been graven there for life'.[77] The novel does not divulge which Welsh hymn Margaret sang, but given the intensity of the characters' concern with religious conversion, the likelihood is that it belonged to the tradition of Methodist hymn-writers, with its strong emphasis on the conversion experience, and frequent metaphorical references to the Welsh landscape.

In contrast to *World Worship*'s Welsh heroine Margaret, Clara Smedley has been frozen and denatured by the sophisticated conventions of nineteenth-century English society. Though barely out of girlhood at the commencement of the tale, she has already succumbed to 'world worship', corrupted by her mother's ideas of what constitutes success in life for an attractive, and therefore potentially upwardly mobile, marriageable young woman. She is miserably aware that to associate as an equal with the lower classes who make up the ranks of Low Church congregations is likely to result in loss of status in the highly competitive middle-class marriage market. In *World Worship* becoming a Christian means breaking bread with the humblest in social rank: the existence of High Church establishments, in which one might not necessarily be kneeling and making one cause with 'poor, working people', is never mentioned.[78] All converts must accept that they will never socially be 'counted-up among the elite' because 'their indifference to the world's maxims' and 'their marked attention and hospitality to the most humble followers of their religious faith' will always alienate the upper echelons of their world, unless of course they too are of an evangelical bent.[79] Just as there was no real church except the Church of England in Ames's fiction, in *World Worship* there is no Church of England that is not Low Church.

In its insistence on the overriding importance of the moment of grace which constitutes the conversion experience, *World Worship* reads more like an early Welsh Methodist memoir than a conventional English-language novel of the period. Its persistent focus on rural Wales as the 'natural' landscape of true conversion, and on Welsh society as one in which, unlike in England, the heinous artificialities of social class have not yet entirely distorted the capacity of individuals to respond directly to their experience, also emphasize Welsh cultural difference, with authorial approval here being accorded to the Welsh rather than the English. That Clara, the novel's English anti-heroine, should become mad because she has resisted a very Welsh type of religious conversion, is particularly telling, given the propensity of women in other English-language novels about Wales, even those written by Welsh women, to run mad after their acceptance of strong religious experience, rather than because of their rejection of it.[80] In complete contrast to Margaret Charlotte Jones's novella, *World Worship* suggests that a sojourn in Wales can provide a much-needed corrective to the spiritual health of the English.

The preface to Eleanor Griffiths's novel tells us that it was written in Llandeilo Fawr, in Carmarthenshire, and that many of its characters are modelled on Welsh clergy of her acquaintance and their parishioners. In that it represents the Welsh as differing from the English because they are more virtuous, rather than less so, it accords closely with the view of themselves that the Nonconformist leaders of Welsh society sought sedulously to promote after 1847. But in this unusual anglophone text, the Welsh are praised for having turned their backs on the values of a more secular England, not for having been influenced by English mores. Eleanor Griffiths venerates the type of Welsh woman who lived only for her religion, not for the good name of her nation or her own reputation for respectability. The regular recurrence of religious revivals in nineteenth- and early twentieth-century Welsh life kept the tradition she admires alive to some extent, but ironically enough, even as she wrote, acquiring esteem in the eyes of the English, as a national cause, was for many women writers gaining predominance over the religious cause. As the next chapter indicates, some anglophone writers contributed to that national cause, too, though for others the increasingly overt clash between Wales and England led to bitter repudiations of Welshness.

4 Rebels and Reactionaries

The 1847 Report rankled as a live and still inflammatory issue for decades after its publication. In England, a stereotype of Welsh women as easily seducible proved particularly long-lasting, perhaps because it provided English audiences whose own sexual behaviour was being increasingly repressively policed by the strictures of Victorian morality with a source of vicarious relief: they were able to imagine that in Wales a lower level of sexual control still persisted. This type of reaction has been described by Edward Said, in his seminal study *Orientalism*, as one common to the relation between imperialist states and their colonies. According to Said:

> [F]or nineteenth-century Europe, with its increasing *embourgeoisement*, sex had been institutionalized to a very considerable degree ... [T]he various colonial possessions ... were useful as places ... where one could look for ... a different type of sexuality, perhaps more libertine and less guilt-ridden.[1]

Said, of course, is describing the West's relation to the East, and it may seem far-fetched to apply his account to Victorian England's relation to Wales. Yet English observers of nineteenth-century Wales are markedly persistent in associating Welsh women with promiscuity, for all the Nonconformists' attempt to combat such prejudice. Elizabeth Gaskell, for example, seems incapable of introducing a Welsh woman into her short stories without making her libidinous, if subsequently contrite. 'The beauty of Pen-Morfa', in a story which Gaskell published in *Household Words* in 1850, soon acquires an illegitimate child and a 'sad, wild, despairing look'.[2] Nest Pritchard in 'The Doom of the Griffiths' is also 'very giddy': 'She coquetted, and flirted, and went to the extreme lengths of

Welsh courtship, till the seniors of the village shook their heads, and cautioned their daughters against her acquaintance.'[3] Though Welsh elders are beginning to exert control over their womenfolk here, Gaskell's sense of the difference between the Welsh and the English idea of acceptable sexual behaviour no doubt lay behind her choice of a Welsh village as a setting for the heroine's betrayal in her full-length fictional study of the 'fallen woman', *Ruth* (1853). Ruth is not herself a Welsh woman, but in the 1850s it must have seemed appropriate to site a scene of seduction, pregnancy and abandonment in Wales. The 'extreme lengths of Welsh courtship' meant that the natives were used to such barbarities there. In his 1867 essay *On the Study of Celtic Literature* Matthew Arnold attributed to the Celt an 'undisciplinable, anarchical, and turbulent' nature,[4] and such traits when they manifested themselves in Celtic women seem in English novelists' eyes easily to translate into sexual irregularities.

So, at any rate, another 1867 publication, Ellen Wood's novel *A Life's Secret*, would suggest. Ellen, or Mrs Henry Wood (1814–87) was in the 1860s on her way to becoming one of the most popular novelists of her day: 200,000 copies of her best-seller *East Lynne* had been sold before the close of the nineteenth century. *A Life's Secret* concerns the evil ploys of two Welsh villains, Lawyer Gwinn and his sister Agatha. Lawyer Gwinn has established a practice in the English town of Ketterford, but his venture is not proving a success: 'Ketterford reviled him ... "A low, crafty, dishonest practitioner, whose hands couldn't have come clean had he spent his days and nights in washing them," was amidst the complimentary terms applied to him.'[5] His sister Agatha, who takes up her abode with him, is from the first presented as eccentric: 'The little boys call after her "the mad Welsh woman"'. The local doctor believes that, on the contrary, she is sane, but 'is one who can allow angry passion to master her at moments,'[6] in a manner characteristic of the Welsh, according to popular stereotype. In particular, Agatha is angry with an English gentleman, James Hunter, who she believes ruined the life of her sister, Emma. Emma had proved all too susceptible to the fresh charm of the young Mr Hunter when, on a visit to Wales, he lodged with her family: 'in the first dawn of manhood' he had paid 'that unhappy visit to Wales, which had led to all the evil'. The 'evil' is premarital sex, Wales's besetting sin as identified by the Blue Books, and here again, as in the Report, the female bears the blame: not only did Emma Gwinn permit

Mr Hunter to 'make acquaintance with her, but she allowed it to ripen into intimacy'. 'The blame lay with her', says the narrator, unequivocally.[7] After a secret marriage, James Hunter has to return to England alone; in his absence, Emma contracts a fatal illness and dies, but not without having confessed to her sister her married state and her husband's identity. Believing Emma dead, Hunter marries again, into a well-off English family, but his middle years are tormented by the return into his life of the repressed Welsh 'secret', in the shape of Emma's revengeful sister. Agatha persuades him that he had been misinformed as to his first wife's death, and that it is Emma herself who still lives, a lunatic in a London mental asylum, and not – as is in fact the case – a third Gwinn sister, Elizabeth, of whose existence Hunter had always been unaware. Having heard from his sister of the revenge she has taken, Lawyer Gwinn, seeing 'a glorious opportunity of enriching himself . . . went up to London, and terrified Mr Hunter out of five thousand pounds'.[8]

Bigamy – or, as in this case, suspected bigamy – novels were popular in the mid nineteenth century, and *A Life's Secret* sold well when it appeared as a volume, with its sales over the 200,000 mark by 1912. Its representation of the Welsh is of particular interest in the light of the likelihood that its author herself had Welsh antecedents. Mrs Henry Wood was born Ellen Price, the daughter of Worcester glove-maker Thomas Price and his wife Elizabeth Evans. Given their Welsh surnames ('Price' is derived from 'ap Rhys'), and the fact that the west Midlands city of Worcester, on the banks of the Severn, is not far from the Welsh border, it is likely that both Ellen Wood's parents hailed originally from Wales, though this possibility is not explored by her biographers: her probable Welsh ancestry appears to have been Mrs Wood's own 'life's secret'. Reasons for repressing any possible association of oneself with the Welsh as a race are evident in her novel's catalogue of stereotypical Welsh characteristics, all of which were familiar to readers of popular English-language novels in the second half of the nineteenth-century. In *A Life's Secret*, the Welsh are liars, cheats and money-grubbers, as they were in the 1847 Report, and their women cannot resist sexual temptation.

Another popular novelist of the period who deplored the Welsh and took pains to distinguish herself from them was Rhoda Broughton (1840–1920). Born in Denbigh, the daughter of an English clergyman, Broughton was living with a married sister in Rhuthun, Denbighshire, between 1864 and 1878 when she wrote her early novels, a number of which are located in Wales, much to their English heroines' chagrin.[9] In her first novel, *Not Wisely But Too Well* (1867), Welsh scenery has lost the appeal it had for an earlier generation of Romantic novelists: 'of the few people who know Pen Dyllas, most have an ill word for that small, dull, North-Wales watering place', says the narrator of that village in which she first introduces her heroine, Kate Chester.[10] Kate is reluctantly holidaying in Pen Dyllas, repulsed by the 'slovenly', 'unintelligent' locals, 'chattering harsh Welsh – the ugliest of all ugly tongues', when she enters upon the ill-advised romance with a visiting English officer which makes up the central plot of the novel.[11] Similarly, Broughton's third novel, *Red as a Rose is She* (1870), also opens in Wales, with a harvest scene spoilt for Esther Craven by drunken harvesters 'gabbling to one another . . . in that deplorable tongue which, we trust, will soon be among the abuses of the past'. Drunkenness is presented here as 'the normal condition of the Welsh';[12] the narrator asks her readers, 'Have you ever seen how drunk the masculine Cymri can be on market days, or what grievous old hags the feminine Cymri become towards their thirtieth year?' At one point she apologizes for making any reference to the Welsh at all: 'why am I drivelling on', she says, 'on the manners and character of this, to my thinking, not very interesting nation?' The answer is that 'the few men and women whom I am going to tell you about . . . are not Taffies, only they happen to have stuck up their tent poles in Taffy-land'.[13] Broughton's negative representations of the Welsh also appear to have been popular with English audiences, who between 1870 and 1877 snapped up twelve thousand copies of *Red as a Rose is She*.

Writers like Broughton and Ellen Wood abuse the Welsh with such a driven ferocity that they would appear to be motivated by a personal dread, the fear, perhaps, that unless they make their abhorrence very clear they will themselves be identified as Celts – a fate which has indeed befallen Rhoda Broughton, who, because her family 'stuck up their tent poles in Taffy-land', is included in Meic Stephens's *Companion to Welsh Literature*. But they were by no means the only mid nineteenth-century English writers to look askance at the Celtic connection: in his poem 'Hail, Britons!' the poet laureate, Alfred Lord Tennyson, advises his fellow countrymen to 'fear the neighbourhood / Of that unstable Celtic blood / That never keeps an equal pulse', warning the Briton against the 'Celt within'.[14] Celticity is more prized in Arnold's *On the Study of Celtic*

Literature, but only as a trace from the past embedded in the genes of the British, adding a strain of sensibility to their dominant Germanic sturdiness. Though he, unlike Broughton, is not so uncouth himself as to judge any language 'ugly' or 'deplorable', yet Arnold, too, declares that 'the sooner the Welsh language disappears . . . the better for England, the better for Wales itself', and argues for 'the fusion of all the inhabitants of these islands into one homogeneous, English-speaking whole' as a 'consummation to which the natural course of things irresistibly tends'.[15] But before the close of his *Study*, it becomes clear that Arnold, too, in his plea for a more appreciative recognition by the English of the past treasures of Celtic literature, is motivated by a dread, in his case the well-founded fear that the Celts, in particular the Irish, were in fact bent on repealing their union with England.

In Ireland, as in many other areas of Europe, the middle decades of the nineteenth century were marked by bitter struggles for national independence. In 1848 the leaders of the Young Ireland movement were engaged in an abortive rising, and in 1867 a larger, nationwide movement, led by the Fenians and financed by Irish-American backing, had to be crushed. On the Continent, 1848, the year of revolutions, saw nationalist uprisings in Poland, Czechoslovakia, Hungary and, in particular, Italy, where the longevity and eventual triumph of the Risorgimento compelled widespread recognition of the strength of that urge towards independence which can grip a people once they have conceived of themselves as a nation without self rule. Recent critical studies have examined the ways in which news of European nations fighting for freedom against imperial dynasties affected Victorian England, at a time when the British state was not only heavily embroiled in colonial expansion but threatened with regard to Irish unrest.[16] Given this historical climate, it is not surprising that from 1849 to the 1860s a number of Welsh writers, too, took a strong interest in such developments. What is surprising is that while the more reactionary works of novelists like Mrs Henry Wood and Rhoda Broughton are still today in print, those anglophone novels of the same period focusing on Welsh rebels and on Welsh nationalist fervour have almost completely dropped from sight, as if they never existed. It could not perhaps be expected that English readers would have shown much interest in them, though there were English women amongst their writers, but, given the scarcity of pre-twentieth-century English-language material sympathetic to the Welsh point of view, their revival in Wales is certainly long overdue. Accordingly, the first section of this chapter investigates the work of six mid nineteenth-century female novelists who were either Welsh and wrote of European nationalist uprisings, or who wrote historical novels fictionalizing earlier Welsh attempts to gain independence.

But these novels were being published at a time in which, more generally in mainland Britain, the resurgence of interest in national unification appears to have led to an increased desire to strengthen the coherence of Great Britain as a whole. Many anglophone texts located in Wales, if they do not, like those of Broughton and Wood, straightforwardly disparage the Welsh, are engaged in that subtler Arnoldian manoeuvre of praising Welshness as a phenomenon which has contributed richly to British culture in the past but is now entering the twilight zone. The passing of the Celt is accepted, if mourned, in the work of certain Welsh as well as English women writers in the 1850s and 60s, and the second section of this chapter examines their work. In other cases, particularly when the writer's publishing career was long-lived and spanned the decades, a shift in attitude towards the Welsh, from mid nineteenth-century abhorrence to greater acceptance, is discernible, accompanied by romantic plots which repeatedly close with the happy-ever-after mixed marriages of Welsh and English characters: the final section of the chapter examines instances of such fictions. In fact, it could be said that in the middle decades of the nineteenth century a cultural struggle was taking place within anglophone women's writing on Wales among, first, those who followed the very negative line of the 1847 Report on Wales; secondly, those who accepted the inevitable demise of Welsh difference but wished to mark its passing with a suitable tribute; and, thirdly, those who recorded Welsh struggles for independence and sought to reanimate Wales as a modern nation. It is with this last group of writers that the next section begins.

i. 'The war was holy – a war of independence ever is such'

The historical novelist Margaret Eliza Roberts (1833–1919) was born in Llanynys near Rhuthun in Denbighshire, of a Welsh father and English mother, but moved to England with her mother after her father's death and was educated primarily by her stepfather, Henry Latham, a Sussex vicar.[17] No doubt experiencing herself as uprooted, she did not settle in Britain in adulthood, but spent much of her life abroad, in Italy, France, Germany and Switzerland, and set most of her numerous fictions in those countries. She first came to fame with the publication in 1860 of her novel *Mademoiselle Mori*, set in Rome during the years leading up to and including the failed revolt against Austrian rule of 1848–9. Giuseppe Mazzini, the founder of the Young Italy movement, and Giuseppe Garibaldi, the military hero of the Risorgimento, have roles in the novel, though its central characters are a group of fictional young patriots, tragically caught up in the history of their times. Apart from one establishment spy in disguise in their midst, all the protagonists fervently believe that Italy's war against the Austro-Hungarian empire is 'holy': 'a war of independence ever is such', says the narrator.[18] For the novel's heroine, Irene Mori, Italy is 'the Sleeping Beauty . . . laid in a magic trance . . . and now . . . about to wake', and for Irene's lover Leone, soon to be killed in the siege of Rome, his country is 'the queen of kingdoms, long a bondslave', who 'holds out her chained hands imploringly to her children!'[19]

According to Gillian Avery, in her introduction to one of the children's stories by Margaret Roberts republished by Longman Press in the 1960s, her books are 'of unfailingly high quality, and have a quiet distinction about them which makes them stand head and shoulders above most of their contemporaries'.[20] Why her work for adults has suffered such a long neglect is unclear, but it may have to do with the fact that as a Welsh woman who wrote primarily of continental Europe she was of little interest to mainstream English criticism. But she should be of particular interest to Welsh readers who wish to acquire that sense of the past which, according to Roberts's characters, must be central to each individual's understanding of his or herself. At one point in *Mademoiselle Mori*, Irene complains to Leone of those Romans who refuse to involve themselves with the national movement, 'They have taken no interest in Italy's past, so they cannot understand the present.' He agrees: 'Exactly – a man cannot put his heart into a cause that he knows nothing about – the present would be a blank, or rather we should seem madmen, if we were set down in the midst of it without the past, out of which it has grown.'[21] Margaret Roberts's fictions emphasize the importance for every individual of developing an understanding of his or her origins and history, and of the history of the nation to which they belong.

From 1849 to the 1860s a group of women novelists were doing the best they could, in some detail, to inform Wales of some of the more turbulent episodes of its own origins and history. Though they made detailed use of the earlier work of the Welsh antiquarians and historians, their genre was the historical novel. In a recent study of twentieth-century women's historical fictions, Diana Wallace argues that a woman writer uses a historical setting in part 'as a fantasy space in which she can centralize a female consciousness and explore female fears and desires', in defiance of that more orthodox history largely constructed by males and generally singularly lacking in female figures.[22] Her argument is very pertinent to the majority of Victorian women's historical novels set in Wales, but as well as inserting a female consciousness into history many of them seem intent in their fictions on shifting Wales, too, out of the shadowlands it usually occupies in British histories.

In 1849 and 1858 two fictionalizations of the story of the fourteenth-century freedom-fighter Owain Glyndŵr issued from women's pens; both insist that Glyndŵr was no rebel but fought for a legitimate cause, and both create a romantic interest by focusing on the chieftain's daughters. The historically recorded predilection of Glyndŵr for using his daughters as bargaining points, in one case at least binding a powerful hostage to his cause by making a son-in-law of him,[23] captured these novelists' attention, and led them to imagine with some sympathy the inner emotional life of the daughters. In the anonymously published *Owen Glendower; or, The Prince in Wales* (1849), Eva, supposedly the chieftain's youngest daughter, is romanced by Edmond (*sic*) Mortimer, the fifth Earl of March, a possible rival heir to the English throne, who was in fact restrained under Henry IV's surveillance in London during the whole period of Glyndŵr's revolt.[24] But in the novel he and his younger brother Roger escape and find their way to Wales, Roger to follow Glyndŵr as his loyal page, and Edmond to fall in love with and eventually win Eva. The novel's author was Elizabeth Hardy (1793/4–1854), an Irishwoman, of whom little is known apart from the fact that she died alone and impoverished in a London debtor's prison;[25] startlingly, her end is prefigured in one of the most sensational scenes in her novel, when the sister of Lieutenant Poins, Prince Hal's companion in Shakespeare's play, *Henry IV*, dies betrayed, abandoned and starving in the rat-ridden dungeons of Rhuthun Castle. Hardy's novel abounds with such Gothic episodes, involving disguise and cross-dressing, with many references to bardic lore and superstition, often derived, or so it would appear from the book's careful footnotes, from Thomas Pennant's *Tour in Wales*, to which she also appears indebted for the less fictional aspects of her account of the revolt. Glyndŵr's only flaw in this text is his excessive superstitiousness; otherwise he is presented as 'brave, impassioned, and sincere', and very nearly successful in his attempt to restore to Wales its liberty, against enormous odds.[26] Though Eva and Edmond Mortimer decide they have seen too much of the suffering of civil war to wish to prolong the revolt, the text closes not with them but with the heroic unconquered chieftain: the narrator declares that it is 'no violation of truth to call the Cambrian chief unconquered; or represent him as making, till the last hour of his eventful life, a resistance unparalleled against the power of England'.[27]

If little is known of Elizabeth Hardy, even less is on record on Alice Somerton, author of *Ida: or, The Last Struggles of the Welsh for Independence* (1858); from her other publications she would appear to be an Englishwoman, but in her fictionalization of Glyndŵr's revolt she, too, sympathizes strongly with the Welsh cause. 'Who of us can turn to the last struggle made by the Welsh to recover their independence, and not see in it something both noble and mighty', asks the novel's narrator.[28] Somerton employs the same type of language and terminology to deplore the fate of Wales as Margaret Roberts's characters used to lament the history of Italy before its unification. In *Ida* the Welsh are the 'unwilling subjects of a country that enslaved them'; 'suffering the deepest oppression' they are ready 'to throw off the chain of servitude'.[29] The novel provides a blow-by-blow account of Glyndŵr's historical campaign, again enlivened by some fictional forays into the love-lives of some of the younger female members of his entourage. Its heroine is not in fact Ida Gwyn; though her name provides the novel with its title, she does little except swoon when her soldier lover unexpectedly returns. But Glyndŵr's daughter Jane has a central role and is fiercely patriotic, considering herself 'the daughter of a race more ancient, and far more noble, than those who oppress us'.[30] Given in marriage by her father to the treacherous Lord Grey, the Earl of Rhuthun, as part of the terms of a peace treaty, she remains loyal to the Welsh cause, and manages personally to secure the freedom of the text's two young heroes, Gilbert Ddu and Evan, both followers of Glyndŵr, when they are cast into prison by Lord Grey.

Alice Somerton appreciates that her nineteenth-century English audience may have difficulty empathizing with her characters' point of view: 'it is impossible for English hearts fully to appreciate the justice of that enthusiasm with which the Welsh people hailed the advent of a champion who was to lead them once more to struggle for their freedom', she says.[31] Nevertheless, though 'centuries have rolled by' and Wales 'has at last become so completely incorporated with England, that we feel loath to look back upon it as a nation distinct', yet the rebels' cause is presented as just and noble.[32] At one point, Glyndŵr, in despair at the collapse of his support, cries out, 'Oh! my country, I would have raised thee from a cruel subjection, and made thee again what thou once wert, but thy own children seem to love the chain that binds them, betraying even those that would set them free.'[33] In 1859, when Italy was once again in arms for its freedom, and Mazzini's Young Europe move-ment was gaining popularity across the Continent, such words must have had a strong resonance. Given the imagined nature of all nation-construction, and the degree to which it depends upon a sense of shared history, particularly shared grievances, it is likely that Somerton's work left whatever Welsh readers it found with a greater propensity to think of Wales as a 'nation distinct', all the more in chains because the English were by now 'loath' to see it as such.

Neither Somerton nor Elizabeth Hardy appears to have won a large readership as novelists, however, but one writer who did, the Suffolk-born novelist and journalist, Matilda Barbara Betham-Edwards (1836–1919), also published a paean in praise of Glyndŵr and emphasized the justice of his cause. In her *Holidays among the Mountains: or Scenes and Stories of Wales* (1860) readers are introduced to the story of that 'great man and patriot, who may well be classified with William Tell, with Robert Bruce, and with William Wallace', Glyndŵr, when a group of English tourists in modern-day – that is, mid nineteenth-century – Wales befriend a young inhabitant of the mountains, Jenny Roberts, and are told the chieftain's history in some detail by Jenny's father.[34] At one point the English first-person narrator, Beatrice, asks Jenny whether or not she thinks 'that Owen Glendower was in the right, you little patriot?' To which Jenny replies, 'Every one ought to be free . . . and if I had lived then, I should have helped him all I could.'[35] Such texts are not only informing English readers of past Welsh struggles for independence, but telling them that the patriotic desire for freedom is as alive in Wales in the mid nineteenth-century as it ever was, and that women and girls can be equally fervently inhabited by that longing as men.

Within the same decade, 1849–59, at least three other women writers published fictions on another historic Welsh rebel against the English throne, Henry Tudor. For all his success on Bosworth field, Henry VII is of course a far more complex figure in terms of Welsh patriotism than Owain Glyndŵr, given that in the event he did little for Wales except induce some of his supporters amongst the Welsh gentry to follow him to England and Anglicization. Nevertheless, the mid nineteenth-century texts which revive his memory all stress the Welsh patriotic fervour of his associates, if not of the man himself. *Owen Tudor: An Historical Romance* (1849), a highly adulatory account of the early life of Henry VII's father, appeared anonymously, but its author was Emma Robinson (1814–90); the daughter of a London bookseller, Robinson published a number of historical and contemporary novels before her death in London County Lunatic Asylum. Henry Tudor, like Owain Glyndŵr, was a 'Son of Prophecy' (*Mab Darogan*), according to the Welsh bards – that is, a hero predestined to fulfil the old prophecies and lead the Welsh to victory over the Saxons.[36] In *Owen Tudor* his father shares the same status: the novel begins with a scene in which Owen Tudor learns that Glyndŵr, before his final disappearance, had prophesied of him that 'sons of Kings thy sons shall be, / Kings of the waves and freer free!'[37] In his animosity towards the English, due to the humiliations they imposed upon his forefathers for their support of Glyndŵr's rebellion, Owen naturally enough takes this as a promise of a Welsh victory over the Saxons, rather than a reference to his role as the founding father of a British royal dynasty. Buoyed by such hopes, he journeys to France to try to raise French support for a Welsh fight for freedom, and ends up pitting himself against Henry V at Agincourt. Though his military prowess is not presented as outstanding, he is still destined ultimately to defeat Henry V by virtue of his superior strength in another capacity, as a lover. The novel closes with Henry V's betrothal to Catherine of France, but Owen, we are told, has already won Catherine's true love – as, indeed, he wins every female heart he encounters: the novel gives him the face and figure of a Welsh Adonis, capable of inciting in all women who behold him an 'electric shock' of irresistible desire.[38] Female sexual desire determines the destiny of dynasties, according to this novel, and, after Owen's eventual marriage to Henry V's widow and the birth of their son Henry Tudor, Welsh blood on England's throne will revenge the centuries of conquered shame.

Wales's humiliations and the rightness of her cause also feature in Frances Georgiana Herbert's far more sober *A Legend of Pembroke Castle* (1853). Relating in some detail the vicissitudes of Henry Tudor before Bosworth, Herbert emphasizes the fact that Henry was of Welsh blood and owed his eventual triumph to the Welsh nobility who supported him as the 'Son of Prophecy'. Sir John Savage tells his chosen prince that 'Wales waits his coming, as those who watch for the dawn of light: he is her son, and she longs to welcome him as a fond parent'. And Henry replies by assuring him that his 'first footstep upon British ground, shall assuredly be in the land of his fathers. From my own native home I will go forth to seek and win a crown.'[39] As well as emphasizing the significance of Wales, Herbert also gives a central role to a woman in her novel: a female recluse, apparently of Druidic origins, the 'descendant of that ancient and mysterious race who, from one generation to another, have made the secrets of hidden wisdom their chief study',[40] prophesies eventual victory for Henry, and intervenes semi-magically at various points in the text, saving him each time from certain death.

A similarly helpful supernatural figure, called the *Dewines* (female wizard), also haunts the pages of another novel set in Henry Tudor's times, *Gladys of Harlech, or, The Sacrifice* (1858), the first published work of a writer who usually signed herself L. M. S. Louisa Matilda Spooner (1821–90) was the daughter of the railway engineer James Spooner, who came to Wales from Birmingham to work for north Wales slate-quarry owner Samuel Holland.[41] Born in Maentwrog, Meirioneth, Louisa never married, but after her father's death settled with her brother Charles Spooner and his family in nearby Tremadog.[42] Her novel provides a lively example of what can be done in terms of re-imagining the past by inserting women as central agents in history. In *Gladys of Harlech*, a disinherited young Welsh woman proves pivotal both to the success of Henry Tudor, and to the righting of Welsh wrongs after his ascension to the English throne. The Tudor monarch himself is by no means the hero of this narrative, and would have done little or nothing to help Wales, had it not been for Gladys's campaign. Hers is the 'sacrifice' alluded to in the novel's title: with the plaintive cry of 'Ethelred, Ethelred, would that you were not a Saxon!'[43] she gives up her English lover in order to devote herself to Wales and 'her people', hard besieged as they are by the 'cursed Saxons'.[44]

Rightful heir of Harlech Castle, Gladys has been displaced by its evil English warden, Edward Stacey, who says of the Welsh, 'I abominate the whole race, were I king of England I would extirpate every living man of them from the soil.'[45] But the enterprise and forethought of a living Welsh woman prove his downfall. Before the battle of Bosworth, Gladys travels to France to beg Harry Tudor to remember his Welsh blood once he is made king:

> 'Henry, future King of England!' cried she, 'you who are blood of our blood, you who have felt our oppression, you who have witnessed tears shed in secret for our daily wrongs, I implore you to promise that when the day comes, which will come, you, in mercy, will issue a charter to emancipate our people from that painful Saxon yoke, a yoke loathsome to every noble, true-born Cambrian heart.'[46]

It is thanks to Gladys that the Red Dragon flies over Bosworth field; while awaiting the happy hour of Wales's release from Saxon thraldom, and aware of the old prophecy of the red dragon representing Wales and its eventual ascendancy over the white dragon representing England, she had in secret, 'worked the Red Dragon banner, upon a ground of green and white silk'.[47] On the eve of the battle she sends the banner to Henry, and he duly bears it aloft to victory. Once Henry is crowned, he restores Harlech to Gladys, but that alone does not satisfy her: her sacrifice was for 'her people' rather than for herself, and they too must have their former rights restored to them. Eventually, in the face of some reluctance from the king, Gladys wrests from him a charter by means of which 'her people would be secured in their privileges on the same footing as the Saxons before the law',[48] a reference to the historical charters which Henry VII, during the last years of his reign, did eventually bestow upon a few north Walian areas, eradicating the heavy penalties which had earlier been imposed upon them after their involvement with Glyndŵr's campaigns. When Gladys returns from London to 'her people' with the charter, it is to wild acclaim:

> The brave men of the Cwm bearing the Red Dragon banner . . . hailed her with shouts of joy that rent the heavens . . . The Saxon yoke was no more, for Cambrian and Saxon were one . . . 'Cambria is free,' they shouted . . . 'Cambria is as it was in the days of our forefathers. He who sits on England's throne is the child of our soil, of our own true blood. Cambria, thou art free! thou art free!'[49]

The contradictions in their response – for how can Cambria be 'as it was in the days of our forefathers' when the Cambrian is now 'one' with his old enemy the Saxon? – are not heeded in the novel. But its confusion on this point is no different, of course, from the confusions of some Welsh patriots over the centuries as to what exactly Henry Tudor's victory meant and whether it could in any way be connected with the ancient dream of winning back, not simply Welsh freedom, but the Isle of Britain as a whole from the Saxon invader.[50]

The question of national revival is also paramount in Louisa Matilda Spooner's second, modern-day novel, in which a central Welsh character dies fighting for Italy's freedom on the barricades of the Risorgimento. *Country Landlords* (1860) asks, in effect, what kind of leader, or landlord, does Wales need? Three possible candidates are proposed in the text: Owen Herbert Gwynne, the absentee landlord of an estate on the western coast of north Wales; his son Anarawd, reared in seclusion on the estate, who has spent his childhood dreaming of 'old bards and Welsh princes' under the encouragement of a local antiquarian; and Captain Ricardo Lewis, a retired sea-captain of Italian and Welsh descent, who has settled in a neighbouring property. Mr Gwynne senior is a corrupt brute, who spends his time gambling and whoring in London, and bullies his wife and son on his occasional visits home. In particular he deplores his son's attachment to Wales's past, telling him that he must shake off such preoccupations if he is to succeed in life. Anarawd's future, as his father sees it, is an officer's career with the British imperial army; he warns his son that if he persists with his dreams,

> 'you will be a target for all the young fellows in your regiment to pop at, while you will be longing to escape to Wales, your beloved Wales, like a truant schoolboy. That will never do; you must emerge from this chrysalis state, and make up your mind to say good-bye to Wales, and all connected with it, for years to come . . . you have to learn the cry of the present day – Forward, forward!'[51]

But though the antiquarian's tales of Ancient Britain have fostered in Anarawd a 'ruling ambition' to be a hero, his revulsion against his father and his way of life results in his determination to become a male hero of the caring and reforming, rather than physically combative, type. His mission field in adulthood becomes the estate on which he was reared, with its neglected local town, the curiously

named Angharad,[52] and the novel stresses that this choice is ultimately more progressive, more to do with the real 'cry of the present
day' in Wales, than any imperial glory.

In fact, the glory of empire is consistently disparaged in this text,
particularly through the actions and sayings of its anarchic third
landlord. Ricardo Lewis sees the English social order as one that
'pampers and favours the nobility – a plebeian is powerless. England calls herself free. She is not free; she is chancery-ridden,
law-oppressed.'[53] His Anglophobic convictions have led him in
earlier life to abscond with an orphaned child, left in his care after
her parents' sudden death in Australia. Although charged with the
responsibility of returning Gertrude to her father's aristocratic
English relatives, the Fitzhammons, Lewis brings her back to Wales
instead and rears her as his daughter, convinced that he can provide
her with 'a happier existence than that of a dependant upon
brain-less high-born relations'. As he explains to Gertrude, 'I would
not take you to England to be contaminated and blighted by the bad
atmosphere which surrounds high life.'[54] When her relatives discover the truth, and insist on Gertrude's return, Captain Lewis flees
to Italy, where he joins an anarchist secret society and fights for
Italian unification. Gertrude follows, determined to rescue him, but
cannot prevent his death in the struggle for Italy's liberation.
However, the reader is assured that before disaster struck in the
form of the vengeful English aristocracy, Captain Lewis had been in
many ways the perfect landlord: 'during the years he had lived in
Wales, he had done more good to the small town of Angharad than
had ever been done before ... He had infused new ideas there,
established new rules, and had been the means of promoting the
education of the youth, as well as a friend to the poor and needy.'[55]
And such is his influence, that after his death, a newly independent
Gertrude, heiress of his estate, chooses to make Wales, not England,
her home, and in due course marries Anarawd; together they
become the best possible local leaders, to some extent by default,
the more glamorous and progressive option having immolated
himself in the cause of Italy's freedom.

In this reversal of the earlier child-kidnapping plots discussed in
the first chapter of this book, where Welsh children were abducted
by Englishmen, it would appear that a child's 'blood' family is well
lost if, instead of corrupting English upper-class ways, they acquire
instead the communitarian values of Welsh rural life, retired from
the world of imperial power-mongering. A lifetime spent dreaming

of the wrongs of ancient Wales, or fighting for the freedom of stateless nations from imperial rule, is here presented as a better preparation for good leadership in modern-day Wales than a career in the British army or within the upper echelons of English society. For many other mid nineteenth-century anglophone writers concerned with the question of Wales, however, that alternative world of Welsh difference was already doomed – a happy never-never land, soon to exist only in dreams of the past without relevance to the modern age.

ii. 'Treading to music the dark way of doom'

Representations of the Welsh as a dying breed surface in a number of mid nineteenth-century English-language texts, nowhere more strikingly than in a verse play included in the collection *Twilight Hours: A Legacy of Verse* (1868) put together after her early death by the friends of the London-Welsh poet Sarah Williams (1841–68), or 'Sadie', as she called herself. Sadie's parents were sufficiently well-off to provide her with a middle-class education, but she was forced to leave school early due to illness, and died suddenly after undergoing medical surgery.[56] She attributed her poetic abilities to bardic traits inherited from her Welsh father, and had published a few of her poems in such journals as *The Argosy*, *Sunday Magazine* and *Good Words* before her death. A melancholy note predominates in her verses, particularly those related to Welsh issues. In 'The Doom of the Prynnes', the Prynnes are an extended family of Welsh exiles, living together in a London mansion 'that, like the fortunes of our family, / Had shrunk and withered to pathetic age'.[57] Their story is narrated by the youngest daughter of the family, Elin, who observes the developing attraction between her two cousins, Mark and Agnes. Her father, Cadwallader, is lost to the world in his antiquarian library, and her aunt, Mark's mother, is even further removed from everyday affairs by her growing insanity. In one Gothic scene, the aunt makes a dramatic appearance to pronounce 'the doom of the Prynnes':

> A Prynne can only love a Prynne:
>   Doom one.
> The Prynne who weds a Prynne, weds Death:
>   Doom two.
> The Prynne who weds not Death goes mad, like me:
>   Doom three.[58]

Doom two becomes the destiny of the two lovers, who are both killed by the literal fall of the house of the Prynnes. One stormy night, the winds uproot a mountain ash which the family's forefathers had brought from Wales and transplanted in their London garden 'to share / The changes in the family estate'.[59] The falling tree brings the whole house down with it, and kills Mark and Agnes, the family's hope for the future. But the Prynnes were a doomed race from the outset, particularly in comparison with the English. At one point Mark comments,

> 'We have our special weaknesses, we Prynnes,
> Our angers, fantasies, and ghostly fears,
> No Saxon courage of tenacity;
> We spring, and rush, and suddenly fall back:
> Sometimes I almost hate to be a Prynne.'[60]

As the Prynnes obviously represent the Welsh in this poem, it would appear that for Mark, as for Matthew Arnold, instability is of the essence of Welshness. 'The Doom of the Prynnes' generally presents the Welsh as impractical and over-emotional, compared to the Saxons with their 'courage of tenacity'. Though Agnes, the poem's heroine, does her best to control the stormy passions of her family and to behave like a proper lady, even she cannot deny the overheated Welsh blood which fuels her fantasies, as it does the damaging obsessions of her relatives. She tries to discipline her weaknesses through prayer, but in vain; she has to confess,

> What though I kneel like marble saint,
> My very soul grows sick and faint
>   At thought of such repose;
> My hands may clasp in stony calm,
> But, each on each, the throbbing palm
>   In burning anguish glows.[61]

The implications are that the Welsh, and particularly Welsh women, are excessively passionate and ultimately uncontrollable; only her early death, it would appear, has saved Agnes from that third 'Doom' of madness, which has overcome her aunt.

At the same time, the strength, of Sadie's feeling for her Welsh roots is conveyed touchingly in many of her poems, nowhere more so perhaps than in one piece, to which she gives a Welsh-language title, 'O Fy Hen Gymraeg' ('O, my dear old Welsh'). Those words, which function as a refrain in the poem, are spoken by its Welsh narrator to his child as he lies dying in London: the poem was probably inspired by the death of Sadie's father, which occurred some months before that of Sadie herself.

> No, there is nothing I want, dear,
>   You may put the candle by;
> There is light enough to die in,
>   And the dawning draweth nigh.
> Only the want remaineth,
>   Gnawing my heart away –
> Oh, for a word of my mother's tongue,
>   And a prayer she used to pray!
>   *O fy hen Gymraeg!*
>
> I wish I had taught you to speak it
>   While the light was on my brain;
> It has vanished now, with the thousand things
>   That will never come back again.
> Only a vision of waters,
>   Rising towards the flow,
> Cometh instead of the countless hills –
>   The hills that I used to know.
>   *O fy hen Gymraeg!*[62]

In this poem, the refrain, which would, of course, have been unintelligible to the majority of Sadie's readers, conveys the immeasurability of the narrator's loss, and his loneliness in a culture where no one speaks his language: his recollections of his birthplace, and with them his sense of his own identity, are drowned under a weight of dark water. Wales and the Welsh are dying in Sadie's poetry, but even in death they are imbued with an intensity presented as being beyond the comprehension of the more enduring but also more prosaic English. Though one cannot doubt the authenticity of Sadie's feeling for her Welsh roots, the image of Welshness she presents, as unstable and dying but adding poetic colour to British culture, is very close to that disseminated by Matthew Arnold a year earlier in his *On the Study of Celtic Literature*.

The Welsh are similarly represented as exiting from the world stage in another long poem, published a little later in the century, Emily Pfeiffer's *Glân-Alarch: His Silence and Song* (1877). Pfeiffer, née Davis (1827–90), from Montgomeryshire on her mother's side, married in 1850 a London-based German manufacturer, Jurgen Edward Pfeiffer. Few of her poems are currently in print, though she does make an appearance in one recent anthology of Victorian women poets, and is also, like Sadie, included in Brennan and Gramich's *Welsh Women's Poetry*.[63] But when *Glân-Alarch* was first published, the *Caernarvon Herald* announced that 'Every Welshman who loves his race and its history is bound to read the poem'. It was also highly praised in the *Welshman*, which welcomed Pfeiffer as the long-awaited, true voice of Wales: 'It would seem as if our wealth of historical and legendary lore has at length found a poetical interpreter worthy of the name.' A *Carmarthen Journal* reviewer went one step further, and suggested, of this poem on the troubled existence of a noble Welsh family in post-Roman Britain, that it might well be 'fated to be an only bright monument of Welsh name and fame when the race, now "treading to music the dark way of doom", shall have disappeared as a separate people'.[64] The ease with which the *Journal* in 1877 foresees the demise of Wales is indicative of the temper of that Arnoldian era, within Wales as well as without it. The quotation given in the review is from the close of *Glân-Alarch*: after singing the praises of the chieftain Eurien, who has just led his people to victory over 'the brutal Saxon, Ethelfrith, the leader / Of the vile scum which makes our wholesome borders / A foul morass',[65] the poet Glân-Alarch turns prophet, and foresees the future of his country after the fall of Llywelyn. Though Eurien has won this battle, the Welsh will not ultimately conquer the Saxon, says Glân-Alarch, yet they will still have a special role to play, for they will remain closer to God than the English. 'In the far time', when the light of faith is faltering in England, the Welsh 'still in the darkness shall lift up the hymn'; it will be their destiny to replenish English 'altars whose light burneth dim', with the 'flame' of their faith, though as a separate people they will themselves be 'Treading to music the dark way of doom'.[66] No wonder that *Glân-Alarch* was well received by that generation for whom it was written; in it Pfeiffer succeeded in combining both the Arnoldian view of the Welsh, as a poetical and musical nation which had contributed its strong colour to the building-up of Britain but was now on the brink of disappearing, and the Welsh idea of Wales, as a country which had received special favour in the eyes of God, and had special religious duties as a result.

But the Welsh are not fighters in her account: engrossed in internal wrangling, they do not rush to defend their country from Ethelfrith's attacks, until they are eventually shamed into so doing by Mona, an orphaned Irish woman who accuses them of betraying their brothers the Irish as well as, in effect, committing suicide themselves through their delay:

> Die! with the sound in your ears of the Sassenach laugh,
> And the requiem, tuneful for ever, of Cymric sighs . . .
> So leave ye to Sassenach mercy the lover or friend,
> And to slow heart-sickness your brothers on alien strand . . .
> Let Cambria fall like a stronghold that treason assails,
> And in tears of your shame shall your land be rechristened wild Wales![67]

The name 'wild Wales' is a shameful title in this poem, and a sign of Wales's pathetic inability either to defend its civilized inheritance from the pagan hordes, or to offer assistance to its Celtic brethren in Ireland, who in 1877, when *Glân-Alarch* was published, had sixty Home Rule League MPs in the British Parliament.

The Welsh are referred to as a race doomed to speedy perdition not only in this poem but also in Pfeiffer's verse play *The Wynnes of Wynhavod* (1881), in which the brother and sister Winifred and Mostyn Wynn are struggling to win back their estate in Wales, lost to the English through the negligence of their forefathers.[68] It is only through Winifred's marriage to the Englishman Norman Thorne, son of the banker who bought Wynhavod, that the brother and sister return to their estate in the last scene of the play. The work's conclusion underlines the importance of the symbolic marriage with the English as the only way in which the Welsh can survive: as a separate people they are doomed, and have no choice but voluntarily to pledge themselves anew to the act of union with England. In both Sadie and Emily Pfeiffer's poetry the Welsh are a twilight race, which must accept Anglicization or perish. Many of the fictions of the 1860s to 1880s similarly focus on the importance of the act of union with England, as the last section of this chapter indicates.

iii. Acts of union

Anne Beale (1815–1900) had an unusually long career as an author: she published her first book, a poetry collection, in 1842 and was still regularly contributing serialized fiction to women's journals in the 1890s. A native of Somerset, Beale came to Carmarthenshire in 1841 to work as a governess in a Welsh clerical household, and settled in Llandeilo: she never married, but her publishing success enabled her to give up her teaching post and become a full-time writer. About eight of her numerous novels were set at least partly in rural Wales, and spanned the half-century: her first fictionalization of Welsh life, *The Vale of the Towey; or, Sketches in South Wales*, was published three years before the 1847 'Treason of the Blue Books', while her last did not appear until the 1890s, during the peak years of the Young Wales movement. According to the entry on Beale in the Welsh *Dictionary of National Biography*, few English writers have written so sympathetically of Wales, and her contemporary Gwilym Teilo, in his volume *Llandeilo-Vawr and its Neighbourhood*, commended her as 'a minute and clever observer of men and manners, and particularly of domestic life'.[69] At the same time, a persistent strain of sensationalism runs throughout her Welsh romances, suggesting that she gained her popularity with English audiences in part through exploiting their appetite for reading material depicting ways of life less inhibited than their own. When set in wild Wales, the fantasy elements in her writings could be accepted by her English readers as credible, but in feeding them such material she reproduced racial stereotypes in a manner which can hardly have been of much real assistance to the Welsh in their endeavour to redeem the nation's 'good name'. Further, many of her fictions through their romance plots lay heavy emphasis on the appropriateness of the union between Wales and England.

The text with which Beale opened her career as a novelist was very much written in well-meaning 'white settler' mode, with an English narrator intent on helping the Welsh natives out of their darkness to the light of a superior civilization. The inhabitants of Towey Vale are often portrayed in very negative terms, which prefigure the criticisms of the 1847 Report. Welsh people are slovenly and primitive in their living habits, according to the narrator: 'The insides of the Welsh cottages are generally as wretched as their outsides', she says, 'there is no indication of taste'. She has 'seen two old women living together in a room that many a dainty, well-styed pig would grunt and turn up his nose at'.[70] Neither are the Vale's inmates prepossessing in personal appearance: 'the lower classes of Welsh women are not, generally speaking, pretty', the narrator explains, and her neighbour, Mrs Davies, 'had passed their good-looking age, which is from fifteen to twenty, after which, either from hard labour in the fields, or because the round-faced ruddy bloom that characterises them is not lasting, they begin to go off'.[71] But a more serious racial flaw in the narrator's view is the incorrigible laziness of the Welsh, another failing much emphasized in the Blue Books. 'They require a sharp eye,' she says of her new neighbours, 'for when they are not vigilantly watched, they will never injure themselves by hard work'; 'there seems to be a spirit of procrastinating amongst these people, and a want of steam when they are set going, which retards their improvement'.[72] The Welsh are also a race of liars in Beale's book, again as they were in the Blue Books: 'Welsh servants are not always conscientiously addicted to truth', the narrator informs her readers, and goes on to remark of the race generally that 'their fertility of invention is wonderful, as is their boldness in persisting in a fact which you have clearly proved cannot be true'.[73] Her sharpest words of criticism, however, are reserved for Dissenters: just as Nonconformist meetings in Wales were presented in the Blue Books as an incitement to sexual immorality, so in the *Vale*, the 'listeners are assembled from curiosity and the pleasures of idleness' and often 'finish the day in drunkenness and riot'.[74]

In later years, however, Anne Beale rewrote her *Vale of Towey* sketches, in ways which indicate her changing view of the Welsh. She republished the book twice under different titles, virtually unchanged as *Traits and Stories of the Welsh Peasantry* in 1849, but very much changed and heavily edited as *Seven Years for Rachel, or, Welsh Pictures Sketched from Life* in 1886. By then, nearly forty years later, the elements of racial indictment and stereotyping in the text are almost wholly eradicated. The sentence which reads 'The insides of the Welsh cottages are generally as wretched as their outsides' in the original is changed to 'the insides of the cottages are not much smarter than their outsides' in 1886,[75] while the reference to Welsh women living like pigs is omitted. Mrs Davies remains unattractive in the 1886 novel but she no longer represents her race: no reference is made to Welsh females of the lower classes lacking in physical charms. Again, the account of the Welsh spirit of procrastination given above is deleted altogether from the 1886 version of the story, and it is now servants generally as a class who 'are not always conscientiously addicted to truth',[76] thus discreetly removing the slur on the Welsh. Beale is systematically deleting all pejorative racial comments from her 1886 edition, where the war between church and chapel is no longer a feature of the text; her fictions in general are much warmer towards the inhabitants of what had by that time become her adopted country, no doubt primarily because greater familiarity with actual Welsh individuals has made it more difficult for her to produce stereotyped generalizations on their racial attributes.

Once established as a popular novelist, however, particularly a writer of serialized fiction for Victorian periodicals, an element of sensationalism was an expected component in her work, and Beale makes use of the image of Wales as 'wild' to give her stories that required spice. *The Pennant Family* (1876), for example, is a 'wrecker' novel, that is, like other novels of the period, it provides a fictional account of the practice of luring ships on to dangerous rocks by means of false lights, in order to loot the resulting wreck. Many Welsh seaside communities, particularly in Anglesey, were rumoured to be wreckers;[77] Sadie has a poem in *Twilight Hours* in which Anglesey is described as having 'rocks so red, / For the sins of the wreckers who preyed there once'.[78] Frances Parthenope Verney (née Nightingale, 1819–90), the sister of Florence Nightingale, published a 'wrecker' novel set in Anglesey, *The Llanaly Reefs* (1873): Lady Verney became acquainted with Wales after her stepson, Edmund Hope Verney, married Margaret Maria Williams of Rhianva in Anglesey in 1868. In her novel the English orphan Winifred Caladine, whose father falls victim to the Llanaly wreckers, is cared for compassionately by the village's more virtuous inhabitants. Winifred, in her discomfiture at her destitution, had hardened her heart, and 'very nearly wrecked her life', but as she slowly grows to realize that the strength of the disinterested care that succours her is greater than the greed which destroyed her father, she herself acquires 'the capacity of caring for others'.[79] When her father's property is finally restored to her by the wreckers she uses it to save the villagers who befriended her from destitution, and marries her local Welsh sweetheart. As if in a reversal of the Blue Books, in this text the Welsh are initially presented as barbarous and immoral, but later, on better acquaintance, revealed to be full of human kindness. Here, too, though, as in Pfeiffer's *Wynnes of Wynhavod*, they survive only through the marriage with English wealth, in which they lose their monolingualism: Winifred initially refuses to learn Welsh, and though reconciled to it before the close of the novel, does not appear at any point to become proficient.

Beale's *The Pennant Family*, published three years after Verney's novel, has a similar plot; as a result of the local wreckers' activities, Daisy Walpole is shipwrecked on a rural Welsh shore in infancy, only to be cared for by a local farming family, the Pennants. Eventually Daisy is revealed to be the daughter of General George

Walpole, a 'nabob' who had 'made one of those fabulous fortunes amassed in those days by men in the [East India] Company's service in India'.[80] His ill-gotten gains succour the survival of the Pennants, who regain Craigavon castle, the long-lost stronghold of their Ancient British family, through their son Caradoc's marriage with Daisy. The General buys Craigavon from its Earl, a descendant of the Norman knight who first took it from the Pennants, after the Earl has been exposed as the organizer of the local wreckers; in his greed he has corrupted the villagers and turned them into illegal harvesters of their rocky seashore. By dramatic irony, therefore, Craigavon returns into Welsh ownership through the iniquity of the Normans and the practical, wealth-acquiring virtues of the modern-day imperial English: *The Pennant Family* is another tale of Welsh humiliations redeemed by their share in the spoils of Empire, once they have agreed on an act of union with England. Again, all the Welsh are required to give up in the process is their monolingualism. When Daisy is first washed up on their shores, and the young Caradoc realizes that she cannot speak Welsh, he resolves 'I will learn English at once – this very day . . . I am ashamed that I know so little of it.'[81]

If the practice of wrecking added the necessary sensationalism to *The Pennant Family*, cross-dressed rioting contributes an equivalent frisson to Beale's *Rose Mervyn, of Whitelake* (1879). This novel, too, features a marriage between the Welsh and the English, this time specifically referred to in the text as an act of union which can serve as a model for Britain's newer imperial colonies to follow. *Rose Mervyn* is set in rural Wales at the time of the so-called 'Rebecca' riots of 1839 to 1843, in which gangs of men disguised in women's clothes attacked and pulled down the toll-gates at the time proliferating along country roads in south-west Wales: the leaders of the gangs were addressed by their followers as 'Rebecca'.[82] In Beale's novel, Major Faithfull is the officer in charge of the English forces sent to suppress the riots, who finds himself lured by one of the natives, Rose Mervyn, the daughter of a local Welsh squire and his upper-class English wife. Rose takes after her mother in manner, but her sister Edwyna is less ladylike: her 'exuberant laughter and jokes were altogether Welsh, and she often made very disparaging remarks upon her mother's country-people, which greatly amused her father'.[83] Evidently, the union of England and Wales in this instance has not produced a contented marriage: Edwyna and her father are 'altogether Welsh', and grate upon the sensibilities of the refined Mrs Mervyn. Major Faithfull has her mother's backing in his wooing of Rose, but her father favours another suitor for her hand, a local farmer called Alfred Johnnes. Given the wilfulness of Johnnes's courtship, it comes as no great surprise to the reader when he is eventually revealed to be none other than 'Rebecca' herself. Though Rose rejects him as incompatible from the start, he is a persistent suitor: one particularly sensationalist scene sees him combining the roles of rebel and demon lover when, in the guise of 'Rebecca', he kidnaps Rose. But Major Faithfull, true to manly English form, succeeds in defeating the rioters, and 'Rebecca' has to flee for her life, thus leaving the field clear for the Major, who manages to win Rose's hand with both her parents' consent. One of the final scenes of the book places their coming marriage, by implication, in the general context of English/Welsh relations. Major Faithfull is regaling his betrothed and his prospective father-in-law with tales of the English army's exploits in India, but his audience is not entirely sympathetic to the aims of the imperialists:

> 'With our 25,000 men we routed the Sikh army of 60,000, and Shere Singh had only 8000 left when he escaped to the Salt Range Hills. He has been obliged to surrender unconditionally at last.'
>
> 'I cannot help feeling sorry for him,' said Rose. 'We call them rebels, but it is their own country after all.'
>
> '*Was*, you mean, Rose! Possession is nine points of the law,' said Mervyn. '*We* had a king and a country once, but the Saxon got the better of us. Look at old Penllyn with its many ancient memories.'
>
> 'And its modern ones of Rebecca, father,' she responded; and both thought of Alfred Johnnes, still a wanderer.
>
> 'But the Welsh and English are united now, and live in happy confidence,' said Major Faithfull, looking at Rose, from whose fair face, indeed, he turned with difficulty.
>
> 'We will hope that the Punjaub, also, will gradually find peace and contentment under British rule.'[84]

Here the message of the text as a whole becomes unequivocal. Rose has chosen the English officer rather than the Welsh rebel, and her marriage serves as a symbol not only of the happy future relation between Wales and England, but of the contentment which will come to all English colonies once they have peacefully acquiesced to British rule. At the same time, the references to Welsh history and to the contemporary Welsh 'rebel' complicate Beale's representation of both the union between England and Wales and British imperialism generally. In her later novels, at any rate, Beale's increasingly pro-Welsh perspective can suggest a critique of imperialism, although she never openly challenges it.

In another anglophone 'Rebecca' novel of the period, however, English rule is represented as not necessarily desirable for Wales. In *The Rebecca Rioter: A Story of Killay Life* (1880), by the Swansea writer Amy Dillwyn (1845–1935), a young farm labourer, Evan Williams, the first-person narrator, joins the local Rebeccaites and remains loyal to their cause even after his transportation to Australia, and long years in exile and captivity. He does not repudiate the political awakening which he experienced on one market-day in Carmarthen during his youth, when Rebecca's speeches first fired him with positive rather than negative images of the wildness of the Welsh. Stirring the meeting to a hatred of the turnpikes, Rebecca had cried:

> 'England – miserable, servile, down-trodden England – may submit to such things if she chooses; but she is no guide for us. We are not cold-blooded English! We belong to Wales, to that wild Wales, which, in days gone by would be ruled by none but her own native princes, and long flung back every attempt of the English tyrant to grind her under his heel ... let us rise against our oppressors ... cry shame on whoever is willing to be down-trodden, on whoever flinches from the task of helping his country to shake off her chains!'[85]

Evan was captured and transported because, after inadvertently killing Squire Tudor during a riot, he returned to the scene of the crime with the intention of attempting to explain his actions to the squire's daughter, Gwenllïan, who had once showed him kindness. But not even the memory of Gwenllïan's humane compassion can reconcile him to the system which ordered their separate spheres. He transcribes his life's history, that is, the novel, in Australia after transportation, but remains unrepentant and still convinced of the injustices of English rule for Wales and the English class system. 'No doubt Miss Gwenllïan did do something for me', he admits at the close of his narrative, 'but one person cannot make up for the evils of a whole system, and it is the system that is to blame – the system of narrowness and of pride, and of exclusiveness'.[86] No compromise marriage, or even forgiveness, softens the close of this text. Its narrator may be as much defeated as earlier historical Welsh freedom-fighters, like Glyndŵr, but he also remains just as defiant.

It is in part through her choice of narrator that Dillwyn in *The Rebecca Rioter* succeeds in presenting the Welsh experience of the mid years of the nineteenth century more vividly than many of her competitors. She herself was born into the privileged sector of that system which Evan Williams condemns, as the daughter of Liberal MP Lewis Llywelyn Dillwyn, who had himself as a local Justice of the Peace captured and punished some of the Rebeccaites, and his wife Elizabeth De la Beche, whose forefathers had owned slave plantations in Jamaica.[87] But Amy Dillwyn was singularly unsuited to the life of the Victorian gentlewoman in her gilded cage of enforced passivity, and wrote her novels in part to offset her deep-rooted frustrations, saying at the time that, 'I haven't any genius for literature or literary composition and only take to it as a *pis-aller*; using my brains because I can't use my muscles, which last I should greatly prefer.'[88] Two of her later novels, also in part set in Wales, similarly critique the culture of the upper classes. In *Chloe Arguelle* (1881), Chloe, the sister-in-law of the Welsh MP Sir Cadwallader Gough, experiences herself as stifled by the mores of upper-class English society, which she condemns as corrupted by a 'dangerous and seductive' humbuggery. 'When once a person begins by blunting his moral sense of truth and honesty with endless conventional pretty speeches,' she says, 'from that he slides down hill to deliberate lies at express pace and grows utterly dead to any feeling of shame at them.' The novel closes with Chloe determining to launch a campaign to eradicate such social artifice: 'let's get up a crusade against humbug!' she pleads.[89]

Dillwyn's third novel, *A Burglary: or, Unconscious Influence* (1883), also features a spirited heroine, much frustrated by her social role as the daughter of a landed Welsh MP. The inveterate tomboy Imogen fervently believes that it is 'better to be free than to be broken into harness of any kind',[90] and fears marriage as an impending restraint upon the 'stunning lot of go' that she experiences in herself: 'the popular idea that it was the natural destiny of all women to get married if possible, seemed to her to be an insult to her sex'.[91] Amy Dillwyn herself never married, but, after her father's death in 1892, was afforded the opportunity to manifest her own 'stunning lot of go': she took over his business interests, redeeming them from debt, and became a successful public figure of some influence and renown. A supporter of the suffragette campaign, she argued, 'All I say is, give women a chance. Don't despise them without knowing what they can do. A woman's duty, like a man's, is to serve her generation in the way she can do it best.'[92] But her novel-writing took place during those long years of her earlier enforced inactivity, in which she appears to have felt as trapped within the class system, and its particular role for gentlewomen, as her fictional heroines and Rebecca rioters.

The Rebecca Rioter also expresses, of course, an explicit dissatisfaction with English rule as well as with the class system, and in so doing accords closely, in political terms, with the work of the earlier historical novelist Louisa Spooner. In both cases the authors' connection with the growth of radicalism within Welsh Liberalism may well have influenced the course of their narratives. Spooner's domestic circle in Meirioneth was, like Dillwyn's, closely involved with the Liberal politics of her day; and it was from within the circle of Meirioneth Liberals that the *Cymru Fydd*, or Young Wales, movement was formed. T. E. Ellis was elected MP for Meirioneth on the Cymru Fydd ticket in 1886, and Dillwyn's father had become a supporter of the movement before his death. Both novelists, therefore, may arguably be presented as writing texts which act as forerunners of Cymru Fydd, a movement influenced by the Italian Risorgimento and the Irish Home Rule campaign. Such influences, in the case of these two women writers at any rate, resulted in English-language texts which are at least as, if not more, radical in their Welsh politics than many of the writings produced by Welsh-language women writers of the period. But that aspect of Welsh culture which suffered most directly from the Treason of the Blue Books, the Welsh language itself, is not defended in their texts in the same way as it is in the work of the earlier antiquarians and historians: the anglophone poets and novelists seem resigned to its death. In fact, however, the last two decades of the nineteenth century witnessed a renaissance in Welsh-language culture, in which women writers participated strongly. The next chapter of this volume traces the history of that development.

5 Developing Women's Welsh-language Print Culture

In 1896, as he welcomed the second periodical for women to be entitled *Y Gymraes* (The Welsh Woman) O. M. Edwards drew attention to the dramatic increase in the numbers of Welsh-language women writers since the publication of *Telyn Egryn* in the 1850s. In an editorial in his journal, *Cymru*, he announced that a revolution had occurred:

> Pan ymddangosodd *Cymraes* Ieuan Gwynedd yn Ionawr, 1850, nid wyf yn cofio am yr un Gymraes yn ysgrifennu iddi ond Elen Egryn; ond yn awr, ar ail gychwyniad y *Gymraes*, gwyr Cymru'n dda am Granogwen, S. M. Saunders, Morfudd Eryri, Winnie Parry, Ellen Hughes, Ceridwen Peris, a llawer ereill.

> [When Ieuan Gwynedd's *Cymraes* appeared in January, 1850, I don't recall that one Welsh woman contributed to it apart from Elen Egryn; but now, at the second launching of the *Gymraes*, Wales is well acquainted with Cranogwen, S. M. Saunders, Morfudd Eryri, Winnie Parry, Ellen Hughes, Ceridwen Peris, and many more.]

Wales by now knows, he says, that its women are amongst its best writers.[1] But for all his appreciation of their contribution it was not O. M. Edwards, or Ieuan Gwynedd, or, indeed, any other male who launched Cranogwen (Sarah Jane Rees, 1839–1916), Ellen Hughes of Llanengan (1862–1927), Ceridwen Peris (Alice Gray Jones, 1852–1943), and a host of other Welsh-language women writers of the second half of the nineteenth century on their authorial careers.

Insofar as this remarkably rapid development can be attributed to the influence of one person, then that person was Cranogwen herself: accordingly, this chapter begins with an account of her career and in particular her work as editor, from 1879 to 1889, of the periodical *Y Frythones* (The Female [Cambro-]Briton), the second Welsh-language magazine for women. However, by the last decade of the century it was not Cranogwen alone, or the generation of women writers she had virtually hauled into existence, that were providing inspiration for new female authors. The temperance movement was the main promoter of the careers of a number of *fin de siècle* Welsh-language women writers, poets like Buddug (Catherine Jane Prichard, 1842–1909) and Myfanwy Meirion (Margaret Jones, 1847–1931), and short-story writers like Ruth (Annie Catherine Prichard, 1858–1938). Under the editorship of Ceridwen Peris, the second *Gymraes* was the mouthpiece of the Welsh-language women's temperance movement; its pages were filled with articles, stories and verses, mostly authored by women. As well as praising temperance reformers, *Y Gymraes* was able to praise a new school of women missionaries. In 1887 the Calvinist Methodists had finally accepted that the segregated nature of Indian society, in particular the barring of men from the women's domestic quarters, the 'zenanas', obliged them to ordain women as missionaries in their own right as well as sending them out as wives and helpmates to male evangelists. The idealistic women they sent out also became heroines to readers at home, and contributed to the extraordinary enthusiasm for missionary activity which marked late nineteenth-century Wales. In the second and third sections of this chapter, I consider the impact these two movements had on the development of women's print culture in Welsh.

i.   Cranogwen and *Y Frythones*

In the lengthy series of articles entitled 'In the company of Cranogwen' which appeared in *Y Gymraes* from 1923–5, Ellen Hughes provides a vivid picture of what Cranogwen meant to a young embryo writer like herself. She describes herself, at eighteen years of age, dropping and breaking a bowl of sugar in her happy confusion on hearing that her first attempts at poetic composition were to be published in *Y Frythones*.[2] A number of other women writers also began their careers through winning the literary competitions established by Cranogwen, on the best 'Welsh Novel', for example, or an such essay topics as 'Which of the two sexes showed most love for Jesus Christ, when he was here on earth?' The author of the winning essay on that question was a young woman from Rhydlewis in Cardiganshire, Anne Rees (1860–87), who proceeded to publish further serial fiction in Y *Frythones* before dying of tuberculosis at twenty-seven. Mary Oliver Jones (1858–93), one of the Liverpudlian Welsh, won the first 'Welsh Novel' competition; when her story 'Claudia, or, Let us do our duty and all will be well' ('Claudia, neu, Gwnawn ein dyledswydd a daw pob peth yn dda') appeared in Y *Frythones* in 1880, she was launched on a highly successful career as a novelist. She went on to publish eight further novels as serial fiction in *Cymru* and Y *Genedl Gymreig*, but it was Y *Frythones* and its competitions which first encouraged her, and gave her the opportunity and inspiration to become an author.[3]

Y *Frythones*' literary contests were open to both sexes, but its editor confessed that encouraging female talent was her main aim. As well as the competitions for adults, she also ran essay-writing competitions for children under sixteen, but she had to scold her young female readers after receiving the first batch of contestants' work. 'Come on, girls, where are you?' she said; 'Most of the writers are boys, and you know that it was to *you* chiefly that we looked' ('Deuwch, ferched, yn mha le yr ydych? Bechgyn yw y rhan amlaf o'r ysgrifwyr, a gwyddoch mai arnoch *chwi* yn benaf yr oedd ein golwg').[4] Yet she ensured that there was at least one female name in the list of each competition's winners: though the work of 'Blodwen' in the first children's competition was only in the second class, she was given a prize of two shillings, notwithstanding, in order to encourage her, and to allow the magazine to print her name as a prizewinner. Lydia Hughes of Llanengan was 'Blodwen', and by June 1879 she had succeeded, after this encouragement, in rising to the top of the class of child competitors; Lydia was the younger sister of Ellen Hughes, and that explains, perhaps, why Ellen started to write and to send her work to the editor of Y *Frythones*. She knew that her attempts would be welcomed by Cranogwen and given a sympathetic reading, if only by virtue of her sex.

In 1900, Cranogwen, as she looked back on Ellen Hughes's successful career, took pride in her early discovery: 'I felt like one who had gained much booty when, years ago ... Ellen Hughes came into view', she wrote in the second *Gymraes*, adding,

Teimlwn fel un wedi cael ysglyfaeth lawer pan, flynyddoedd yn ol ... daeth Ellen Hughes i'r golwg ... Ni wyddwn, waeth i mi gyfaddef, fod yr ohebyddes ddyddorol o Lanengan i dyfu cyn y byddai hir o amser, i fod yn un o wroniaid meddyliol ei hoes, a hyny, pe y byddai bwys i'w ddweyd, heb gyfrif rhyw.[5]

[I did not know, I might as well confess, that the interesting correspondent from Llanengan was to develop before very much time had passed to become one of the intellectual heroes of her age, and that, if it is of any significance to say so, without counting gender.]

By 1900 there was less need to place emphasis on gender: Welsh women had proven their literary ability. But in 1880 in the early years of Y *Frythones*, the sex of the contributors was a very important consideration. Through openly and enthusiastically favouring female talent in this way, Cranogwen succeeded in producing for ten years, between January 1879 and February 1889, a substantial monthly journal (some thirty pages of small double-column print every month), with nearly as little work by men in it as there was of women's writing in Ieuan Gwynedd's *Gymraes*. She created a network of Welsh-language women writers who knew one another, wrote about and for one another, and received inspiration and encouragement from one another, and particularly from 'the Ed.' ('Yr Ol.'), as Cranogwen liked to refer to herself.

She herself rose to fame during the aftermath of the Blue Books, when the fact that she was a woman – a talented, articulate and profoundly religious Welsh woman – appealed to audiences who saw in her further proof of the iniquity of the 1847 Report. In this context her rural lower-class upbringing was a positive aspect of her image. Reared in Llangrannog, a small fishing-village on Cardigan Bay, across which her father sailed his ketch, she herself had worked as a sailor initially, before acquiring further education and becoming a teacher at the village school. She shot into the Welsh limelight through winning a poetry competition in the 1865 National Eisteddfod at Aberystwyth; the glory of the win was increased by the fact that two of the leading male poets of the day, Islwyn and Ceiriog, were amongst the defeated contestants. Cranogwen started on her career as a lecturer immediately after this victory, and by 1866, when she was twenty-seven years of age, she was making enough money from public speaking to give up teaching and turn to full-time lecturing, preaching and writing.

Few role models were available amongst Welsh women of her generation for such a career, and virtually none from the same class as herself. During the 1860s the essayist Eliza Peter (1833–89) published occasionally in sectarian periodicals, but though she was born in New Quay, just a few miles down the coast from Llangrannog, the circumstances of her upbringing were very different from those of Cranogwen. Soon after her birth in 1833, Eliza's wealthy father moved his family to Liverpool, where she received as good an education as her age could offer women, according to her biographer.[6] Married to an Independent minister, she belonged to the Welsh middle classes; nevertheless, when she started to contribute to the contemporary debate on woman's roles, Peter's voice was radical in its insistence upon the importance of women's mental independence. 'The starting place of a woman's intellectual abilities is *independence of mind*', she writes in an 1863 essay on 'Women's culture' ('Cychwynfa galluoedd deallawl benyw ydyw *annibyniaeth meddwl*').[7] She believed women should be educated not only in the Bible and in domestic science, but also in politics, geography, history, mathematics – 'there is nothing better than Mathematics to strengthen and establish the mental faculties', she wrote ('Nid oes dim tebyg i Feidroniaeth am gryfhau a sefydlu y galluoedd meddyliol') – and even astrology. All women should fight for a good education, whatever their social class: 'if your education has been neglected by those who should be looking after you,' Eliza Peter advises her female readers, 'lose no time in making up the deficiency; conserve your time, and endeavour to the utmost of your abilities to win knowledge, in the face of all adverse circumstances' ('os esgeuluswyd eich addysg gan y rhai a ddylasent ofalu am danoch, na chollwch ddim amser i wneud y diffyg i fyny; cynilwch eich amser, ac ymdrechwch hyd eithaf eich gallu i enill gwybodaeth, er gwaethaf pob amgylchiad gwrthwynebol').[8] Eliza Peter's essays no doubt helped to prepare the way for Cranogwen, and her contribution was acknowledged in the first number of *Y Frythones* in 1879, which published one of her last articles, on 'Health and beauty'. In it, Peter adds physical education to the list of subjects which should be taught to each and every young woman: a training in the rudiments of physical education is necessary, she says, in order to develop strong female bodies, capable of enjoying their own existence and becoming worthy temples of the living God.[9]

The high moral tone of her essay strikes the key note for much that is to follow in *Y Frythones*, which inhabits a different world from that of the first *Gymraes*, with its abundance of female delinquents in every Welsh county. Only in one place in *Y Frythones* is there any reference to 'courting on beds'. In 1885, Gwladus Ruffydd of Penrhos wrote to the editor's 'Questions and Answers' column to enquire 'Why does the *Frythones* not speak against night associations?' ('Paham na ddywed y *Frythones* yn erbyn cyfeillachu y nos?') – that is, courting on beds. Cranogwen replies, 'Because she does not assume that any of her readers practise it . . . Is there much of that to which you refer still carrying on? We are so ignorant in these matters' ('Am nad yw yn tybied fod un o'i darllenwyr yn arfer hyny . . . A oes llawer o'r hyn y cyfeiriwch ato eto yn parhau? Yr y'm mor anwybodus yn y materion hyn').[10] Recent historical studies of the lovemaking habits of the Welsh have shown that these 'night associations' did in fact continue into the twentieth century: only slowly between 1920 and 1930 did the practice of 'courting on beds' die out in rural Wales, according to Catrin Stevens.[11] But there is no need to assume that Cranogwen was responding hypocritically to her correspondent's question, and denying what she knew to be the case. Rather, the heterosexual lovemaking habits of the rural labourers amongst whom she had been reared may indeed have lain outside the field of her awareness, for reasons which are not unrelated, perhaps, to her success as a leader in the campaign to raise the image of Welsh women.

Cranogwen evinces very little interest in the customary love problems of her sex: no 'agony aunt' ever showed less patience with the courtship and marital anxieties of her correspondents. She does not take them seriously, and as a result the 'Questions and Answers' column is the most entertaining section of the journal. On the whole, she advises those in doubt not to marry, but always emphasizes the fact that she is no expert in such matters. In April 1880, for example, the answer which 'Claudia' from Aberporth received to her question 'What age do you think is the safest for women in general to enter into the state of matrimony?' was 'Such a question is not appropriately addressed to us, but we'll take the freedom to reply that the safest thing for those who can't decide this question for themselves is not to enter that state at all' ('Pa oedran tybed, yw y dyogelaf i ferched yn gyffredin fyned i'r ystad briodasol ynddo?' 'Nid atom ni, bid sicr, y cyfeirid y gofyniad hwn; ond cymerwn ein rhyddid i ateb mai y dyogelaf i'r rhai y byddont yn methu penderfynu y cwestiwn ar eu rhan eu hunain, yw peidio myned o gwbl').[12] Neither is it likely that the anxieties of 'R.A.' from Gwmceri were eased by the brusque answer she received to her question 'Are there not many more girls in the world than boys? How then is it possible for them all to be given in marriage?' ('Ai nid oes llawer mwy o ferched yn y byd nag o feibion? Sut gan hyny y mae yn bosibl iddynt oll gael eu rhoddi mewn priodas?') The 'Ed.' replied, 'No, the number is pretty equal. Not "all" of them choose marriage presumably . . . Be comforted, sisters, and try to find something to do. A little *singing* could be a happy admixture' ('Nac oes; y mae y rhif yn bur gyfartal. Nid ydynt "oll" yn dewis hyny dybygid . . . Byddwch gysurus chwiorydd, a cheisiwch rywbeth I'w wneyd. Gallai ychydig o *ganu* fod yn gymysgedd hapus').[13] This impatience with female anxieties about marital prospects cannot in Cranogwen's case be related misogynistically to the supposed bitterness of the unmarried; on the contrary, the readiness with which she welcomes questions on the single life shows her satisfaction with her chosen state. In October 1881 she was asked by a male correspondent, Gwilym Jones, 'At what age do women go over the boundary to become old maids?' ('Pa bryd y mae merched yn myned dros y terfyn i fod yn hen ferched?') – a most discourteous question, but Cranogwen responds with gusto:

> Cwestiwn o bwys a dyddordeb neillduol; ac yn ffodus, yr ydym yn hollol hyddysg yn yr achos hwn. Yr un pryd ag y bydd bechgyn a phobl yn gyffredin, sef yw hyny, pan ddechreuont dyfu yn rwgnachlyd, yn anhawdd eu 'plesio', ac i ofyn llawer o sylw. Ond fel rheol, gellir ychwanegu fod y rhai y cyfeiriwch atynt yn dal y tu yma i hyny yn hwy na phobl briod.[14]

> [A question of extraordinary importance and interest; and fortunately we are fully informed on this matter. At the same time as men and people in general do, that is, when they start to become grumblers, and difficult to 'please', and ask for too much attention. But usually one can add that those to whom you refer keep to this side of that state longer than married people.]

But on other occasions, Cranogwen can reply with kindness to her correspondents, particularly to those who are clearly in genuine perplexity about the appropriate role of women in society. In September 1881, she was asked by a correspondent who signed herself simply 'Meg', 'Is it through marrying or through not doing so that a woman best answers the purpose of her existence?' ('Pa un ai wrth briodi ai wrth beidio yr etyb merch ddyben ei bodolaeth yn oreu?'). No doubt Cranogwen was pleased by this refusal to take it for granted that reproduction was a woman's fate. In giving her answer, she emphasizes, as she does regularly throughout her editorial contributions to *Y Frythones*, that the differences which exist between one individual and another make it impossible to generalize on such matters:

Anwyl chwaer, pwy yw y ferch yr ymholwch o berthynas iddi? . . . Y
mae merch fan yma ar ein pwys yn cyfrif, meddai, ei bod hi yn ateb
dyben ei bodolaeth yn dda iawn trwy beidio, ond nid hi yw pawb; y
mae y fath wahaniaeth rhyngom a'n gilydd, wyddoch.[15]

[Dear sister, who is the woman about whom you ask? . . . There is a
woman here by our side who considers, she says, that she answers the
purpose of her existence very well by not doing so, but she is not
everybody; there is so much difference between us and one another, you
know.]

The 'woman here by our side' was probably Jane Thomas, an
'interesting character' ('caricter diddorol') according to Cranogwen's biographer, the Reverend D. G. Jones, and a lifelong partner
of Cranogwen.[16] While her parents lived, their house in Llangrannog was Cranogwen's home, but Jane moved to live in the house
next door, and after the death of her parents Cranogwen sold her
family home, and lived with Jane for the last twenty years of her life.
In one of the most personal of her poems, 'Fy Ffrynd' (My Friend),
she attempted to explain what such a relationship meant to her.
Although she is careful in the opening verses to categorize the
attraction as a romantic friendship rather than a love affair, as the
poem proceeds its tone becomes unambiguously lover-like:

> Ah! anwyl chwaer, 'r wyt ti i mi,
>> Fel lloer i'r lli, yn gyson;
> Dy ddilyn heb orphwyso wna
>> Serchiadau pura'm calon
> [. . .]
> I seren dêg dy wyneb di
>> Ni welaf *fi* un gymhar . . .
> Mae miloedd eraill, sêr o fri,
>> Yn gloewi y ffurfafen;
> Edmygaf hwy, ond *caraf* di,
>> Fy Ngwener gu, fy 'Ogwen'.[17]

> [Ah! dear sister, you are to me
> as the moon to the sea, constantly;
> following you restlessly are
> my heart's purest affections
> [. . .]
> To the fair star of your face
> *I* see no equal . . .
> A thousand other stars of distinction
> brighten the firmament;
> I admire them, but I *love* you,
> my beloved Venus, my 'Ogwen'.]

Here, particularly with the reference to 'Ogwen', the female love-object in a popular romantic ballad of the period, Cranogwen places herself unequivocally, and without any apparent embarrassment or self-consciousness, in the male lover's role. This is the explanation perhaps for the emphasis laid in the 'Questions and Answers' columns of *Y Frythones* on the differences between individuals; Cranogwen knew she was different from the majority of her sex. It was women rather than men who were important to her, emotionally at any rate, if not also sexually.

A passage from the diary she kept in 1870, while on a lecture tour of the United States, gives a droll sense of the manner in which the intensity of her relations with women could at times prove a torment as well as a delight. During her visit to Nortonville, California, in July 1870, she was much pained by the cold response of the local women to her, and had to find expression for her feelings, if only in her diary:

> gadawer i mi enwi yr hyn y sydd lawer pryd megys yn fwyaf o boen i mi ... Wel, *menywaid beilchion, hunanol, digydymdeimlad, drwgdybus, eiddigeddus, mursenaidd* – y rhai hyn y sydd yn boen ... Unrhyw siom, neu boen, neu syrffed yn hytrach na hyn, – merched a gwragedd heb megys galon o'u mewn yn unlle ...Y mae *merch* ddideimlad, ddigalon yn hagrwch a siom annyoddefol; y mae – wel nid oes genyf air ... y mae yn gostwng tymheredd cysur un yn isel iawn – islaw *Zero* gryn lawer; wel y mae yn gymaint a fedr un ddal heb rewi o hono yn delpyn.[18]

> [Let me name that which many times gives me most pain ... Well, *proud, selfish, unfeeling, suspicious, jealous, affected women* – it is these who are a pain ... Any disappointment, or pain, or surfeit rather than this, – girls and women without as it were a heart anywhere inside them ... An unfeeling, heartless *woman* is an unbearable blight and disappointment; it is – well, I have no words for it ... it lowers the temperature of one's comfort very severely – considerably below *Zero*; well, it's all one can bear without freezing solid.

As much as the poem 'My Friend', this diary entry conveys Cranogwen's dependence on her emotional relation with women. To be in the company of an unfeeling woman is for her an 'unbearable disappointment', but she does not at any point in her writings comment one way or the other on her emotional responses to men. Women are her all-in-all, in a manner which no doubt made her all the more effective as the inspirer and leader of a new wave of women writers. Maybe she was not, as a result, knowledgeable in every aspect of her contributors' relationship problems, but not one of them could doubt the wholeheartedness of her concern and dedication to their progress as women.

Neither does it appear that her difference in any way affected her popularity. On the contrary, by rejecting men, and maintaining an entirely 'pure' image in the heterosexual context, Cranogwen was meeting the needs of her age and her society. There is no indication in her writings or in her memoir that she was at any time made to feel ashamed of the fact that her strongest emotional feelings were for women. She was criticized by some for looking like a man, for speaking like a man and for speaking from public platforms like a man,[19] but there is no evidence of her ever having been accused of loving like a man. Of course, in an age when the royal head of state repudiated the possibility of its existence, lesbianism was barely an acknowledged concept. Unlike male homosexuality it was not a criminal offence; 'defiling the marital bed' by becoming pregnant outside it was the act which caused a woman to 'fall'. Only at the close of the nineteenth century, with the publication of studies like Havelock Ellis's *Sexual Inversion* in 1897, were suspicions generally raised about the nature of 'romantic friendship' between women.[20] As in the case of the Ladies of Llangollen, before then such relationships were accepted and, indeed, admired as proof of the fact that women could love faithfully on a level above the physical.[21]

Nevertheless, there is much in Cranogwen's writing which indicates her understanding of, and sympathy with, women placed at the margins of their society, at odds with their world. The work for which she was by many most esteemed during her lifetime, the essay series 'Esther Judith', which appeared in *Y Frythones* between October 1880 and July 1881, is one such portrayal.[22] Esther Judith, a neighbour of Cranogwen during her childhood in Llangrannog, had worked throughout her life as a farm labourer, and in old age was dependent upon the parish. But Cranogwen solicits respect for her memory as one who had 'exceptional *talents of expression*' and '*intellectual strengths*' ('*dawn ymadrodd* nodedig' and '*chryfder deall*').[23] 'She would have made an orator without compare,' she says ('gwnaethai areithiwr o'r bron digymhar'), and should have been a preacher or a poet.[24] For all her poverty, had Esther Judith been male she might well have been afforded the opportunity to train for the ministry; within her chapel community her talents would not have gone unnoticed, and could well have gained her a

community-funded place at a Calvinist Methodist theological college. But the talents of young women, as opposed to those of men,
were not promoted by their chapel communities in the same way.
Cranogwen's portrayal of Esther Judith emphasizes the manner
in which women's abilities were wasted, and their potential under-
developed, much to their culture's loss, and to their personal
frustration. The series 'Esther Judith' is a lament for the lost women
preachers and writers of Wales.

It is also a protest against the human obstruction of divine
purposes, as Cranogwen saw them, for Esther Judith was clearly
not created to fill the conventional female role. 'Whoever else was
called upon to "keep house" and look after a family, Esther was
not', says Cranogwen; 'she possessed as little aptitude and ability in
that direction as John the Baptist or one of the early prophets' ('Gan
nad pwy a alwyd i "gadw tŷ" a thrin teulu, *ni* alwyd Esther; ni
feddai fawr fwy o gymhwysder a gallu i hyny nag a feddai Ioan
Fedyddiwr, neu un o'r proffwydi cynnar').[25] But Esther was a
prophet in the wilderness, without an audience. Cranogwen
describes her as habitually carrying her family Bible out into her
garden to read it aloud, discoursing on it as she read, but with no
hearers apart from the gulls. 'The loss was', writes Cranogwen,
'that neither Esther nor any of her contemporaries understood the
particular mission her gifts could have accomplished in the world'
('Y golled ydoedd na ddeallodd Esther, na neb arall ydoedd yn fyw
ar unwaith â hi, y neges arbenig y gallasai y ddawn ydoedd ynddi hi
ei chyflawnu yn y byd').[26] But the editor of *Y Frythones* understood
her own mission: in order to prevent the repetition in subsequent
generations of that loss which Esther represented, her readers must
be made aware that the time had come for the women of Wales, as
well as its men, to speak to and for a more responsive audience than
the rocks and sea-caves of Llangrannog.

But by the last decades of the nineteenth century Cranogwen and
her journal were not alone in providing inspiration for Welsh
women. In an elegy on Cranogwen, the poet Nantlais refers to her
role as one of the leaders of the Welsh women's temperance
movement:

> Ganwyd hi i arwain byddin,
> > Blaen y fyddin oedd ei lle;
> Rhoddodd Duw ei byddin iddi,
> > Byddin Merched dewr y De.[27]

[She was born to lead an army,
the front line was her place;
God gave her an army,
the army of the brave Women of the South.]

The 'army' to which Nantlais refers was the South Wales Women's Temperance Union, founded by Cranogwen in 1901; she led it as its secretary for the next fifteen years until she had to give up the work in 1916 because of ill health. But the South Wales Women's Union was the successor of the massively successful North Wales Women's Temperance Union. The temperance movement would have succeeded in Wales without Cranogwen, for all the value of her contribution to it. And even without her example it would have succeeded, as it did, in making many of its female members into public figures, as protesters, organizers, lecturers and writers. The next section of this chapter assesses the contribution of female temperance campaigners to Welsh-language print culture.

ii.   The battle against Bacchus

In a seminal article on the history of the Welsh women's temperance movement, Ceridwen Lloyd-Morgan recorded how quickly the North Wales Women's Temperance Union grew from its formation in 1892: by 1896 it had 106 branches and 11,821 members, many of them inspired by the movement to take a far more public role than hitherto in their society.[28] From 1892 to the outbreak of World War I, throughout the towns and villages of Wales, women strengthened one another in the cause in public meetings; marched through their local streets under temperance banners to picket popular taverns; established refuges to save and succour weaker sisters in danger of succumbing to alcoholism; attended law courts to try to prevent new public-house licences being granted, and invaded taverns en masse to sing temperance hymns and harangue the customers directly. Such was the enthusiasm for the cause that had Wales won its independence in the 1890s and given women the vote, as the Cymru Fydd movement pledged itself to do, then in all probability the United States would not have been the only country to introduce Prohibition. Because of the rapid and unregulated growth of the coal, iron and steel industries in south and north-east Wales, leading to work stress, overcrowding and social upheaval, alcoholism had indeed become a pressing concern by the second half of the nineteenth century. As it was also connected with the stereotype of the Welsh as barbaric – the 1847 Report had listed drunkenness amongst the sins of the Principality – to regulate the consumption of alcohol became one of the first priorities for those who wished to 'raise' Wales. In an 1889 address to the Women's Liberal Association in Penllyn, Meirioneth, Anna Ionawr (Annie Vaughan) told her audience that all Welsh patriots should pledge themselves to support the temperance movement as one of the chief measures by which to rid Wales of its shameful image.[29] Attacking the great 'Seductress' that lured their men into disgrace and poverty was seen as a particularly appropriate role for those pillars of familial and religious good order in Wales, its Dissenting women. 'Let us temperance women vow to point our arrows at her', wrote Buddug (Catherine Jane Prichard, 1842–1909): 'No doubt some will say that it is not suitable for women to shoot, but our profound belief in this present campaign against the "Seductress" makes us aware of the necessity of taking up the bow and shooting' ('Ymdyn-ghedwn ninau ferched dirwestol i anelu ein saethau ati. Dichon y dywed ambell un nad gweddus i ferched saethu, ond y mae ein dwfn argyhoeddiad yn yr ymgyrch bresenol yn erbyn yr "Hudoles", yn ein gwneyd yn ystyriol o'n rhwymedigaeth i osod ein llaw ar y bwa, a saethu').[30]

Few Welsh-language women authors writing in the last two decades of the nineteenth century failed to produce a temperance hymn or prose tract. One exception, but one which in a sense proves the rule, was Mair Eifion (Mary Davies, 1846–82), ordained a bard in the National Eisteddfod at Pwllheli in 1875. A profoundly patriotic poet, no less zealous for the good name of Welsh women than any other contributor to the *Frythones* or the second *Gymraes*, Mair Eifion repeatedly begs her readers to do all they can to shed reflected glory on their race and gender. 'Insist on a name worth carving', she tells her audience, 'and prove indisputably / that women are gifted' ('Myn enw gwerth ei gerfio . . . A dyro brawf yn eglur / Fod merch yn meddu dawn').[31] But temperance is not one of her themes, for the simple reason that she was the daughter of a tavern-keeper. Her parents kept the Tregunter Arms in Porthmadog, and that inn was her home throughout her short life. She never contributed to the women's periodicals, perhaps because of the particular emphasis placed in their pages on temperance. 'I'd rather see you in your coffin / than see you as a curse to your country', sang the daughter of the Tregunter Arms to her Welsh sisters ('Gwell genyf a fyddai dy wel'd yn dy arch / Na'th weled yn felldith i'th wlad'),[32] but for a Welsh woman to have any contact whatsoever with the demon drink, let alone owe her livelihood to it, would have been in itself a national disgrace for many of them, however virtuous and patriotic she might be in every other aspect of her life.

Her contemporary Myfanwy Meirion (Margaret Jones, 1847–1931) lived a much worthier existence, according to the notions of the period: she consecrated her energies to the Bridge of Hope Mission, then at work in darkest London saving 'girls of a shattered character' ('merched o gymeriad drylliedig') from the grip of both the seductress alcohol and male seducers.[33] From the Bridge of Hope, Myfanwy Meirion sent home to her compatriots many heartening messages on the success of the movement. In the *Frythones* in 1885, for example, she wrote of the Mission's transformation of an East End tavern into a Christian refuge, its 'Public Bar' now a prayer room, adding 'I am certain that many Welsh hearts will rejoice in contemplating this victory for virtue and religion' ('Yr wyf yn sicr y bydd llawer calon Gymreig yn llawenhau wrth feddwl am yr oruchafiaeth i rinwedd a chrefydd').[34] Such was her faith in the character of her countrymen that it was to her a bitter disappointment to meet a Welsh person who did not share her principles. She gives the history of one such unfortunate encounter in her poem 'May He Who Reads Consider' ('A Ddarlleno Ystyried'); a Welshman, professedly a patriot, greeted her cheerfully, but his breath smelt of spirits. Myfanwy Meirion tells him,

> Dy garu yr ydwyf o eigion fy nghalon
> 　　Er mwyn yr hen iaith, ac er mwyn yr hen wlad,
> Nis gallaf ymatal, rhaid ydyw im' lefain,
> 　　O! gochel y cwpan, O! gochel y frad.[35]

> [I love you from the depths of my heart
> for the sake of the old language, and the old country,
> I cannot hold back, I must cry out,
> O! beware of the cup, O! beware of the betrayal.]

The influence of such writers as Myfanwy Meirion depended to a great extent on the connection between their literary productions and what their readers knew about them: their personal story, as women who had given their lives to fight the demon drink and save its victims, was an important aspect of the effectiveness and popularity of their writings. Another author with a similar reputation was Annie Catherine Prichard, one of the Liverpool Welsh who became well known as the hard-working secretary of the North Wales Women's Temperance Union from 1900 to 1925. The minute-books of the Union meetings she kept for a quarter of a century often make interesting reading, for the Union felt itself empowered to comment on moral issues of the day generally, insofar as they applied to women. On one occasion, for example, the Union at its Annual Council presented a strongly worded declaration to the Royal Court on divorce, arguing against testimonies put forward to that Court 'that a different standard of morality should rule the lives of men and women' ('y dadganiad cryfaf yn erbyn . . . eu tystiolaethau . . . fod safon gwahanol o foesoldeb i lywodraethu bywyd meibion a merched').[36] The continuing acceptance of the double sexual standard for men and women was anathema to women like Annie Catherine Prichard: rather, men must learn to keep as strict a check on their physical desires as women were expected to do.

Highly respected as an organizer, Prichard was offered the job of editing the second *Gymraes*, but refused it; nevertheless, she contributed extensively to the periodical, publishing in it, under the pseudonym Ruth, a stream of short stories and articles. She was an expert at combining in popular fiction the principles of temperance with romance; one cannot but admire her creative inventiveness in writing so many stories on the same theme. All the varied aspects of the temperance cause were mirrored in her fictions. As might be expected, she has victorious stories of the drunkard's wife succeeding in winning him back from the clutches of the 'seductress' by admirable feminine devices, as well as tales of warning about innocent young women taking jobs as barmaids and falling into ill repute.[37] These are set in working-class contexts, but Ruth also composed fictions with more middle-class settings, which deal with such issues as the connection between the stock market and the production of alcohol.

In a story published in the *Gymraes* in May 1899, for example, Grace Hughes, the young mistress of a substantial property, Y Fron, is appalled to learn where her dead father invested the family funds. When paying a missionary visit to the local village, she is told by one old sinner, John Morris, 'you can't teach me about drunkenness, while you live on the profits of alcohol. Your father knew where he could get the highest interest for his money, and it is us drunkards you must thank for that high interest' ('nid chwi sydd i'm dysgu i yn nghylch meddwi, tra yr ydych yn byw ar arian y ddiod.

'Roedd eich tad yn gwybod lle i gael y llog ucha' am ei arian, ac i ni sydd yn meddwi y rhaid i chwi ddiolch am y llog uchel yna').[38] Of course Grace must now sell the dirty shares, but at first she has difficulty persuading her brother Ogwen that they must do so, though he is a chapel deacon. He tells her defensively, 'We only do as hundreds of religious people do, some of them preachers of the gospel too' ('Tyden ni ddim ond yn gwneyd fel y mae cannoedd o grefyddwyr yn gwneyd, a rhai o honynt yn weinidogion yr efengyl hefyd').[39] But Grace succeeds in her aim at last, though she and her brother have to move from Y Fron to a lowly cottage in the village after losing the high interest on their shares. However, the story is a romance as well as a temperance tract, and all ends happily. Before its close, not only has John Morris turned teetotal under the influence of Grace's sacrifice, but the interesting widower who bought Y Fron is doing his best to persuade Miss Hughes to take up her old position as the house's mistress once again. In this way Ruth sweetened the pill of the temperance message to her readers: the romantic framework of the stories meant that her principled heroines received their reward in this life as well as in the hereafter.

Another diligent worker for the North Wales Women's Temperance Union who also gained fame as a writer was Buddug, the Union's Anglesey secretary.[40] Her *Yr Arholydd Dirwestol* (The Temperance Catechism, 1905) was praised by O. M. Edwards as proof of the fact that a catechism could be a work of art.[41] At times, however, it is difficult to believe that Buddug was not deliberately writing with her tongue in her cheek when she composed some of her temperance verses: 'Yr Eneth a'r Gasgen' ('The Girl and the Barrel'), for example, is an absurd exchange between a girl and a talking beer-barrel. The humble wood is profoundly distressed and apologetic about the role enforced upon it, but the girl assures it that its moral stature must be higher than that of 'weak men' who voluntarily 'give up their bodies so easily / To become barrels in their thousands' ('rhoi eu cyrph mor rhwydd / Yn gasgiau wrth y miloedd'). Nevertheless, she sympathizes deeply with the disgraced barrel, telling it that

Rwy'n teimlo dros dy angen
    Fel pe baet imi'n frawd;
[. . .]
Mil gwell fuasai'th dynged,
    A mwy fil mil dy barch,

Pe byddet yn ddi arbed
   Yn gwneyd i ddyn ei arch.[42]

[I feel for your need
as if you were my brother;
[. . .]
A thousand times better would be your fate,
and your respect a thousand thousand times higher,
if you were without delay
to make for man his coffin.]

But at other times, Buddug's seriousness and her appetite for victory in the great fight is undeniable. In her war-song 'The Battle of Temperance and Bacchus', Welsh women are exhorted to arm themselves against an enemy which is for once recognized as a temptation for women themselves, as well as for men. The only armour they need in order to defeat the seductress is the word 'No' and the strength to '*stop* taking, *stop* giving' ('*peidio* cym'ryd, *peidio* rhoddi'):

Peidio, ferched, dyna'r rhyfel
   Drosodd, heb ddim tywallt gwaed,
Peidio, dyna froydd tawel,
   A dynoliaeth ar ei thraed.[43]

[*Stop*, girls, there's the war
over without loss of blood,
Stop, there's quiet regions,
and humanity on its feet.]

'Stopping', for a temperance woman, meant not only foregoing alcohol personally but also not socializing with – and certainly not marrying – anybody who was not also an abstainer, as well, of course, as not doing anything which would in any way promote the market in alcohol. The narrower, more negative aspects of the movement are evident here: for all the emphasis put on actively working for temperance, saying 'no' was, of course, at the core of the fight against Bacchus. Temptation had to be resisted and controlled in the self, first of all, before going out on the streets to evangelize for the cause. In the literature of some of these abstainers, alcohol seems to become a symbol of the body's dangerous desires generally, desires which had to be defeated if the body was to become a temple to God and an honour to the Welsh nation.

This stance accorded well, of course, with the general campaign to regulate and purify the Welsh body, ongoing since the 1847 Report, but it deflected the blame for physical transgressions from sexual desire (which was always, as we have seen, represented as the woman's fault and responsibility) to alcohol. Since Eve's fall, men could blame women for all heterosexual weaknesses; but with alcohol as the most potent 'bad influence', women were also now offered a scapegoat. And when it came to drink, it was obvious that women belonged in fact to the gender most capable of abstaining: men were by far the most overt and public drunkards, though there might be a few sad cases amongst the women. By testifying against drunkenness, Welsh women were thus symbolically rejecting the world of the flesh and all its temptations, and throwing the guilt of unregulated desire from their own shoulders on to those of the men in the taverns they campaigned against. No wonder, then, that the temperance movement in Wales worked to promote women's self-respect.

Changes in the characteristic themes of Welsh-language literature by women between 1870 and the last years of the nineteenth century evince their growth in self-esteem. In 1879 Ceridwen Peris, for example, published in the *Frythones* a tale conveying very negative views of Welsh women: 'Alegori – Blodau Pleser' ('Allegory – The Flowers of Pleasure') portrays its central female character as prey to her own appetite; she lives only to satisfy her lust for the 'flowers of pleasure', and loses her life in the selfish quest for them.[44] But Welsh women are presented as positively heroic in Ceridwen Peris's later pieces, such as, for example, her long quest poem 'Y Fun a'r Faner Wen' (The Maiden with the White Banner), published in the *Traethodydd* in 1893. The Maiden with the White Banner is a pilgrim on an allegorical journey through a nightmare territory, with temptations ranged on each side. But her military purity enables her to conquer each and every foe, and she plants a white banner to mark the site of each successful combat, in order to inspire the sisters who will come after her. Temptation conquered means heightened self-respect: 'In the skeleton of temptation she found reviving structures', says the poem of its heroine ('Yn sgerbwd temtasiwn cadd ddiliau adfywiol').[45] Welsh temperance women appear generally to have found their defeat of the devil drink reviving: it created heroines which the nation as a whole could pride itself upon, and women were informed of them in great detail in the journal that Ceridwen Peris went on to edit, the second *Gymraes*.

To a far greater extent than the *Frythones*, the aim of Ceridwen Peris's *Gymraes* was to create Welsh heroines.[46] In poems such as 'Ferched Cymru, Ymwrolwch' (Women of Wales, Take Heart) Ceridwen Peris assures her readers that 'Great is the history of Welsh women' ('Gwych yw hanes Merched Cymru'), and praises in particular women of the Puritan period and the early Methodist movement who 'stood up for truth / like pillars of steel' ('sefyll dros wirionedd / Fel pileri dur').[47] But Welsh female courage was not something which belonged only to the past; on the contrary, the biographical articles in the second *Gymraes* provided a host of portrayals of contemporary heroines who were also worthy to be emulated. Authors, lecturers, Liberal Women's organizers, Band of Hope leaders, temperance movement fighters, Sunday-school and day-school teachers – they were all an honour to their sex and their nation. In an article on Ruth and her contribution, Ceridwen Peris could proclaim with pride 'Whatever nation can boast of its wise, talented, religious young women, pure of character, Welsh women must be placed first' ('Pa genedl bynnag a all ymffrostio yn ei merched ieuanc call, talentog, crefyddol, pur eu cymeriadau, rhaid rhoddi menywod Cymru ar y blaen').[48] But the group of women that the *Gymraes* admires most profoundly is that small though increasing band who went out as missionaries to the far corners of the British Empire. Many of the female missionaries, too, wrote on their experiences, often in order to raise funds for foreign fields from the chapel members back home; their first-hand experiences of new worlds meant that they brought a new dimension into Welsh-language women's writing, a dimension explored in the next section of this chapter.

iii.   Welsh women's mission and the British Empire

On 19 October 1816, Ann Evans, née Jones, from Llanidloes, seventeen years old and just married to Calvinist Methodist minister Evan Evans from Llanrwst, set sail on the *Alacrity* for the Cape of Good Hope, at that time part of Britain's most recently established colony. Motivated by the need to secure for the merchant ships of the East India Company a safe resting-place on the sea

route to India, the British Crown, after a series of bloody engagements with both the indigenous people of the Cape and its Dutch
settlers, was finally able to fly the Union Flag over Cape Colony in
1814. Where the soldiers went, the missionaries followed. Under
the auspices of the London Missionary Society, Evan Evans was
appointed to minister the gospel to the Hottentots, or, rather, to the
Khoikhoi, to give the people of the Cape their indigenous name
(Hottentot, which apparently denotes 'stutterer', was the name the
Dutch settlers gave to the natives they encountered, whose language
included an expressive pattern of clicking sounds). Eight months
after she had embarked, Ann Evans, from her new home in
Bethelsdorp near Cape Town, set about the task of attempting to
convey to her family at home some impression of the world in
which she now found herself. Her long letter, which was subsequently published in Wales as a fund-raising missionary pamphlet
(though there is no suggestion in the letter that she herself intended
it to be put to such use), vividly evokes the high romance of the
enterprise, and presents a markedly egalitarian view of the people
she encountered: she took them as her equals, in a manner rarely
found in other writings home to Britain from the Empire.[49] But
when she returned to Wales ten years later, Ann Evans accompanied
a dying husband, worn out at the age of thirty-five as much by his
struggles with the obstructive Cape colonists as by his work
amongst the indigenous people and the diseases and hard life of the
hinterland. She buried him in Llanidloes shortly after their arrival
home, along with one of their children who had sickened on the
voyage; the bodies of two more of her children were left behind in
African graves.[50]

Such a close to her adventure was not anticipated in 1816, when
she and her husband were cheered on their way by the prayers and
good wishes of their friends and co-religionists. At least two poems
were written in their honour: 'Ffarwél i Evan Evans' by Mary Evans
of Llanrwst commends the 'suitable wife' ('priod addas') the missionary has chosen, and Eleanor Hughes, in her poem 'Ar ymadawiad Evan Evans' (On the leaving of Evan Evans), dismisses her
own grief at losing her friends by reminding herself of the 'heavenly
purpose' ('nefol ddiben') of their mission.[51] These poems are
anthologized in Cathryn Charnell-White's edition of early Welsh-
language women's poetry, along with another poignant piece of the
same period, in which Mary Bevan, of Pen-yr-Allt-Wen in
Ceredigion, bids farewell to her friends before setting out in 1818 to

the Madagascar mission field with her husband, Independent minister Thomas Bevan. Within a year Bevan, her husband and their child were dead, but her poem eloquently encapsulates the high romance of her brief life. 'As I swam the river of corruption / I was caught in the net', she says of her conversion experience at the age of seventeen ('Wrth nofio afon llygredd, / Fe'm daliwyd yn y rhwyd'). Subsequently, she yearned to become an evangelist, apparently hopelessly because of her gender, but God answered her prayer through her marriage, enabling her 'to go to Madagascar / with the pearls of Calvary' ('I fynd i Madagascar / Â pherlau Calfari').[52]

As texts arising out of missionary activities, these poems, along with Ann Evans' letter, are representative of that type of discourse in which are to be found by far the most numerous references to the British Empire in Welsh-language nineteenth-century writing. Before the close of the nineteenth century, gospel-bearers had been sent out from Welsh chapels to every corner of the Empire, to Natal, Sierra Leone, the Sudan, Ceylon, Malacca in South East Asia, Australia, Fiji, Jamaica, Trinidad, the West Indies, British Honduras, Newfoundland, Gibraltar (to convert the Papists) and throughout India. Major bases had also been established by the Welsh Nonconformists in territories – such as China, Madagascar, northern Africa and Tahiti – which were affiliated to Britain through trading agreements though not actually annexed under the British Crown. The numbers and the costs involved in such enterprises were substantial: by 1897, the Welsh Calvinistic Methodists had sent out fifty-six ordained ministers to the Khasi Hills alone. And with the missionaries went, of course, their wives and children, and later doctors, schoolteachers and nurses as well. A well-developed late nineteenth-century missionary base contained schools, hospitals, domestic dwellings for the converts as well the British-born (for the converted were often rejected from their own families and had to be housed and supported by the mission), and maybe a printing-press too, as well as the church itself, of course, all of which had to be maintained by voluntary contributions from the congregations back home.[53] In order to encourage their readers in the impetus to give, the Welsh denominational journals of the day filled their pages with letters and reports from missionaries, and articles, stories and poems about missionaries.[54]

The secular press, too, insofar as nineteenth-century Wales can be said to have had a secular press, also naturally enough reflected the same preoccupation. *Llon a Lleddf* (Joyous and Plaintive, 1897), a collection of tales about Welsh village life by Sara Maria Saunders (1864–1939), for example, is replete with references to India: a penniless girl sells her abundant hair in order to contribute her mite to the missionary collection; a widow so successfully dissembles her grief as she bids her only child Godspeed to the mission fields that he thinks she hardly cares, but the neighbours know that it's always been part of her generosity to give as if the gift meant nothing to her, and that she'll never recover from this loss; a deacon who has never left his village is more familiar with every detail of the topography of the Khasi Hills than he is with his own backyard.[55] Such fictional characters were modelled on figures like Elizabeth Evans of Llanwrtyd, of whom Cranogwen wrote that 'the names of the missionaries and native converts are as familiar to her as those of her neighbours' ('enwau y cenhadon a'r athrawon brodorol mor gynefin iddi ag ydoedd eiddo ei chymdogion ago-saf').[56] Elizabeth Evans had once placed a sovereign in the hand of the missionary Jermyn Jones, asking him to use it to open up a new mission field in India; as a consequence, the Bhoi tribe first heard the words of the Lord, and Elizabeth Evans was referred to as Mrs Evans, Bhoi, for the rest of her days. She named her home in Llanwrtyd 'Bhoilymbong', and followed the doings of the mission-aries so closely that she virtually lived in Khasia, for all that she never in fact set foot in India. Every penny she could she gave to the cause, and she collected funds assiduously from her neighbours, as well as publishing poems exhorting her brothers and sisters amongst the Calvinist Methodist congregations to become mission-aries, as the highest calling open to man and (after 1887) to woman.[57] The imperial fields of the Lord were such people's romance, the missionaries their knights in shining armour, and each black convert a pearl that would shine forever in their heavenly crown.

The intensity of Welsh people's involvement with missionary activity is such as to suggest that the missionaries had redemptive roles to play as saviours, not only of the indigenous people of the British colonies, but also of Welsh pride. By the mid nineteenth century, given the mortifications it had endured at the publication of the Blue Books, Welsh self-esteem would have been considerably lower had it not been able to glory in the figure of the Welsh missionary, as representing a far, far better mode of relating to the world at large than that of the English imperial officer or soldier.

Overt disapproval of the soldiers of the Empire and their methods is expressed in a number of early accounts of Indian travels. Emma Roberts (*c.*1793–1840), who hailed from a landed Denbighshire family, travelled to India in 1828 with her sister, the wife of a British officer serving in Bengal. After her sister's death, she settled in Calcutta and for a period in 1831–2 acted as editor of the *Oriental Observer*, according to the 'memoir' which accompanies the post-humous publication of her *Notes of an Overland Journey through France and Egypt to Bombay*.[58] In that volume, her family connections with the imperial army do not prevent her from recording in detail one incident she observed in Cairo:

> I . . . saw a drunken Englishman, an officer of the Indian army, I am sorry to say, beat several natives of Cairo, with whom he happened to come in contact in the crowd, in the most brutal and unprovoked manner . . . I regret to be obliged to add, that it is but too commonly the habit, of Englishmen to beat the boat-men, donkey-men, and others of the poorer class, whom they may engage in their service. They justify this cowardly practice – cowardly, because the poor creatures can gain no redress – by declaring that there is no possibility of getting them to stir excepting by means of the whip; but, in most cases, all that I witnessed, they were not at the trouble of trying fairer methods: at once enforcing their commands by blows.[59]

In the early years of the nineteenth century, when empire-building was understood as being pre-eminently about increasing overseas trade, there was often open antagonism between the militia and the missionaries of the Empire. The ethos of trade was, of course, clearly distinguishable from that of Christian evangelism. It was the evangelists largely who had aroused public protest in Britain against slavery and brought about the abolition of the British slave trade in 1807, and the freeing of slaves on British territory in 1833, with the loss, of course, of much trade revenue. But the Indian uprising of 1857, which nearly brought to an abrupt close Britain's rule in India, changed the way in which Britain conceived of its empire. The trading interest saw the mutiny as in part brought about by the natives' fear of the Christianizing presence, but the missionaries pointed out, with greater effect, that in those Indian provinces in which they had succeeded in making their presence felt fewer natives had rebelled. No Christian convert had raised arms against the British; had the East India Trading Company allowed them more scope, said the missionaries, and put Bibles in the hands of every Indian schoolchild as they had requested, the uprising might never have taken place. After Britain regained full control of India in 1858, its purposes in furthering its empire were now presented to the world in explicitly Christian terms: the British ruled for the good of the colonized, it was now to be understood, not for personal gain. According to one influential politician of the period, for example,

> the authority of the British Crown is at this moment the most powerful instrument under Providence, of maintaining peace and order in many extensive regions of the earth, and thereby assists in diffusing amongst millions of the human race, the blessings of Christianity and civilization.[60]

The missionaries, it would appear, had won the public opinion battle, but in another sense, they had lost it, for from now on they and all they stood for would be seen as part and parcel of the ethos of British imperialism, and as the providers of its overt moral justification.

In devoutly Nonconformist nineteenth-century Wales, responses to the Empire in the second half of the century are consequently diverse and ambivalent. Some commentators appear to have swallowed wholesale the ideology of the British Empire's Christianizing mission. The travel writing of Margaret Jones of Rhosllanerchrugog, a Welsh Nonconformist maidservant, serves to provide a more conventional comparison between the 'heathen' and the Christian than Emma Roberts's more radical perspective. Margaret Jones found employment within the household of a family of converted Jews who participated in the Christian mission to the Jews, first in Paris, then in Jerusalem, and lastly in Morocco. In a characteristic passage from the second of the two books she published on her travels and experiences, she comments on the people she observed through her Moroccan window:

> Gwelais hwy o ffenestr fy ystafell yn curo troseddwr am bum munud; dyrnent ef fel dyrnu ŷd. Yr oedd fy nheimladau yn gymysgedig o dristwch a gorfoledd. Tristwch am gosp y pechadur, a llawenydd fy mod yn gwybod am wlad well, am weinyddiaeth well, am fy mod wedi fy ngeni a'm magu yn y wlad, ac wedi fy nysgu yn y grefydd sydd yn *mainspring* cyfiawnder y wlad hono. Prydain am byth![61]

> [I saw them from the window of my room beating an offender for five minutes; they thrashed him like thrashing corn. My feelings were a mixture of sadness and rejoicing. Sadness at the punishment of the

sinner, and joy because I knew of a better country, a better administration, because I was born and bred in that country, and educated in the religion which is the mainspring of its justice. Britain for ever!]

She closes her commentary by assuring her audience that the only hope for the restoration of law and order in Morocco is its speedy assimilation into the British Empire and a thoroughgoing Protestant Christian mission.

At the same time, the Welsh-language women's periodicals often opposed imperial wars: looking back over the year 1884, Cranogwen says in *Y Frythones*, 'our readers know that the intervention in Egypt is still in process . . . it is a disastrous business, involving much shame and loss' ('hysbys yw i'n darllenwyr fod yr ymyrraeth â'r Aifft o hyd yn parhau . . . helynt drychinebus yw, gyda sarhad a cholled ryw gymaint').[62] A decade later in *Y Gymraes*, Ellen Hughes asks, 'When will England recognize that a lust for territory and authority is not praiseworthy, and that it is the basest craving which is satisfied by singing "Rule, Britannia"?' ('Pa bryd y daw Lloegr i weled nad ydyw chwant am diriogaeth ac awdurdod yn glod iddi, ac mai y nwyd iselaf a foddheir wrth ganu "Rule, Britannia"?').[63] But both journals are unquestioningly supportive of the 'Romance of our Foreign Mission' ('Rhamant ein Cenhadaeth Dramor'), as Sara Maria Saunders called it, and of course both were fully aware that the majority of the Welsh missionaries worked in fields which had only been made accessible to them by British guns, and that their security while at work was largely attributable to their identity as British subjects, as 'Christian soldiers' in the army of the Great White Queen.

The career of another Ellen Hughes, not the essayist but a missionary, illustrates the manner in which missionary activity was caught up in imperial government, so that they could not easily be separated. Born in 1872 in Llanefydd, in Denbighshire, to a Nonconformist minister and his wife, Ellen Hughes was appointed as a missionary with the Calvinist Methodists in 1899. She started on her work in Silcar in Khasia, but very shortly, before the year was up, on the strength of her University of Wales degree from Bangor, was appointed headmistress of the Eurasian School for girls in Shillong – a British government school, not a Welsh Methodist missionary one.[64] In the many pamphlets and articles Ellen Hughes published in Wales in order to raise money for the missionaries, she presents the history of her exertions in India and subsequently in

Burma, in a manner which makes it obvious not only that she was still proselytizing Christianity fervently after accepting an imperial teaching post, but that she also took pride in the success of any of her converts who were appointed to posts as schoolteachers or civil servants in the institutions of the Raj. Of course the consequence was that her converts were bound more tightly than before to the Empire, and to acceptance of British rule: Ellen Hughes was clearly working for the Empire as well as for her religion.

At the same time, one cannot doubt that it was saving souls for Christ that was important to Ellen Hughes, not the success of the British Empire in India. In one of her stories, 'The History of Hom Ray and its Consequences' ('Hanes Hom Ray a'r Canlyniadau'), she describes the journey she made in 1899 with Annie Thomas of Merthyr Tydfil, another missionary sent out by the Calvinist Methodists, to a remote area of Khasia, an area she says 'without roads at all, and only narrow tracks along the mountainsides and through the forests' ('heb ffyrdd o gwbl, a dim ond llwybrau culion hyd lethrau'r mynyddoedd a thrwy y coedwigoedd'). The two young women sing hymns as they trudge onwards, and through so doing attract the attention of a crew of shepherd boys, full of curiosity about the sudden appearance of two white women in the middle of the hills. As the boys 'laugh their heads off' the women sing to them the Welsh hymn, 'Dewch, hen ac ieuanc, dewch / At Iesu, mae'n llawn bryd' (Come, old and young, come / to Jesus, it is full time), translated into their language.[65] After the missionaries continue on their journey, one of the boys, Hom Ray, remains curious and starts asking questions of a previously converted neighbour:

'Wel, faint o amser sydd er pan ddaeth y Gwaredwr hwn?' meddai Hom. 'Y mae yn agos i ddwy fil o flynyddoedd welet ti,' meddai'r Cristion. 'Tase hwnna'n wir, mi fase ni wedi clywed amdano cyn hyn,' meddai Hom. 'Na,' meddai'r hen ŵr gan daflu cochl dros y pechod o ddifaterwch gwledydd cred, 'newydd gael hyd i ni mae nhw, yr ydym yn byw mor bell.'[66]

['Well, how long is it since this Saviour came?' said Hom. 'It's nearly two thousand years, you see,' said the Christian. 'If that was true, we'd have heard about him before now,' said Hom. 'No,' said the old man, throwing a veil over the sin of apathy in Christian countries, 'they've only just found us, we live so far away.']

For Ellen Hughes it was straightforwardly a sin that the West had not carried the faith of the New Testament to every spot on the globe long before 1899; Britain's imperial armies, in finally opening up the mission fields, had ultimately been following a divine plan. Yet at the close of the 'History of Hom Ray', the shepherd boy from the hills, after having accepted Christianity and been educated in the missionaries' school, becomes a teacher in one of the British government institutions, and thus a servant of the Empire. Shaped as it was by its place within imperialism, it is difficult to see the encounter between Ellen Hughes and the shepherd boy as one which was unequivocally to his benefit, for all the missionary's evident sincerity and dedication.

At the same time, the allure of this tale to readers back in Wales, particularly its young female readers, is obvious enough. Here were two young unmarried women, adventuring alone over an entirely unknown and potentially dangerous, yet breathtakingly beautiful terrain, confident in the certainty that God was on their side and that to everyone who knew of them in their faraway homes they were already saints. It is difficult to imagine a life further removed than theirs from the narrow round usually allotted to the late nineteenth-century Welsh woman; understandably, to be a missionary was the dream of many of the more adventurously minded Victorian girls of Wales. Unlike their brothers, they could not hope to become a preacher in Wales, but particularly after 1887, when the Calvinist Methodists started ordaining unmarried women as missionaries, to become a missionary was a dream that might be fulfilled.[67] As a child, the favourite activity of the niece of Margaret Jones, *Fy Chwaer*, Sidney Margaret Roberts, from Y Wyddgrug, Flintshire, was playing the game 'Saying Goodbye to the Missionaries'; she grew up to be the wife of the missionary John Roberts and his assistant, with the work of translating the Bible into the Khasi language.[68] Sara Maria Saunders had also longed to become a missionary during her childhood: 'she had a child's partiality to a little missionary book,' said one of her biographers, 'and she quietly hoped that the Lord would use her in the field of the Foreign Mission' ('Yr oedd hoffter plentyn ynddi at lyfr cenhadol bychan, a distaw obeithiai y byddai i'r Arglwydd ei defnyddio ar faes y Genhadaeth Dramor').[69] 'To be a missionary was the life ambition of Miss Williams' ('*Bod yn genades oedd uchelgais bywyd Miss Williams*'), emphasized the biographer of Annie Williams, a member of the Liverpool Welsh community who went out to Shillong as a missionary with the Calvinist Methodists in 1896, at twenty-three years of age, and who died there of cholera within a year, leaving not one but two nations mourning her loss, according to *Y Gymraes*.[70]

Such was the persistent need for funds that, whether or not they felt called to emulate the missionaries, Nonconformist women were given little opportunity to forget about the cause. *Y Drysorfa*, the periodical mouthpiece of the Calvinist Methodists, contained in each number many pages on missionary activities, the columns of which were often towards the close of the century being written by women. In 1890 Elizabeth Williams, born in Penrhyndeudraeth in 1866, described herself in *Y Drysorfa* as preaching to as many as forty women at a time in a cramped zenana in Sylhet, belonging to the family of her Bengali tutor.[71] She asks her readers at home to pray for the neglected women of India, and begs them to send out more female missionaries to assist in the great work of their conversion. In a later letter from Sylhet, Elizabeth Ann Roberts, born in Blaenau Ffestiniog in 1864, draws attention to the fact that the female missionary is a relatively new phenomenon, and blames men for women's previous absence from the field: in the past women had 'not been encouraged by our masters, who preferred rather to keep us dependent and subordinate' ('nad arweinid ni allan gan ein meistriaid, y rhai a ewyllysient yn hytrach ein cadw mewn stad o ddibyniad a darostyngiad'). Roberts argues that every Christian woman should acknowledge her personal responsibility to heal the world: 'she does not have the right to let disorder and cruelty persist, and on earth there is no suffering, injustice, or misery for which she is not responsible' ('Nid oes ganddi hawl i adael i anrhefn a chreulondeb barhau, ac nid oes ar y ddaear ddioddefaint, anghyfiawnder, na thrueni, nad yw hi yn gyfrifol am dano').[72]

In India the missionaries had come to appreciate the power of women: 'it's the women', one missionary is reported as saying, 'who are the true defenders of Hinduism' ('Y marched . . . ydyw prif amddiffynfa Hindwaeth').[73] Now a new self-respect encouraged them to believe that Welsh women, too, could be central to their communities and empowered to uphold their own religion and values. 'With Christ, she is a great power', says Elizabeth Roberts of all her female co-religionists; 'we women have not yet imagined what we can accomplish through him' ('Gyda Christ y mae hi yn allu mawr. Nid ydym ni ferched eto wedi dychmygu yr hyn allwn wneyd trwyddo ef').[74] In these letters back home from the mission field such writers were sounding a new note, of feminism supported by Nonconformist Christian belief in the responsibilities of every individual to fulfill their god-given strengths to the utmost, for the saving of their own soul and of that of as many as possible of God's other children. For women to remain passive and complicit with the dictates of a dying patriarchy was a sin, in the face of such enlightened challenges. But by the 1890s, their message was also receiving support back home in Wales by influences from another quarter as well, as the last chapter of this book indicates.

6 Writing Young Wales

According to William George, David Lloyd George's brother and an early historian of the Cymru Fydd movement, 1886 was a 'very remarkable year in the development of the national spirit in Wales' ('blwyddyn nodedig iawn yn natblygiad yr ysbryd Cenedlaethol yng Nghymru').[1] In that year a group of Welshmen meeting in London under the leadership of Thomas Edward Ellis established the first Welsh Home Rule society, with the aim of securing a Parliament for Wales.[2] A few months later Ellis was elected MP for Meirioneth, after having called for Welsh Home Rule as part of his electoral campaign; he went on after his victory to help develop within the Welsh Liberal Party the Cymru Fydd, or Young Wales, movement. 1886 was also the year in which Michael D. Jones, headmaster of Bala Theological College and founding father of the Welsh settlement in Patagonia, invited one of the leaders of the Irish Land League, Michael Davitt, to a meeting in Blaenau Ffestiniog at which the establishment of a Welsh nationalist political party was advocated. A few years later, in 1890, David Lloyd George, newly appointed MP for Arfon, joined Tom Ellis as leader of the movement, which by 1892 had set up branches throughout the country.[3] In 1894 the Cymru Fydd League was formally established on a national basis, and a year later it merged with the North Wales Liberal Federation, thus dedicating that party in north Wales to the cause of Welsh Home Rule and the disestablishment of the Church of England in Wales. The movement was also supported by an active and committed press: between 1888 and 1891 a bilingual periodical entitled *Cymru Fydd* proselytized the cause, and later in 1895 the English-language journal *Young Wales* was launched. Throughout the period newspapers like *Y Brython* and the Caernarfon weekly, *Y Genedl Gymreig*, reported sympathetically on the movement;

Beriah Gwynfe Evans, editor of *Y Genedl Gymreig* from 1892, only left his post to become secretary of the Cymru Fydd League in 1895.[4]

But as a political movement Young Wales was of brief duration; in 1896, when it appeared to many to be on the verge of achieving its goals, it collapsed virtually overnight. When Lloyd George tried to persuade the South Wales Liberal Federation to join the north Walians and merge with the Cymru Fydd League, his hopes for a united national movement were quickly shattered. The south Wales Liberals, under their leader, the coal magnate D. A. Thomas, MP for Merthyr, were not prepared to unite their interests with those of Cymru Fydd, or accept the north Walians as their political leaders. In a decisive meeting in Newport in January 1896, Alfred Edmunds of Merthyr maintained that 'Glamorgan and Monmouth were not to be dictated to by the isolated county of Caernarvon', and Robert Bird, a Cardiff businessman, declared that south Wales was too cosmopolitan to submit to domination by the 'Welsh ideas' of the northerners. A motion to merge the South Wales Liberal Foundation with the Cymru Fydd League was defeated by 133 votes to 70.[5] Yet though that meeting effectively brought Cymru Fydd as a political force to a close, a renaissance in Welsh culture which had been born with the political awakening of the 1880s, and had progressed side by side with it, continued to prosper up until the First World War.

For the first time in the history of Wales, women had now a significant part to play in that cultural renaissance; some of the strongest and liveliest women writers of the century belong to its last decade. With a new-born confidence, these authors gave a voice to a new type of Welsh woman, more sophisticated and more aware of the worth of her contribution to her country than hitherto. But the Wales their writing represented was a fragmented one; those divisions which brought the Young Wales movement to an abrupt end also feature in women's poetry and prose of the period. In this final chapter I examine, first, the developments which went towards the making of the new Welsh woman; secondly, the politically awakened radical Wales portrayed in women's writing of the period; and thirdly, some of the forces which divided Welsh opinion, as evinced in women's writing.

i. The new Welsh woman

From the first the Cymru Fydd movement supported women's suffrage, or so Nora Philipps, a suffragist herself and the founder and first president of the Welsh Union of Women's Liberal Associations, announced in 1896 in the journal *Young Wales*. 'The national movement in Wales has identified itself in the woman's cause', she states, and, quoting from Cymru Fydd's manifesto, goes on, 'The national organisation has pledged itself to "promote legislation with a view to secure equal rights of citizenship for women with men" as one of its objects.'[6] Through their zeal for the cause of independence and through their acceptance of positions in the new parish councils established in 1894, women had shown their readiness to take responsibility in fields other than the domestic, and the leaders of the Home Rule movement took it for granted that they would be able and eager to share with Welsh men the task of ruling an independent Wales. In listing the most important aspects of the new order which Cymru Fydd sought to realize, the MP W. Llewelyn Williams places women's suffrage first on his list: 'the growing power and influence of women in our public life', he says, is a fact which demonstrates that Wales is ready for Home Rule.[7] The periodical *Young Wales* devoted a number of pages each month to accounts of women's social, political and educational development, pages which were written for the most part by female contributors.[8] In the article quoted above, Nora Philipps takes particular pride in the fact that, 'The women of Wales who, only a few years ago, were supposed to be behind the women of England, and were so in many respects, can now uplift their own standard to encourage their sisters across the border.'[9] Other female columnists comment similarly on the strength of the suffragist cause in Wales, and on the readiness of Welsh men to support it, and show Young Wales to be more radical than an England that was not yet willing to see women receiving the vote, let alone a share in government. In 1897 the Welsh-language novelist Gwyneth Vaughan, councillor for Gwyrfai, suffragist and Home Rule campaigner, rejoiced in her countrymen's support:

> it is with a glad heart that I feel that the men of my own land are in the vanguard of reform ... The men of Wales encourage their mothers, wives, sisters, and daughters in their highest aspirations ... and rejoice with them in all their achievements. We have John Bull as usual lagging behind in his own thick-headed fashion.[10]

Moreover, it was not only Welsh women who saw their position in such glowing terms: an international 1909 appraisal of women's standing in various countries also refers to the Welsh woman as one who enjoys greater equality with the males of her nation than does the Englishwoman. According to T. Athol Joyce and N. W. Thomas in *Women of All Nations: A Record of their Characteristics, Habits, Manners, Customs, and Influence*, 'unlike Englishwomen who are silent when their husbands talk, the Welsh join in equally':

> The Englishwoman, it has been said, lags behind her husband, the American woman strides ahead, the French woman walks beside him. Of the American and the French woman the reflection remains true. Of the English woman it is becoming less true and of the Welsh woman apparently hardly true at all.[11]

In certain areas Welsh women had indeed made very rapid progress since the middle years of the century: in particular, the success of a movement to further the education of Welsh women was to a large extent responsible for this swift rise to greater equality with men. The historian W. Gareth Evans, in his work on Welsh women's education after 1847, shows how quickly the situation changed in the last decades of the nineteenth century. In 1864 only 48 per cent of women in north Wales and 43 per cent in the south could sign their names, compared to 64 per cent of males in Wales as a whole, and in 1881 only 2,133 of Welsh girls attended secondary school, compared to 3,827 boys. But in 1889 the Welsh Intermediate Education Act ensured that girls were afforded the same secondary school opportunities as boys, and also that the education they were given at school was the same; this was long in advance of similar measures in English education. As a result, by the end of the century the numbers of boys and girls in Welsh secondary schools were more or less equal.[12] In higher education, also, Welsh women were in the vanguard of reform: newly opened colleges of the University of Wales – Cardiff when it opened in 1883 and Bangor in 1884 – accepted women as students from the outset, awarding them full degrees, and so from 1884 did Aberystwyth as well. By 1888, 33 per cent of University of Wales students were women, a far higher percentage than in English universities at the time.

These achievements were the result of a long and strenuous campaign, fought mainly by Welsh women themselves. In arriving at their progressive position with regard to gender equality, the founders of the University of Wales were influenced by such figures as Frances Hoggan (1843–1927). The daughter of a Brecon curate, Frances Morgan, as she then was, became the second British woman to graduate as a doctor, taking her degree in Munich at a time when British medical schools were closed to women.[13] The 1871 Census includes a striking and at that time most unusual entry, in which a twenty-seven-year-old Frances Morgan, then employed at the New Hospital for Women in London and not yet married to fellow doctor George Hoggan, lists herself as 'Head of Household', with her widowed mother and a niece as dependants, and gives as her occupation 'MD of Zurich'. Though she worked in London for much of her life, Frances Hoggan did not forget her Welsh roots, and fought to make the route towards higher education an easier one for Welsh women coming after her than it had been for her. Her pamphlet *Education for Girls in Wales* advocates developing women's education in order to build a strong Wales in which 'the full measure of national prosperity, of national happiness and usefulness, and of national growth can be attained'.[14] Another influential London-Welsh activist in this cause was Dilys Davies, later Dilys Glynne Jones, a teacher at the North London Collegiate School for Girls; in 1886 she became one of the first two Honorary Secretaries of the Association for Promoting the Education of Girls in Wales, and campaigned assiduously on its behalf. Her co-Secretary was Lady Verney, who later served for decades as a member of the University of Wales Council and was awarded an Honorary Doctorate of the University in recognition of her contribution to its development.[15] Born Margaret Hay Williams of Bodelwyddan, Flintshire, Margaret Verney was the step-daughter-in-law of Frances Parthenope Verney, and the reason why Florence Nightingale's sister wrote fiction located in Wales.

The main influence on the establishment of the Association for Promoting the Education of Girls in Wales was not Dilys Davies or Lady Verney, however, but another progressive and enlightened Welsh woman, Elizabeth Phillips Hughes (1850–1925), a doctor's daughter from Carmarthen who became the first head of the Cambridge Training College for women teachers, later named Hughes College in her honour.[16] In 1884, in the Liverpool National Eisteddfod, Elizabeth Phillips Hughes's essay on 'The higher education of girls in Wales, with practical suggestions as to the best means of promoting it' was judged by Lord Aberdare and William Gladstone's daughter Helen to be 'by far the ablest of the competing

Essays' and was duly published.[17] It recommended the establishment of a committee to further women's education in Wales; co-education for the sexes in schools and at the University of Wales; hostels for women at the University's colleges; and the use of the Welsh language in Welsh education at all levels. Above all, the essay stresses that 'our education must be national, and therefore must be in our own hands'.[18] Hughes delivered a similar message in the columns she wrote for *Young Wales* in the 1890s: 'I do not believe that there is any force strong enough to keep our nationality for us except the force of education', she wrote; 'If we accept the education of England, in due time we should be Anglicised.'[19] Like the other female columnists of *Young Wales*, Hughes also in a later article praises Welsh men for their support of women, saying of them,

> their message to us, their fellow country women to-day is this, – 'We admit you on terms of absolute equality to all University privileges. We dare to do what the older Universities have not done. Now, in the morning light of our Welsh renaissance, we open every door to you, admit you freely to every office and to every privilege, we feel that you at your best are necessary for the real and rapid development of our country.'[20]

Her enthusiasm reflects the fact that influential male figures, like Tom Ellis and Isambard Owen, did indeed work alongside women campaigners in the Association for Promoting the Education of Girls in Wales, and with them won for Welsh women many advances, such as the enhanced opportunities for girls' intermediate education offered by the 1889 Act.[21] Hughes acted as the Association's secretary from 1898; she was also the only woman on the committee which drew up the charter of the University of Wales in 1893.

New horizons were opening up before the women of Young Wales, and many made much of their extended opportunities, rising to professional, middle-class positions, often from working-class backgrounds. In 1851 only 2.1 per cent of Welsh women were in professional posts – usually as nurses or schoolteachers – compared to 4.2 per cent in England. But by 1901 the percentage of women in the professions was higher in Wales than in England – 8.2 per cent in Wales compared to 7 per cent in England. And by 1911, 9.1 per cent of Welsh women workers were in professional jobs (such as the civil service, local government, banking and insurance, as well as education and health care) compared to only 7.2 per cent in England.[22] These differences may not seem very momentous, perhaps, but they indicate that the enthusiasm of the *Young Wales* contributors on the topic of Welsh women's ascendancy was not unsupported by hard evidence. In the last half of the nineteenth century Welsh women had made very swift progress in material and cultural terms, and were better educated and more likely to gain professional posts than the mass of their sisters in England.

Not surprisingly, this new strength finds reflection in the self-confidence and radicalism of a new generation of Welsh women writers. Although the North Wales Women's Temperance Union did not as an association officially support the suffragist cause,[23] many of its individual members did so, and the campaign for the vote was positively represented on the pages of Y *Gymraes*, as it had been in Y *Frythones*. Cranogwen was a strong supporter of female suffrage, confidently predicting in 1886 that 'we know it is only a question of time before it becomes a fact' ('*Gwyddom nad yw ond cwestiwn o amser iddo ddyfod yn ffaith*').[24] Votes for Women also frequently featured as the topic of debate in Y *Gymraes*'s dramatized dialogues, a by-now-defunct genre aimed at arousing discussion on key issues of the day, with the suffragist advocate invariably winning the debate. In a 1900 dialogue, for example, an aptly named Mrs Tawel (Mrs Quiet) initially resists her more forceful neighbour Mrs Gwyn's insistence that the world will not be put to rights (particularly with regard to its abuse of alcohol) until women have the vote and become MPs. But when Mrs Gwyn points out to her that the University of Wales's degree results provide clear proof that women's mental abilities and their capacity for hard work are often superior to those of men, and yet they cannot vote though the dullest of males can, Mrs Tawel finally starts to wonder and protest at the injustice of her society. From that point on she makes rapid progress, and is looking forward to a social revolution in gender roles before the close of the dialogue.[25]

Perhaps the strongest piece Y *Gymraes* published on the suffragist cause, however, was not these dialogues, which always have a comic, entertainment element to them, lessening their intensity, but an article on 'Women and Representation' ('Merched a Chynrychiolaeth') that appeared in 1910. In it Ellen Hughes asks, 'if a woman is a reasoning and moral being, with the waves of eternity beating in her nature, how can she lack the qualifications to take part in governing her country?' ('Os ydyw dynes yn fod rhesymol a moesol, a thonau tragwyddoldeb yn curo yn ei natur, tybed ei bod islaw meddu y cymhwysder i gael rhan yn neddfwriaeth ei gwlad.')[26] Ellen Hughes is arguably the Welsh-language author of the period who comes closest to being a feminist in the modern sense.[27] For thirty years she was a regular columnist in the *Gymraes*, and her monthly contributions added substantially to the journal's progressiveness. An autodidact who received very little formal education, she was well acquainted with both Welsh and English literatures and had also taught herself Greek and Hebrew. In 1896 she published an article in the second *Gymraes* on 'The New Woman' ('Y Ddynes Newydd') in which she celebrates the new opportunities being made available to Welsh women in the fields of work and education.[28] And in such essays as 'Angels of the hearth' ('Angylion yr aelwyd') and 'Moral courage' ('Gwroldeb moesol'), she argues against the ideal of womanhood as nothing other than a domestic angel, and insists that virtues are not gendered: courage is a quality that should be admired above humility in women as much as in men, she says.[29] She tries to awaken in her readers a consciousness of their independent identity and potential: her message to her female contemporaries is:

> I lwyddo y crewyd ni oll, nid i aflwyddo. Dyna yr hyn y dylem fod yn ei gylch bob dydd o'n bywyd – rhwystro ein hunain ac eraill rhag myned yn fethiant ... Y mae yn anmhosibl i ferch lwyddo ond fel merch, ond nid ydyw hynny yn dweyd nas gall lwyddo mewn llawer cylch a llawer gwaith ag y mae y byd wedi arfer eu gwahardd iddi ... Gelli, ti elli![30]

> [We were all created to succeed, not to fail. This is what we should be doing every day of our lives – preventing ourselves and others from becoming failures ... It is impossible for a woman to succeed except as a woman, but that is not to say that she cannot succeed in many circles and many jobs from which the world has been accustomed to debar her ... You can do it, you can!]

The focus of such writers and campaigners as Ellen Hughes and Elizabeth Phillips Hughes is very much on women's contribution and on opportunities for women, rather than on changes to Wales as a whole during this particularly turbulent period of its history. However, some women writers of the period aspired to the traditionally more masculine genre of the political novel, choosing in their work to represent the changing political face of *fin-de-siècle* Wales; the next section of this chapter examines their contribution.

ii. Representing radical Wales

In the early summer of 1888, newspapers and literary reviews were generous in their praise of a new anonymously published novel. According to the *Scotsman*, the novel *Fraternity*, 'for its liberality of thought, the nobility of its aspirations . . . may be placed in a class of fiction of which now-a-days we have too few examples – that of the earliest productions of George Eliot'. The *Literary World* also felt that, 'The thought and feeling in which the book is steeped to a very uncommon degree is true as well as lofty. The name of an author who writes thus earnestly on a vital question cannot long remain unknown.'[31] Nevertheless, the author's name was not revealed, though a verse collection published in 1892 and a book of memoirs which appeared in 1898 were signed 'by the author of *Fraternity*'. But thirty years later, in 1919, a donated copy of *Fraternity* sent from France to the National Library of Wales was inscribed 'from the author Mabel Holland Grave'. Mabel Holland Grave was, I believe, born Mabel Holland Thomas in 1861 in the parish of Ffestiniog, Merioneth; both the place and the date fit the presumably autobiographical data included in the 1898 book by 'the author of *Fraternity*', *Some Welsh Children*. From the evidence of her poetry, it would appear that Grave lived on the Continent for much of her adult life, but she never forgot Wales; it is the subject of her two prose books and many of her poems. In the poem 'Christmas Eve: In Italy', for example, the speaker experiences herself as estranged from her Mediterranean surroundings through the intensity of her recollections of her homeland: she asks herself, 'What do we here where the flowers bloom . . . / Whose hearts are dark with the wintry gloom / Of the wild Welsh coast where the storm winds blow?'[32]

Her only novel, *Fraternity*, is, indeed, as its reviewers suggested, an ambitious text which calls upon 'young Wales' (directly invoked as such in the novel) to accept the principle of Fraternity, or 'fraternal Socialism', as its guiding light.[33] Edmund Haig, the novel's central character, was reared as an orphan in England, but during the course of the story he learns, much to his satisfaction, that both his dead mother and still living father are Welsh. Following a yearning instinct, he had earlier, before this revelation, arrived in Wales intent upon educating the masses. He learns the Welsh language, writes articles expounding his political beliefs in the local periodicals, and, with the help of a poet called Duwineb (Godliness), has some success in persuading the slate-quarry workers of the Ffestiniog area to turn from their nascent trade unionism to espouse Fraternity. As a system of belief Fraternity spurns trade unionism as too divisive, and is itself derived, not from Marx, but from the more benign aspects of the philosophy of the French Revolution and the inventions of Iolo Morganwg.[34] At one point Haig explains in some detail in a letter to an English sympathizer the way in which the bardic 'Gorsedd' of the Welsh National Eisteddfod constitutes a 'great army' of bonded brothers and sisters who will work to overthrow the English class-system. '[A]t the Gorsedd or initiatory rite', he says, 'men and women are equal, princes and quarrymen meet on the same level':

> The only difference between man and man, 'in the face of the sun, the eye of light,' as the old motto runs, is that between poet and people, inspired and uninspired, though even that last is but a distinction of quantity, not quality ... [T]he strength of Bardo-Druidism lies in the labouring classes; the Ovates are young workmen, farmers, shoemakers, plasterers and plumbers; the Bards are the same men, inspired ... The classes must join the masses here; for in my country, I assure you, the latter are far superior to the former.[35]

Regrettably, the novel does not take much further this heady vision of a combatively socialist Gorsedd; Haig apparently wins many noble hearts to his cause amongst the workmen, but little detail is provided as to what they accomplish.

Instead, it focuses on its romance plot, in which Haig finally weds Blodwen Trevor, an intensely patriotic member of the old Welsh aristocracy, who is initially suspicious of him because of his apparent Englishness. In a manner indicative of the ironic tone of the novel when it addresses its imagined English reader, its narrator says of Blodwen, 'ridiculous as it must seem, dear reader, she was quite as proud of being Welsh as you are of being English'.[36] Living with her aunt in 'the quiet parish of Llanfairydd' in north Wales, Blodwen still follows the old egalitarian way of life of the Welsh squirearchy, sitting down to dine with the family servants in a manner that much impresses her more enlightened visitors, such as Harold Price, Australian-born though of Welsh parentage, and soon to be revealed to be Edmund Haig's brother. When Blodwen's old nurse joins the family and its guests for dinner on Harold's first evening in Llanfairydd, he 'began to understand that fraternity had been very thoroughly understood in Wales in those good old times'.[37] With the looks of 'some proud young British princess',[38] Blodwen is an exemplary, if somewhat idealized, representative of her race, who gladly espouses Edmund and his 'fraternal Socialism', and joins with him at the close of the text in looking forward to a Wales finally freed from the yoke of England – or at least from the yoke of the Anglican Church. Both are confident that the time is quickly coming when 'the English Church in Wales shall rest in the quiet grave of oblivion, with all her flock'.[39]

The disestablishment of the Church of England in Wales is a key topic in another English-language novel published in the same year, Elizabeth Watkin Williams's *Even Such Is Life: A Story of To-day*. In 1888 Lady Williams was the widow of Sir Charles Watkin Williams, late Liberal MP for Caernarfonshire. The text appears to have been written as a form of solace after the loss of Sir Charles, who died suddenly in 1884; its hero, Sir Victor Arvon, whose name presumably refers to Sir Charles's electoral triumph, is obviously modelled on Lady Williams's husband, and its first volume in particular is a very detailed, barely fictionalized, account of the 1880 Caernarfon election, in which Watkin Williams defeated the 'Tory Giant' Lord Penrhyn and his heir. Most of the subsequent events of this three-volume novel seem imagined in order to provide further evidence of the magnanimity, good sense and great-heartedness of 'Sir Victor', and can hardly be said to form any kind of novelistic plot. Nevertheless, read as a political study, there is much of interest in the book's detailed transcriptions of Sir Victor's arguments with his English acquaintance on the nature of the contemporary Welsh character. Charles Watkin Williams, though himself the son of the Anglican rector of Llansannan in Denbigh-shire, was the first MP to put before the House of Commons a motion on behalf of the disestablishment of the Church in Wales.[40] In his widow's novel, Sir Victor, after his election, is plagued by English critics, who suggest that he won his seat purely through pandering to the anti-Anglican bigotry of the Nonconformist ministers. But both Sir Victor and his fictional wife Lady Arvon vigorously and at some length deny such charges, and champion the voters of north Wales as true and enlightened Radicals, as well as loyal Nonconformists. In response to one 'sneering, sceptical' com-ment, supposing that his speeches to his would-be constituents must have been 'almost entirely of the one cry of disestablishment, and down with the clergy', Sir Victor replies,

'No . . . information was as eagerly demanded on education, the burial laws, game laws, equalisation of county and borough franchise, and other matters as on the disestablishment question, vital as that undoubtedly is, and I can only tell you that I needed as much to give my very intellectual best to my speeches among those hard-headed mountaineers as I should need to give it for the House of Commons itself.'[41]

As he sees it, and of course his devoted wife agrees with him, 'dissent and the cry for disestablishment are the result, not the cause, of the people's Radicalism': what has caused the growth of Radicalism in Wales is not Nonconformity but the landlords and squires,

> by their indifferentism to the claims and needs of the people; by their alienation from the national interests and genius of the country . . . and by their want of sympathy with the poetical element and devoted love to language and to country which distinguished that warm-hearted race.[42]

Elizabeth Watkin Williams was an Englishwoman, the daughter of Lord Chief Justice Lush, and at times her text makes it evident that she saw Wales only through her husband's eyes, and had little first-hand understanding of the country. At one point in her novel, Sir Victor's brother Frank, supposedly a Welshman himself, on leave from his post as an engineer in Ceylon and holidaying in the family home of Plas Arvon in north Wales, remarks on 'how delightful the return to such a charming bit of English life has been', and no one corrects him.[43] Neither are Lady Arvon and her creator radicals when it comes to matters which pertain uniquely to them rather than to their husbands; Lady Arvon is strongly opposed to the whole notion of female suffrage, for example, and highly critical of its supporters, as emasculated women 'stalking about like a man' and surrendering 'a wealth of influence for a poverty of rights'.[44] The sacred Victorian doctrine of an Angel in the House's 'influence' remains Lady Arvon's lodestone, as no doubt it was that of her creator. Elizabeth Watkin Williams's commitment is to her husband, first and foremost, and to Wales and Radicalism only through him and not for their own sakes. The contrast between her approach and that of Mabel Holland Grave serves to highlight the far greater originality and independent strength of mind of the 'author of *Fraternity*'.

But neither of these two authors was herself directly involved in the Cymru Fydd campaign, unlike two further political novelists of the period, Gwyneth Vaughan and Mallt Williams, who both worked for Welsh Home Rule and wrote fictions furthering the cause. Gwyneth Vaughan was the pseudonym of Annie Harriet Hughes (1852–1910), a miller's daughter from Talsarnau in Merioneth; after a very elementary education and an apprenticeship in millinery, she married John Hughes Jones, a medical student, but by 1893 was left a widow with four children to support. Becoming a journalist and novelist, she published her fictions as serials in the weekly newspapers, primarily *Y Cymro* and *Y Brython*, and also worked for the temperance cause, as well as serving as the secretary of the Welsh Union of Women's Liberal Associations. Her two best-known novels are historical fictions: *O Gorlannau y Defaid* (From the Sheepfolds, 1905) is set in rural Wales during the religious revival of 1859, and *Plant y Gorthrwm* (Children of the Oppression, 1908) tells the tale of rural families caught up in the traumas of the 1868 election, with its catastrophic aftermath for many tenant farmers, who had voted Liberal against the wishes of their Tory landlords. Her last fiction, the serial 'Turn of the Wheel' ('Troad y Rhod') published in *Y Brython* in 1909 and left unfinished at her death, is set in contemporary Wales, however, and concerns the rise of radical Welsh Liberalism, and its connection with improvements in the education and prospects of the rural poor. Strictly speaking, Gwyneth Vaughan is of course a twentieth-century writer, but the intensity of her involvement with the Cymru Fydd movement, which is very much a nineteenth-century phenom-enon, makes it difficult to omit her from this section.

Though romantic plots and idealized heroines feature in each of her novels, her central concern is to delineate the particularities of Welsh Nonconformist culture, the political ascendancy of the radical lower class, and the need for women's suffrage. Unlike Elizabeth Watkin Williams, Gwyneth Vaughan saw women's rights as central to the Welsh Liberal agenda. In an article in the *Christian Commonwealth* in February 1900, she spoke of her conviction that 'women should have the same rights as men', and repeated the claim that she had made earlier in *Young Wales* that Welsh men were more supportive of women's rights than Englishmen: 'All our great men believe in the equality of the sexes and we would very soon have equal political rights if it depended upon Wales.'[45] Neither did she forget the economic frustrations of her own upbringing; she stresses the need for financial independence for women of the working as well as middle classes: 'Let us not rest content until every girl holds in her own hand a bread winning weapon', she says in a *Young Wales* article.[46] In her second novel, on the 1868 Liberal landslide, she seized the opportunity to include a suffragist protest. In one 'wisdom from the mouths of babes' scene, a young child is horrified to learn that the novel's heroine has no vote in the coming election. Dyddgu protests,

> 'Mae Jerry Jones, Tŷ Nant, ym myn'd i fotio, a mae nhad yn deyd dydi o ddim yn agos yn gall . . . ' Does dim sens fod dyn heb fod yn reit gall yn fotio, a chitha ddim, Miss Rhianon . . . Heblaw hynny, does gin ddim dyn ddim busnes i rwystro ddim dynes . . . Chyma i ddim o'u lol nhw wedi i mi fynd yn fawr.'[47]

> ['Jerry Jones, Tŷ Nant, is going to vote, and my father says he has no brains . . . There's no sense in a half-witted man voting, and you not, Miss Rhianon . . . Besides, no man has any business holding back any woman . . . I won't take any of their nonsense when I've grown up.']

Nevertheless, for all Dyddgu's protest, Rhianon experiences herself as very much held back by men, and frequently expresses her frustration with the limitations the gender system impose upon her, complaining that had she been a man, and able to stand for Parliament herself, she could have done much more to promote democracy and civil rights.[48] Angharad Fychan, the heroine of Vaughan's first novel, similarly rebels against the fact that she is not afforded the same possibilities for education and employment as her cousin Dewi. She lays the blame for this injustice on St Paul, or rather on those who insist on still following the rules on gender roles proffered in St Paul's two-thousand-year-old letters: 'Perhaps I could preach like Dewi if it wasn't for Paul', she says ('Hwyrach y cawswn i bregethu fel Dewi oni bai Paul').[49] *O Gorlannau y Defaid* is a novel on a religious revival and *Plant y Gorthrwm* is an election novel, but in both tales the reader is not allowed to forget that the central female character longs to take a much more active role in the key events, as preacher in the one case and politician in the other, and that she would clearly be well suited for the work from which she is debarred, at a serious loss to her society.

In the contemporary novel 'Troad y Rhod', Gwyneth Vaughan is still protesting against the slowness of change for Welsh women. The childhood of the main protagonists takes place before the 1889

Intermediate Education Act: William Jones the weaver has sacrificed his savings to buy his nephew Nedw a good education, but neither he nor his widowed sister Susan thinks of providing the same opportunity for Siarlot, Nedw's sister. She yearns to share her brother's schooling, but no one considers that 'the girl too could have had a capacity for learning, and it might have been of benefit to her one day' ('y gallai yr eneth hefyd fod yn meddu ar allu i ddysgu, ac y byddai o fudd iddi hwyrach rwy ddiwrnod').[50] Vaughan also provides a radical critique of the traditional Welsh Mam figure, as one who, in her over-zealous self-sacrifice to the needs of the family's males, can harm the psychological development of both her boys and girls, rather than nourish them. If Susan Jenkins had a fault as a mother, 'her tendency to serve in excess, and teach her daughter to do the same thing, was that fault. The two of them – the mother and daughter – appeared to have no other aim in their lives than to serve William Jones and Nedw' ('ei pharodrwydd i or-weini, a dysgu ei geneth hefyd i wneud yr un peth, oedd y bai hwnnw. Yr oedd y ddwy – y fam a'r ferch – fel pe heb un amcan arall i'w bodolaeth ond gweini ar William Jones a Nedw'). But 'making a maid of his sister did much harm to Nedw' ('gwnaeth gwneud morwyn o'i chwaer ddrwg mawr i Nedw');[51] naturally enough, he took it for granted that he could dominate her, and his disregard of her and of his mother coloured his egotistic relations with others generally.

Gwyneth Vaughan's chief aim in this final, unfinished fiction, however, was to depict the ascendancy of the Radical Liberals. At times she writes as if to propose a more violent resolution of Wales's problems than any envisaged by the Cymru Fydd movement. Lack of social justice under a system still ruled by landowners is her village radicals' main rallying cry, rather than the disestablishment of the Church. William Jones fulminates against injustices in the local magistrates' court, in which one man gets sent to prison for a year for poaching a hare, while the next is only bound over for six months after having nearly killed his wife. The weaver explains to his appalled listeners that such errors of justice occur because 'the rich men, the men who own the hares, are also the men who own the right to make the laws – that's why the law is all on the side of the great man and his property' ('y cyfoethogion, y dynion bia'r sgyfarnogod, bia'r hawl hefyd i neud y cyfreithia – dyna pam y mae'r gyfraith i gyd o ochr y gwr mawr a'i eiddo'). One of his listeners comments, 'A change will come one day and a terrible change it will be, when those who seem as if asleep will awaken' ('Mi ddaw tro ar fyd ryw ddiwrnod, a thro ofnadwy fydd hwnnw, pan fydd y rhai sydd megis yn cysgu wedi deffro'),[52] and refers to the French Revolution as pointing the way. Nevertheless, victory with the ballot box rather than on the streets remains the goal of Vaughan's radical characters in 'Troad y Rhod', in a manner which in some ways looks forward more to the rise of the Independent Labour Party, and Keir Hardie's success in Merthyr, than to the fate of the Cymru Fydd movement.

Gwyneth Vaughan's work has not been in print since the beginning of the twentieth century, and the one critical article of any length published on her work condemns it as anachronistic in the attention it pays to landlordism. According to Thomas Parry, she dwells too much on the power of the landlords, though their day was over, and presents too romantic a picture of Welsh rural life.[53] Except insofar as it refers to her overly idealized heroines, his criticism seems misjudged, however: after all, Vaughan's two best-known texts were historical novels, set back in the pre-reform period, when landlords did indeed exert significant control over their tenants. The English-language novelist with whom Vaughan worked as co-secretary of *Undeb y Ddraig Goch* (the Union of the Red Dragon) in 1903, Alice Matilda Langland Williams (1867–1950), was arguably much more of an anachronistic romanticist than the miller's daughter, though she too was dedicated to the nationalist cause. Born to an English-speaking middle-class family in Brecknockshire, Mallt Williams came under the influence of the Llanover circle: she learnt Welsh (or a version of it), adopted the 'traditional' Welsh costume, and contributed very generously over a number of years to every patriotic Welsh cause in existence, including in later years Saunders Lewis's Plaid Cymru and the Welsh League of Youth.[54] Under the pseudonym 'The Dau Wynne', she and her sister Gwenffreda published two novels, *One of the Royal Celts* (1889) and *A Maid of Cymru* (1901); the second of the two appeared as a serial story in *Young Wales* from 1900–1. From 1901 on, Mallt Williams also edited the women's pages in *Young Wales*.

But Mallt and Gwenffreda Williams were the children of a medical captain with the South Wales Borderers, and as such were daughters of the British Empire, and proud of it. *One of the Royal Celts* is an idealized fictionalization of imperial campaigns fought by the South Wales Borderers, that is, the 'Royal Celts'. By devious twists of omission, the book manages to give the impression that the

British Empire was acquired solely through Celtic valour: no English character is introduced throughout the text, and the only regiment to be mentioned by name, apart from the Royal Celts, is the Highlanders' Black Watch. In this curious manner, the Dau Wynne apparently sought to unite Welsh nationalist feeling with an enthusiasm for an empire which becomes in their work Celtic, rather than British. Little emphasis is placed on democracy in their vision of a glorified Wales: Glyndŵr Parry Lloyd, the hero of *One of the Royal Celts*, can trace his ancestry back in a direct line to the last Prince of Wales, and is intensely proud of the fact. At the close of the novel he dies a hero's death in the Egyptian desert, 'alone, surrounded, hemmed in by the dusky foe', though his 'trusty sword' has 'piled a wall of dead about him . . . ere with a strange gray shadow on the kingly face, he falls to the ground'.[55] Well may there be a 'strange gray shadow' on this last of a noble line, when the only way he can salve its honour is by eagerly embracing the colonizing ethos which brought about its downfall in the first place. His 'dusky foe', the Mahdi and his followers in the Sudan in 1884, were involved in a last-ditch endeavour to defend their freedom and faith after the conquest of Egypt by the armies of the Empire. Glyndŵr Parry Lloyd's heart bleeds for his own country after the death of Llywelyn: 'Our brave, lost Prince!' he cries, 'If I had but lived in those stirring times when my good sword could have fought for king and country, and my vengeance fallen on the craven wretches that betrayed him to his death!'[56] But he does not think of connecting the history of Wales in the medieval period with that of contemporary Sudan, although the Sudanese are fighting for independence from the same foe. Rather, the battlefields of the imperial army become the sites on which the Welsh regain their tarnished honour, and redeem their humiliations.

In a recent article on Mallt Williams, Marion Löffler suggests that her sister Gwenffreda's views strongly influenced their first jointly written fiction, but that Mallt Williams worked on the second novel, *A Maid of Cymru*, alone, and produced a much more patriotically Welsh fiction.[57] *A Maid of Cymru* is not free, however, from the snobbery and class consciousness very apparent in the pages of *One of the Royal Celts*. Supposedly a contemporary novel, *A Maid of Cymru* anachronistically portrays the Welsh landed gentry as enjoying an easy ascendancy over the popular radicalism of the period. Its heroine Tangwystl Hywel, whose first name derives from that of a fifth-century Brecknockshire princess, is persistently addressed by her acquaintance as 'Foneddiges' (that is, 'lady' or 'honourable one'), and has no difficulty retaining her influence over 'her people'. At one point in the novel she manages to bring to a halt a local strike, of which she disapproves, as it may result in English-speakers being brought into the area as replacement workers. She attends union meetings to sing patriotic songs to the strikers: 'She sang songs of the Great past – of the Future Hope' until 'a cry broke from a hundred throats, "Cymru dros byth! Cymru dros byth!" and she knew that she had conquered.' Tangwystl may have mastered the men, but she, or rather her author, has not mastered the Welsh language; here the aroused strikers are shouting 'Wales over ever!' rather than 'Wales for ever'. Nevertheless, her triumph affords her an ominously fascistic thrill: 'She knew then the feeling – the thrill that stirs the hearts of those few who hold magnetic power over the throng.'[58] This 'feeling' is in no way questioned within the novel, but rather entirely condoned: it is industrialization, and in particular the mobilization and politicization of the working class, that is the enemy of Welshness in *A Maid of Cymru*, rather than the class system.

But in the early 1900s it was Gwyneth Vaughan's fictions, not those of her co-secretary, which were hailed as embodying the new Welsh political spirit, and as such influenced a new wave of women writers. In September 1905, Eluned Morgan wrote from her home in Trelew in Patagonia to thank her correspondent William George for his gift of a copy of *O Gorlannau y Defaid*, which she had found inspiring: she predicts that

> Tra pery'r iaith Gymraeg, bydd coffadwriaeth Gwyneth yn gynes yn nghalon y Werin ... a'i gwelediad eglur-iach i guddiad cryfder y Genedl fechan fynodd fyw drwy bob gorthrwm – yn destun syndod ac edmygedd Cenedlaethau.[59]

> [while the Welsh language survives, Gwyneth's memory will be warm in the heart of the people ... and her lucid vision into the hidden strength of the little nation which insisted on surviving through all oppression – will be a topic of wonder and admiration for generations.]

That this prediction should, in the event, have been so ill-founded, given the speed with which Gwyneth Vaughan and all she stood for was forgotten, is indicative of the changes and internal divisions that confounded *fin-de-siècle* Wales, and brought to an abrupt close its first Home Rule movement in five centuries. The final section of this book explores further the nature of those divisions, as represented by Wales's women writers.

iii. A divided nation

In 1893 Eluned Morgan wrote from Patagonia of her joy at hearing of the growth of the Cymru Fydd movement, and her pride in the Welsh Liberal MPs who were 'fighting so bravely and unitedly' ('yn ymladd mor ddewr ac unol').[60] Like other supporters of the movement, however, she was soon to be disappointed at its collapse, but that was only one of the many setbacks Eluned Morgan suffered with regard to her hopes for Wales during the last decade of the nineteenth century. Christened Eluned Morganed (that is, sea-born) Jones,[61] she was born in 1870 on board the *Myfanwy*, the second ship to take a group of Welsh emigrants to what is generally referred to as the 'Welsh colony'. But of course Patagonia was never an imperial colony, or at least not a Welsh one; it was part of an independent Argentina ruled and Christianized by descendants of Spanish colonists. The Welsh emigrants were fleeing from a country in which English was the only official language and the language of education, and in which small tenant farmers found themselves increasingly squeezed by rack-rent landlords and an Established Church from which they had dissented, but to which they still had to pay tithes. In Patagonia, though they did not find the fertile land they expected, they acquired the right to live according to their own religious beliefs and to use their own language: until the end of the nineteenth century, Welsh was the sole language of the settlers.[62] But they had no colonial relation to the indigenous people of the area and were expressly forbidden by the Argentinian authorities from proselytizing their religion to them.

In her account of her Patagonian childhood, Eluned Morgan describes the ties formed between the emigrants and their nomadic neighbours, with the Indians frequently requesting the Welsh to intercede on their behalf against the Spanish Argentinians' attempts to drive them out of their traditional territories. *Dringo'r Andes* (Climbing the Andes), initially published in 1899 as a series of travel articles in O. M. Edwards's *Cymru*, describes a chance encounter with one such persecuted Indian, who had received support from Eluned's father:

179

Wrth ymgomio yn y babell daeth y gair 'Cristianos' i mewn, a gofynais iddo pwy feddyliau wrth y 'Cristianos' hyn.

'Yr Hispaeniaid,' meddai.

'Eithr onid ydym ninau hefyd yn Cristianos?' meddwn.

'O na, *amigos de los Indios* ydych chwi.'⁶³

[As we talked in the tent the word 'Cristianos' came up, and I asked him whom he meant by this 'Cristianos'.

'The Spaniards,' he said.

'But are not we [that is, the Welsh settlers in Patagonia] also Cristianos?' I said.

'Oh no, you are *amigos de los Indios*.']

'How painful to think that the word which used to be so sacred was coupled in the pagan's heart with every cruelty and barbarism', Eluned Morgan comments; 'The Spaniard is not one jot worse than the Yank or the Englishman in this respect; destroying natives and small nations is the characteristic vice of each of them' ('Mor chwith meddwl fod y gair fu gynt mor gysegredig wedi ei gyplu yn nghalon y pagan â phob creulonderau a barbareiddiwch ... Nid yw'r Hispaenwr un gronyn gwaeth na'r Ianci a'r Sais yn hyn o beth; difa brodorion a chenhedloedd bychain yw pechod parod pob un o honynt').⁶⁴ According to its founding father, Michael D. Jones, 'to keep our nation from extinction' ('cadw ein cenedl rhag difodiad') was the primary goal of the Patagonian scheme.⁶⁵ Involved with that cause as she was, it is no wonder that Eluned Morgan should have become particularly sensitized to the destructiveness of colonialism; at the same time, it is of course true, paradoxically enough, that through settling on lands which the Argentinian Indians had once held as their own, she and all the Welsh emigrants were participating in the long history of European imperialism.

Nevertheless, in her letters and essays Eluned Morgan castigates the Welsh for condoning British imperialism and supporting its wars: 'quite apart from the injustice of war', she writes to William George in 1901, the fact that small nations were fighting for freedom against imperialist forces 'should be enough to make every Welsh heart burn with sympathy, remembering that the land of old Wales has been sanctified with the blood of braves who fought for the same thing against the same nation' ('ar wahân i anghyfiawnder rhyfel dylai y ffaith fod cenedl fechan yn ymladd am fam-wlad a rhyddid, fod yn ddigon i roi pob calon Gymreig ar dan o gydymdeimlad, gan gofio fod daear hen Gymru wedi ei chysegru a gwaed y dewrion fu'n ymladd am yr un peth yn erbyn yr un genedl').[66] Not their history alone, but also their religion should incite the Welsh to oppose all warmongering, she argues. To read of Welsh preachers justifying war 'with all its cruelties' perplexes her; she advises her friends in the mother country to 'study Mazzini', and defy 'John Bull', but fears that 'the Welsh have been servile through the ages' ('gwaseiddiwr fu'r Cymro ar hyd y blynyddoedd'),[67] and are now still mystified by the glamour of the British Empire in its heyday.

However, it was in part the independent circumstances under which Eluned Morgan was reared in Patagonia which gave her a perspective from which she could so straightforwardly denounce Victorian Britain: the complexity of the relation between Wales and England was not part of her make-up. 'Servility' does not seem an obvious characteristic to attribute to writers like Buddug, Ruth or Ellen Hughes, yet all three of them published articles in *Y Gymraes* praising that most potent symbol of British imperialism, Queen Victoria. The cult of the 'Great White Mother', ubiquitous as it was in anglophone writing of the period, also affected late nineteenth-century Welsh women's writing, and must have muddied their perception of their national loyalties and their attitude towards the Empire. It was Victoria's much-trumpeted virtue which appears to have constituted the chief stumbling-block for those who might otherwise have been reluctant to accept her rule. Ellen Hughes comments on the Queen's life, 'As we analyse it, that is the element which is most apparent in it until it swallows all the others into itself, – "*I will be good*"' ('wrth ei ddadansoddi, dyna'r elfen a ganfyddir amlycaf ynddo nes llyncu'r lleill oll iddi ei hun, – "*Mi a fyddaf yn dda*"').[68] The Welsh women writers respected the image of Victoria so effectively circulated by the spin-doctors of the age because of the similarity between it and their highest ideals for themselves: according to the hype, Victoria was diligent, hard-working, responsible and self-disciplined, and at the same time extraordinarily warm-hearted, able to sympathize with the lowliest of her subjects. Buddug writes in all seriousness of Victoria in 1887, on her fiftieth anniversary, that 'there beats under her precious crown, / The best heart in the world' (A chura dan ei choron ddrud, / Y galon oreu yn y byd').[69]

In 1897, the year of Victoria's Diamond Jubilee, the Welsh-language presses, like the English-language ones, were swamped with adulatory messages to the queen. Loyal addresses were translated into Welsh; 'Buddugoliaeth Buddug', for example, a translation of Catherine E. Phillimore's 'Jubilee Ode', rhetorically asks 'For whom . . . / Beats the heart of the people?' and answers 'For her who made man's cause / Her own', that is, of course, for Victoria ('I bwy . . . / Y cura calon gwerin? / I'r hon wnaeth achos dyn / Yn eiddo iddi ei hun').[70] Ruth at least begins her 1897 essay by asking whether the Welsh are not betraying themselves by celebrating an Englishwoman's rule, only to decide that 'We can honour her without dishonouring ourselves or our religion' because 'there are excellencies pertaining to Victoria which the Welsh can appreciate, perhaps, more thoroughly than any other nation' ('Gallwn ei hanrhydeddu heb ein dianrhydeddu ein hunain na'n crefydd . . . y mae yn perthyn i Victoria ragoriaethau y gall y Cymry eu gwerthfawrogi, feallai, yn fwy trwyadl nag odid un genedl arall').[71] That is, Victoria is too good for the English; only the Welsh can truly recognize and appreciate her virtues. The Queen's virtues were celebrated in every genre, including in the macaronic verses of Mair Hydref, or Mary Jane Williams, née Owen, from Treffynnon, in Flintshire, a bilingual poet who changed her language according to the needs of the occasion. Her 'Welcome to Wales', written on the occasion of a royal visit, has a Welsh-language refrain:

> Our hearts are enraptured with joy, love, and pride,
> To hail our good Queen, and fair daughter beside;
> The mountains shall ring with our outbursts of cheer,
> For every Welsh subject is true and sincere.
>
>> Hir oes i'n Brenhines, oruchel ei bri,
>> Un anwyl, rasusol, rinweddol yw hi,
>> Duw Iôr a'i bendithio – yw'n taer weddi ni.
>>
>> [Long life to our Monarch, of exalted fame,
>> She is a dear, gracious and virtuous one;
>> May the Lord God bless her – is our ardent wish.][72]

Here, the Welsh-language refrain (the gist of whose meaning is easily enough deducible from the context) works to reassure England's monarchy that the Welsh are loyal subjects in both their languages.

But the Queen, or her image, was central to the British Empire; to revere the one made it difficult straightforwardly to oppose the other. The concept of the Great White Mother was part and parcel of the rationale for British imperial rule as a civilizing, caring system: the Empire was one great family, who shared in the feelings of their 'Mother' as she shared in theirs. Or that, at any rate is the loyal assumption professed in the poem 'Monody on the Death of Albert Victor Christian Edward, Duke of Clarence and Avondale', which was awarded the Gold Medal at the Rhyl National Eisteddfod in 1892. This elegy to Victoria's oldest grandson, Prince Albert, glorifies not only the personal virtues of England's royal family, particularly 'Her whom all our souls revere' (that is, Victoria, of course), but also its imperial conquests. The dead prince is the 'Son of an Empire's sorrow!' and his loss has been felt globally:

> . . . The great wail
> Of anguish, when thy spirit passed away . . .
> Rang not alone within our little isle,
> But o'er the great Atlantic onward borne . . .
> Where India's dusky millions own our sway . . .
>   And, drowning joy and mirth,
> Girded a zone of sorrow round the earth,
> Making of Babel tongues one harmony of woe.[73]

The poem succeeded in pleasing not only the Eisteddfod's judges, but also 'Her whom all our souls revere': having been sent a copy by the adjudicator, Victoria ordered a hundred more for her personal use. Its author was Anna Walter Thomas (1839–1920), or Morfudd Eryri, to give her her bardic name; an Englishwoman, born in Barningham in Suffolk, Anna Fison in 1871 married the Reverend David Walter Thomas, vicar of Bethesda in Caernarfonshire.[74] She learnt Welsh and was an enthusiastic supporter of the National Eisteddfod; English, however, was the language of the two poems with which she won Eisteddfodic fame, the 'Monody on the Death of Albert' and 'Llandaf', a poetic account of the history of the Church of England in Wales which was successful at the 1883 Eisteddfod in Cardiff. It says much about the nature of the Eisteddfod at the time that such topics were chosen for the poetry competitions.

Prose writers as well could prosper through judicious use of the Victoria cult. Marie Trevelyan (Emma Mary Puclieu, 1853–1922) effusively dedicated most of her works on Welsh life and folklore to members of Victoria's family: born Emma Mary Thomas in Llantwit Major in Glamorgan, the daughter of a stonemason, Trevelyan married a French doctor and was living in France when she published many of her writings, but her remove from British shores clearly did nothing to weaken her sense of intense loyalty to England's monarchy. In her preface to her historical novel, *Britain's Greatness Foretold: The Story of Boadicea, the British Warrior Queen* (1900), Victoria is represented as the glorious realization of the Druidic prophecy in which, according to William Cowper's poem, empire was promised to the Ancient British Queen, Boadicea. 'Regions Caesar never knew / Thy posterity shall sway', Cowper's Druid tells the defeated queen to comfort her, and Trevelyan links the two queens of Ancient and modern-day Britain as if the connection were unproblematic. In her preface she tells the reader that she 'felt impelled' to write Boadicea's history because in Wales she was 'accustomed to hear constantly around me the language in which the great queen thought and spoke; accustomed always to hear her called by her British name of Buddig [*sic*], which means Victoria'. This led her to compare 'Victoria, the primitive queen, in whose time the nation was rising' with 'Victoria, our revered monarch, in whose reign the nation is at its zenith, and – let us devoutly hope – bright with a splendour that shall "never see sunset"'.[75] Marie Trevelyan's use of the term 'nation' here is clearly not intended to signify that nation which still spoke the language of the Ancient British queen: its 'splendour' refers to the British Empire rather than to any Welsh lustre, except insofar as Wales participates in Great Britain's glory. For the south Wales Liberal industrialists who voted against unifying under the banner of Cymru Fydd, dreams of an independent Wales could not compete with the possibilities of 'cosmopolitan' growth and progress afforded by the Empire. The cult of Victoria and her virtue must have also have made it difficult for many less worldly-minded Nonconformists to give their full support to a Welsh Home Rule movement, for to accept Victoria was to accept also the unity of that empire of which she was supposedly the 'heart'.

Welsh Dissent's whole-hearted espousal of missionary activity, facilitated as it usually was by imperial conquests, also affected its members' responses to the Empire, as we saw in the last chapter. It might therefore be expected that in Wales the strongest critics of the Empire, and the group most likely to work towards a radical break-up of the United Kingdom, would be that growing minority which, as the nineteenth century drew to its close, was becoming critical of chapel culture and its stifling – as they saw it – grip on the mass of the Welsh population. But Cymru Fydd and Welsh Liberalism generally had always been strongly identified with the Nonconformist cause: the disestablishment of the Church in Wales was, after all, the first aim of Young Wales. Those Welsh women writers who were moving away from their Nonconformist roots were not therefore likely to develop stronger ties with Cymru Fydd; on the contrary, they were more likely to turn away from Wales altogether. This process is exemplified in the career of one of the most innovative Welsh-language women writers of her generation, Winnie Parry (1870–1953), whose best-known novel *Sioned* was first published in serial form in O. M. Edwards's journal *Cymru* from 1894–6. Born in Welshpool, Winnie Parry was sent as a child, after her mother's death in 1876, to live with her staunchly Nonconformist maternal grandparents in Y Felinheli in Caernarfonshire. But she did not succeed in making their religion meaningful to herself: according to her biographer R. Palmer Parry, she attended chapel services only out of habit, and to please her grandparents.[76] In *Sioned* the eponymous narrator satirizes chapel-goers and pokes fun at the pomposity and hypocrisy of their preachers.[77] *Sioned* was received with great enthusiasm by its readers, who were clearly happy to discover a new, alternative Welsh voice. But in 1907 Winnie Parry left Wales for England; she never returned, and published little after that date. She appears to have experienced Nonconformity as so stifling, and so integral to the Welsh way of life, that in order to escape it she was prepared to sacrifice her literary gift.

Criticism of Welsh Nonconformity is also a recurring feature in the work of Anne Adaliza Beynon Puddicombe (1836–1908), who gained international fame as the novelist Allen Raine. The daughter of a Castellnewydd Emlyn solicitor, Allen Raine married an English banker and lived for much of her life near Croydon. She retained close connections with her native land, however, and chose Cardiganshire as the setting for her eleven novels and numerous short stories.[78] Her 1899 novel *By Berwen Banks* presents a Methodist preacher as the source of dissension in a south Cardiganshire village, where the animosity between Nonconformists and Anglicans provides the backdrop for a Romeo and Juliet romance, with the young lovers separated by the bigotry of their parents. Caradoc Wynne, the vicar's son, and Valmai Powell, the Methodist minister's niece, marry secretly before Caradoc leaves for Australia, but in his absence the pregnant Valmai is excommunicated from the *seiat*, and driven from her home by her uncle. This does not cause her much personal grief, however, as she has already decided that her own instinct is 'purer and healthier' than her uncle's religion; according to the text, 'her joyous nature could not brook the saddening influences of the Methodist creed'.[79] And in Raine's *Queen of the Rushes* (1906), Nonconformity, in the heightened form it took during the 1904 religious revival, does indeed prove most destructive of the 'healthier' instincts of young Welsh women, so much so that Nance, one of this novel's more susceptible characters, is driven to madness and an early death by her over-excited involvement in the revival.[80]

Although Caradoc Evans's *My People* (1915) has been critically hailed as the major literary denunciator of Welsh chapel culture, earlier, forgotten, women's texts also developed similar themes; Violet Jacob's novel *The Sheep-Stealers* (1902), for example, is another anti-Calvinist novel. Born in Scotland to a Welsh mother and a Scottish father, Jacob set her historical novel on the Anglo-Welsh border in south Wales: she must have known the area well, for her descriptions of it are detailed and convincing. Her text is centrally concerned with exploring the differences between Wales and England, described here as 'two nations, nominally one since the middle ages, but in reality only amalgamated down to a very few inches below the surface'.[81] Methodism has darkened the lives of the dwellers to the west of the border: Anne Walters, the mother of the novel's central protagonist, undergoes a Calvinist conversion after the sudden death in childhood of her first-born son:

> It was just at this time that an earnest preacher . . . came to hold meetings among the Methodists of the mountain district, and Anne went to hear him speak . . . the hard doctrines and straitened ideas which he preached appealed to her in a way that nothing else could; the wholesale condemnation of sinners which he announced was entirely in accordance with a type of mind that had ever hated the Devil more than it had loved God, and she threw herself wholly into the sea of his relentless Christianity, for there were no half-measures with her.[82]

Her husband Eli, a comparatively weak and irresolute character, does not join her in her new faith, but does not oppose her either. Conventional gender-patterns are thus reversed, thanks to the forces of Calvinism: it is the female who is, or becomes, stern and judgemental, and the male who is subordinated and overawed.

The long-term effect on her son Rhys, the novel's anti-hero, is disastrous; unable to accept his mother's religion himself, and unable to find a suitable role-model in his father, he becomes, in increasing desperation, first a Rebecca rioter, then the sheep-stealer of the title, and finally a suicide. Anne Walters is one of the many equivalents in Welsh literature of the stern female image portrayed in Curnow Vosper's iconic *Salem* (1908), but in Jacob's novel her influence is pernicious. The text as a whole would appear to suggest that if there is no vital life left for the Welsh within Nonconformity, there is no future for them either outside it. The effort of trying to think himself free of Calvinism does not leave the protagonist with the energy or hope necessary to work towards any new conceptualization of what it might mean to be Welsh.

In 1902, however, with the 1904 religious revival waiting in the wings to take central stage in Welsh life, not many Welsh women would have shared Violet Jacob's point of view: more representative of the mass of the population at the time would have been a writer like Sara Maria Saunders (1864–1939), a Methodist minister's wife and Cymru Fydd MP Tom Ellis's sister-in-law, whose bilingual fictions focus on the conversion experience.[83] And yet S. M. S. (as she signed herself) is also radical, in the strength and the influence she attributes to her female characters. Typically, she wrote a series of tales linked by the same narrator, locality and community, and those communities without exception are dominated by strong and intelligent women who are their backbone and saving grace. The authority of the deacons of Salem chapel in Pentre Alun is nothing compared to the power of Mrs Powel, Tynrhos, for example: 'Mrs Powel moved through the neighbourhood like a flame of fire', says the narrator ('Yr oedd Mrs Powel yn symud trwy'r gymdogaeth fel fflam o dân').[84] Similarly, Shani Jones, who is full of good 'sense from her heels to the crown of her head' ('synwyr o'i sowdl i'w choryn'), is the chief upholder of the chapel of the Cwm in Llanestyn.[85] The influence of these women in no way depends upon their husbands: on the contrary, 'marriage was the only foolish move' ('priodas oedd yr unig dro ffôl') in Mrs Powel's history, 'because Richet Powel was a wastrel, wholly unworthy of his wife' ('oherwydd dyn ofer oedd Richet Powel, hollol anheilwng o'i wraig').[86] And Shani Jones had 'an old rag of a man' ('hen glwtyn o ddyn') as a husband; according to the text, 'the only sensible thing he ever did was to die young' ('yr unig beth synhwyrol wnaeth e erioed oedd marw yn ddyn ifanc').[87]

Nancy Morris, the heroine of S.M.S.'s English-language series, 'Welsh Rural Sketches', is similarly forceful: in such stories as 'Nancy on the Warpath' she is portrayed fighting the battles of her husband and mother-in-law for them, and defeating her merciless and tyrannical father-in-law, William Morris, though he is 'His Majesty of Pentre-Rhedyn', the most powerful man in the locality and the chief deacon of his chapel.[88] Like all S.M.S.'s heroines Nancy also has a sharp wit; to an innocent-enough query on the equality of the two sexes, she responds, 'Oh! I don't know that I've ever thought women were equal to men. I've thought many times that they were a good deal better.'[89] The popularity of S.M.S.'s writings indicate that Welsh readers at the close of the nineteenth century were ready to accept as heroines women who were the moral and emotional superiors of men, and increasingly independent of them. Her success is an indicator of the triumph of the new image of the Welsh woman as strong and principled, the moral backbone of her society, and often its overt as well as covert leader.

But the Nonconformist world within which that new image had been formed was losing its hold on Wales; the 1904 revival proved its swan song. In the 1906 General Election the Liberals won every Welsh seat except Keir Hardie's in Merthyr, but it was his Independent Labour win which was indicative of what was to come. By 1912 the *Rhondda Leader*, a Liberal paper, was deploring the fact that the industrial valleys had become a 'happy hunting ground' for 'evangelists of socialism', not Calvinism. When the central intensity of Welsh life shifted, in south Wales in particular, from Liberalism and the chapels to Labour and the trade-union movement, it proved difficult initially for women to speak for their communities, given their exclusion from the workforce of the heavy industries. The tale of their struggle to make their voices heard within that new culture belongs, however, to another century and another volume.

Epilogue

On New Year's Eve 1900, Sarah Richards of Bridgend, Glamorgan, sat before the dying embers of her fire musing over the end of an era 'brilliant in various forms and ways'. In a poem commemorating the nineteenth century, she lists its achievements, particularly its inventions – 'The Telephone, The Electric Works, and discovery of Mines; / The Railways and Steam Engines . . .'.[1] She also records with pride the 'efforts we have seen' to 'place the Bible in the hands of every tribe', but is otherwise ambivalent about the growth of the British Empire, deploring war and the 'many empty seats to-night' that it has entailed.[2] Interestingly, she associates imperialism with 'guilt', albeit a 'guilt' which has been 'erased' by the 'noble work' of the 'Statesmen, Earls, and Peers, Physicians, Nurses too', who help to rule and, as she sees it, heal the colonies. Sarah Richards does not choose to probe the problems she hints at further: her verses have little critical edge, but characteristically constitute a straightforward record of events in her life and her locality. By far the majority of her poems are commemorative pieces, mourning the death of a neighbour or celebrating the marriage of their children. She is one of the many women who throughout the nineteenth century contributed to a popular culture animated by balladeers and 'beirdd gwlad', or local rhymesters. A recent study of eighteenth-century Welsh-language balladeers shows that women were amongst the ballad-mongers and popular rhymesters of pre-nineteenth-century Wales;[3] in the nineteenth, too, they continued to record in verse local events and occasions important to their communities. Such poets played an important role in maintaining their neighbourhood's social cohesiveness and resilience, helping their audiences to grieve or celebrate their losses and gains.

Elizabeth Davies of Neath, for example, published a series of pamphlets in the middle years of the century on such topics as the opening of the canal at Neath, or the coming of the South Wales Railway: whatever brought new life and resources to her community was celebrated in her verse. She has poems in praise of local landlords if they prove worthy, in which she switches from Welsh to English according to the language of the family;[4] and she also welcomes the coming of industrialization. More than one of her poems are dedicated, not to any local squire or MP, but to Isambard Kingdom Brunel. She tells 'brave Brunel' that, before his engineering triumphs in the Neath area, money was 'scarce in every place / No work was to be had'; the opening of his South Wales Railway means that 'Welshmen bold will earn their gold'.[5] But it is not only the material survival of her community that concerns her; she also composed 'Verses to the Ivorites for their Great Love of the Welsh Language', in which she thanks the antiquarians of the Cambrian Society (called the 'Ivorites' after their founding father Ifor Ceri) for having united 'Like faithful brethren . . . / Their language to preserve'.[6] Every human exertion that helps to preserve her community as it is, or to make it prosper, calls for and gets a praise poem from Elizabeth Davies. From a stylistic point of view, her verse is doggerel in both languages, but her gusto is infectious and her sense of rootedness in her community is palpable, as is her confidence in her capacity to act as spokesperson for that community, despite her gender.

Much the same can be said of the Welsh-language poet Dorothy Jones, or Dora Eifion, as she called herself, whose verses on the doings of her local Caernarfon community were collected and published in one volume in the 1870s. She, too, has poems on such events as the emigration to America of neighbours; local deaths of travellers crossing the mountains in winter; the wreck of the *Royal Charter* off Anglesey; a disaster in a local coal-mine. Her characteristic voice is one more of protest than praise, however; she is more likely to protect her community by satirically protesting against its enemies than by praising its friends. She expresses her fury at a range of local pests, from hypocritical chapel deacons and rack-rent landlords to the ageing process and household vermin. 'Well, come on, deacons, / You must tear out the old weeds' ('Wel deuwch flaenoriaid, / Rhaid tynu'r hen chwyn'), she tells her chapel's leaders in 'Y Blaenor Dau-Wynebog' (The Two-Faced Deacon),[7] and cutting away the dross from her community so as to secure its good health appears to be her chosen role. In another poem, 'Bankrupts' (she uses the English word), she fulminates against those spendthrift social adventurers who pose as rich people and live luxuriously at the expense of local artisans and small traders, whose bills they will never pay. The poem begins, 'Well today, joyous family, I'm going to expound a song, / The world is boiling to a powder of bankrupts big and little' ('Wel, heddyw deulu llawen rwy'n mynd i draethu cân, / Mae'r byd yn berwi'n bowdwr o bankrupts mawr a mân').[8] The fact that Dora Eifion thinks of her audience as 'family' speaks volumes for the place of such poets as herself in the long history of the bardic tradition in Wales, going back to the period of the family bards of the feudal lordships. That she should also think of them as 'joyous', even though she is, in this particular poem, lamenting one of the ways in which they have been unfairly cheated by a sup-posedly superior but in fact inferior class, is also indicative of her role. She is the spokesperson who voices with defiance, and also a robust humour, the harshness of their lot, and in so doing contributes to her audience's sense of being able to face up to their circumstances, difficult as they may be, and protest against them, as a community.

Dora Eifion, Elizabeth Davies and Sarah Richards are representative participants in that popular bardic culture which operated as a continuous choric commentary on the affairs of communities. As such, they and poets like them have not hitherto featured in this study of nineteenth-century Welsh women authors, which has focused largely on the more orthodox female voices of the dominant print culture, and on the women of the Liberal ascendancy, both Nonconformist and, in a few cases, Anglican. An interesting volume waits to be written on the nineteenth-century poets of the oral tradition, but in this book the primary aim was rather to explore to what extent women writers contributed to the changing patterns of the mainstream culture in Wales during the nineteenth century. It is appropriate, however, at its close to look back over the decades, like Sarah Richards did on the eve of the new century, and ask what were the main achievements of women writers as a group, during one hundred years in which Welsh life and the concept of Welshness changed fundamentally.

In 1800, the domination of the aristocracy and landlords over most aspects of cultural and political life was still widespread: Wales could still be described as a 'feudal country' right up until the eve of the Liberal landslide of 1868, according to Henry Richard.[9] The country's claims to being a democracy were merely nominal:

before the 1832 Electoral Reform Act, Welsh parliamentary seats, under the control of local landowners, went generally uncontested in general elections. For all the rapidity of its growth, the Methodist movement did not at first challenge the status quo: the sect remained part of the Established Church until 1811, and its Rule-book pledged its loyalty to the English state and monarch. It was not until 1852, after that state's 'betrayal' of Welsh Nonconformity in the 1847 Report on Education, that a Nonconformist first held a parliamentary seat in Wales. But with the secret ballot and the further expansion of the franchise, a popular, democratic and profoundly Nonconformist Wales rapidly established itself in political as well as cultural spheres: by the end of the century the vast majority of Wales's MPs were Liberal Nonconformists. From their beginnings, Welsh local councils reflected the same influences: in 1889 Nonconformists Liberals swept the board in the first Welsh County Council elections, taking control everywhere except in two Powys counties.[10] Women took their place in those councils alongside the men, showing their readiness to participate as fully as they could in the changes reshaping their country.

As we have seen, particularly in chapters 1, 3 and 5, from the first, women's contribution to the making of that distinctive Nonconformist culture was extensive: the hymn-writers of the first half of the century, the model school and Sunday-school teachers venerated from 1847 on, and the journal editors and contributors, temperance campaigners and missionaries of the 1880s and 90s all helped to form and ground a newly self-respecting awareness of Welsh national identity. In terms of individual influence, Cranogwen's achievement was unparalleled, but as a group the radically progressive female educational reformers of the 1880s and 1890s did most, perhaps, to ensure that the youth of Wales as a whole, and its girls and young women in particular, faced the twentieth century armed with an education, and an energizing confidence in their country's need of their resources arguably considerably in advance of that of their working-class counterparts in England. Wales's women writers helped to inspire such self-belief, through their influence as role models, their willingness to take on communal as well as familial leadership responsibilities, and their literary dissemination of strong images of Welsh women. As their obituary writers so often found cause to emphasize, they and the female followers they inspired were the 'pillars' of their communities, the 'mothers in Israel' whose shining light restored Welsh pride.

Within English-language culture, too, the contribution of women writers was more directly conducive to the development of the new Welsh consciousness than has previously perhaps been recognized. Admittedly, as we saw in chapter 4, some anglophone writers were Celtophobic, and, like the 1847 Report itself, furthered Welsh progressiveness, if at all, more by inciting patriotic opposition against their defamations than by any more positive contribution. But others, like Angharad Llwyd, Lady Llanover, Lady Charlotte Guest and Jane Williams did much to advance a renewed recognition of the richness and value of the Welsh heritage, in terms of its language, its history and its specific literary and cultural traditions. Both the historical and contemporary fictions penned by the anglophone daughters of Welsh Liberalism throughout the last half of the century, from Louisa Matilda Spooner's *Gladys of Harlech* and *Country Landlords* in the 1850s to Amy Dillwyn's *Rebecca Rioter* and Mabel Holland Grave's *Fraternity* in the 1880s, must also have helped to develop their readers' consciousness of the value and distinctiveness of Welsh culture, and sharpened their resistance to English homogenization. Such writers were not merely recording past or present times, but participating in an emergent discourse, constructive of a new Wales, with new opportunities opening for women within it.

That the Cymru Fydd movement, in which, as we saw in the last chapter, many women writers participated, failed in its goal of achieving constitutional independence for Wales does not detract from the vitality of the cultural renaissance it promoted. The glamour of the British Empire in its heyday, and the cult of Victoria in her Jubilee years, may have proved too compelling to allow the majority of the women writers of Wales to imagine their way free of such influences in either of Wales's languages, while the connection between the missionary movement and imperial aspirations overcame other potential resistances to empire-building. Yet a sense of the importance of holding on to and valuing a Welsh identity increased rather than diminished, during a century in which the common-sense expectation of many English cultural leaders, and some Welsh ones too, was that it would pass into history. Both Welsh- and English-language women writers contributed to that unexpected survival, and for that reason, as well as for the intrinsic interest of much of their work, their names and their writings deserve to live on in present-day post-devolution Wales.

Notes

Prologue

1   Catherine Davies, *Eleven Years' Residence in the Family of Murat, King of Naples* (London: How & Parsons, 1841), p. 4.

2   Ibid., pp. 5–6.

3   Ibid., pp. 30–1.

4   Ibid., p. 83.

5   Raymond Williams, 'The Culture of Nations' (1983), in *Who Speaks for Wales? Nation, Culture, Identity*, ed. Daniel Williams (Cardiff: University of Wales Press, 2003), p. 191.

6   Mary Robinson, *Walsingham; or, the Pupil of Nature*, 4 vols (1797), ed. Peter Garside (London: Routledge/Thoemmes Press, 1992), IV, pp. 44 and 49.

7   1536 Act, quoted in Norman Davies, *The Isles: A History* (London: Macmillan, 1999), pp. 492–3.

8   [Mabel Holland Grave], 'My Country', *Some Welsh Children* ([1898] London: Elkin Mathews, 1920), pp. 33–4.

9   [Mallt Williams], The Dau Wynne, *A Maid of Cymru: A Patriotic Romance* (London and Carmarthen: Simpkin, Marshal & Co. and Spurrell and Son, n.d. [1901]), p. 327.

10   [Annie Harriet Hughes] Gwyneth Vaughan, 'Gweledigaeth y Babell Wag', *Cymru*, 22 (1902), 24–8; 'Breuddwyd Nos Nadolig', *Cymru*, 29 (1905), 245–8.

11   Vaughan, 'Gweledigaeth y Babell Wag', 26.

12   See, for example, Nira Yuval-Davies and Floya Anthias (eds), *Woman-Nation-State* (London: Macmillan, 1989); Anne McClintock, '"No longer in a future heaven": nationalism, gender and race', in Geoff Eley and Ronald Grigor Suny (eds), *Becoming National: A Reader* (NY and Oxford: Oxford University Press, 1996), pp. 260–84; Ida Blom, Karen Hagemann and Catherine Hall (eds), *Gendered Nations: Nationalisms and Gender Order in the Long Nineteenth Century* (Oxford and New York: Berg, 2000); and Tamar Mayer (ed.), *Gender Ironies of Nationalism: Sexing the Nation* (London: Routledge, 2000). In the Welsh context, see Kirsti Bohata, 'En-gendering a new Wales: nationalism, feminism and empire in the fin de siècle', in her *Postcolonialism Revisited* (Cardiff: University of Wales Press, 2004), pp. 59–79.

¹³ Kathleen Hickok, 'Why is this woman still missing? Emily Pfeiffer, Victorian poet', in Isabel Armstrong and Virginia Blain (eds), *Women's Poetry, Late Romantic to Late Victorian: Gender and Genre 1830–1900* (Basingstoke: Macmillan, 1999), p. 387.

¹⁴ Catherine Brennan, *Angers, Fantasies and Ghostly Fears: Nineteenth-Century Women from Wales and English-Language Poetry* (Cardiff: University of Wales Press, 2003), pp. 111–69. For a further critique of Pfeiffer, and of other Welsh women poets writing in English in the second half of the nineteenth century, see also Euronia Lucretia Williams, 'Lost in the shadows: Welsh women poets writing in English, *c*.1840–1970' (unpub. Ph.D. thesis, University of Wales, Bangor, 2006), pp. 19–102.

¹⁵ Katie Gramich and Catherine Brennan (eds), *Welsh Women's Poetry 1460–2001: An Anthology* (Dinas Powys: Honno Press, 2003), pp. 70–159.

1. Romantic Wales

¹ Jane Austen, *Catharine and Other Writings*, ed. Margaret Anne Doody and Douglas Murray (Oxford: Oxford University Press, 1993), pp. 76 and 78.

² Ibid., pp. 18–26.

³ Ibid., p. 170.

⁴ Linda Colley, *Britons: Forging the Nation 1707–1837* (New Haven and London: Yale University Press, 1992), p. 156.

⁵ For influential Welsh travel-books of the period, see, for example, Thomas Pennant, *A Tour in Wales*, 2 vols (London: Henry Hughes, 1778–81); Henry Penruddocke Wyndham, *A Tour through Monmouthshire and Wales in 1774 and 1777* (Salisbury: E. Easton, 1781); and William Gilpin, Observations *on the river Wye, and several parts of South Wales* (London: R. Blamire, 1782).

⁶ Moira Dearnley, *Distant Fields: Eighteenth-Century Fictions of Wales* (Cardiff: University of Wales Press, 2001); Francesca Rhydderch, 'Dual nationality, divided identity: ambivalent narratives of Britishness in the Welsh novels of Anna Maria Bennett', *Welsh Writing in English: A Yearbook of Critical Essays*, 3 (1997), 1–17; Andrew Davies, 'The reputed nation of inspiration: representations of Wales in fiction from the Romantic period, 1780–1830' (unpub. Ph.D. thesis, Cardiff University, 2001).

⁷ See Leith Davis, *Acts of Union: Scotland and the Literary Negotiation of the British Nation, 1707–1830* (Stanford: Stanford University Press, 1998), p. 6; and Murray G. H. Pittock, *Celtic Identity and the British Image* (Manchester and NY: Manchester University Press, 1999), p. 95.

⁸ Katie Trumpener, *Bardic Nationalism: The Romantic Novel and the British Empire* (Princeton, NJ: Princeton University Press, 1997), pp. xi and 33. For Welsh bardic material, see Evan Evans (ed.), *Some Specimens of the Poetry of the Antient Welsh Bards* (London: R. and J. Dodsley, 1764); and Owen Jones, Edward Williams and William Owen Pughe (eds), *The Myvyrian Archaiology of Wales, collected out of ancient manuscripts*, 3 vols (London: S. Rousseau, 1801–7). The second collection contains many of Edward Williams's (Iolo Morganwg's) forgeries.

⁹ See Dot Jones, *Statistical Evidence relating to the Welsh Language 1801–1911* (Cardiff: University of Wales Press, 1998), p. 225.

[10] Benedict Anderson, *Imagined Communities: Reflections on the Origin and Spread of Nationalism* ([1983]; rev. edn, London: Verso, 1991), pp. 12–22.

[11] Ieuan Gwynedd Jones, *Mid-Victorian Wales: The Observers and the Observed* (Cardiff: University of Wales Press, 1993), p. 61. For details of the 1851 Religious Census, see also Jones, *Statistical Evidence relating to the Welsh Language*, pp. 413–41.

[12] See E. Wyn James, '"The birth of a people": Welsh language and identity and the Welsh Methodists, *c.*1740–1820', and Geraint Tudur, '"Thou bold champion, where art thou?": Howell Harries and the issue of Welsh identity', in Robert Pope (ed.), *Religion and National Identity: Wales and Scotland c.1700–2000* (Cardiff: University of Wales Press, 2001).

[13] William Williams, *Gweithiau William Williams, Pantycelyn*, 2 vols, ed. Garfield H. Hughes (Caerdydd: Gwasg Prifysgol Cymru, 1967), II, pp. 2–3.

[14] Derec Llwyd Morgan, *The Great Awakening in Wales*, trans. Dyfnallt Morgan (London: Epworth Press, 1988), pp. 56–60.

[15] *Rules and the Design of the Religious Societies among the Welsh Methodists* (Chester: W. C. Jones, 1802), p. 32.

[16] See Cathryn A. Charnell-White, 'Marwnadau Pantycelyn a pharagonau o'r rhyw deg', *Tu Chwith*, 6 (1996), 131–41, and 'Galaru a gwaddoli ym marwnadau Williams Pantycelyn', *Llên Cymru*, 26 (2003), 40–62.

[17] E. D. Clarke, *Tour through the South of England, Wales and part of Ireland, Made during the summer of 1791* (1793), p. 216.

[18] George Lipscomb, *Journey into South Wales in the Year 1799* (1802), p. 12; quoted in Bridget Hill, *Women, Work and Sexual Politics in Eighteenth-Century England* (Oxford: Basil Blackwell, 1989), pp. 35 and 58–9.

[19] See Llawddog, 'Cyflwr cymdeithasol a moesol merched swydd Aberteifi', *Y Gymraes*, i (1850), 358.

[20] 'Morwyn Ffarm', *Y Werin*, 1 March 1890; quoted in David A. Pretty, 'Women and trade unionism in Welsh rural society, 1889–1950', *Llafur*, 5/3 (1990), 6.

[21] Morgan, *The Great Awakening in Wales*, p. 122.

[22] See Luce Irigaray, 'La Mystérique', in *Speculum of the Other Woman*, trans. Gillian C. Gill (Ithaca, NY: Cornell University Press, 1974), for an account of the prevalence of the feminine within religious mysticism: Irigaray suggests that a mortal 'he' becomes a 'she' at the point of penetration by the immortal, and follows 'her' lead towards the 'source of light that has been logically repressed' (p. 191).

[23] John Hughes, *Methodistiaeth Cymru: sef Hanes Blaenorol a Gwedd Bresenol y Methodistiaid Calfinaidd yng Nghymru*, 2 vols (Wrecsam: R. Hughes, 1854), II, p. 27.

[24] Catherine Jones, 'Marwnad er coffadwriaeth am Mrs Barbara Vaughan o Gaerffili, 19 Ebrill 1808', in Cathryn A. Charnell-White, *Beirdd Ceridwen: Blodeugerdd Barddas o Ganu Menywod hyd tua 1800* (Swansea: Cyhoeddiadau Barddas, 2005), p. 315.

[25] See O. Llew Owain, *Cofiant Mrs Fanny Jones, Gweddw y Diweddar Barch J. Jones, Talysarn* (Machynlleth and Caernarfon: Cwmni y Cyhoeddwyr Cymreig, 1907), pp. 31, 29–30.

[26] For a biographical account in English of Ann Griffiths's life and work, see A. M. Allchin, *Ann Griffiths* (Cardiff: University of Wales Press, 1976).

27   Gwyn A. Williams, 'Romanticism in Wales', in Roy Porter and Mikuláš Teich (eds), *Romanticism in National Context* (Cambridge: Cambridge University Press, 1988), p. 26. See Saunders Lewis, *Williams Pantycelyn* ([1927] Caerdydd: Gwasg Prifysgol Cymru, 1991), for the case for William Williams as a Romanticist.

28   Ann Griffiths, *Gwaith Ann Griffiths*, ed. O. M. Edwards Llanuwchllyn: Ab Owen, n.d. [1905]), 44. For a selection of Ann Griffiths's hymns with an English translation by Alan Gaunt, see Katie Gramich and Catherine Brennan, *Welsh Women's Poetry 1460–2001: An Anthology* (Dinas Powys: Honno Press, 2003), pp. 84–93.

29   For a more detailed account of Ann Griffiths's use of the 'Song of Solomon', see Derec Llwyd Morgan, 'Ann Griffiths yn ei dydd', *Pobl Pantycelyn* (Llandysul: Gwasg Gomer, 1986), pp. 56–7.

30   *Gwaith Ann Griffiths*, pp. 41, 35, 43.

31   Ibid., p. 35.

32   See W. Samlet Williams, 'Pegi Shenkin, Trelalas', *Y Gymraes*, viii (1904), 155.

33   Mary Owen, *Hymnau ar amryw destunau* (Caernarfon: P. Evans, 1839; 2nd edn., Llanelli: Rees & Tomos, 1840), pp. 67–8. See also, for further information on Mary Owen, Elfed, 'Mrs. Mary Owen', *Y Geninen* (Ceninen Gŵyl Ddewi: Argraffiad Arbennig, 1903), pp. 17–20; J. Seymour Rees, 'Mary Owen, yr emynyddes', *Y Llenor*, 24 (1945), 68–75; and Branwen Jarvis, 'Mary Owen yr emynyddes', *Y Traethodydd*, 143 (1988), 45–53.

34   Jane Ellis, *Casgliad o Hymnau, Carolau a Marwnadau a gyfansoddwyd ar amrywiol achosion* (Wyddgrug: H. and O. Jones, 1840; 3rd edn. of Jane Edward, *Ychydig hymnau, a gyfansoddwyd ar amrywiol achosion*, Bala: R. Saunderson, 1816), p. 35. I am grateful to Rhiannon Ifans for alerting me to the existence of this third edition of Jane Edward's collection, and to its author's change of surname. Ifans also believes Jane Edward's volume to be the first published in Welsh by a woman, but for the argument that *Casgliad o Hymnau*, 1806, should be considered the first because Ann Griffiths's name appears on its title-page, see E. Wyn James, 'Ann Griffiths: O lafar i lyfr', in Angharad Price (ed.), *Chwileniwm: Technoleg a Llenyddiaeth* (Caerdydd: Gwasg Prifysgol Cymru, 2002), p. 73.

35   Edward, *Ychydig hymnau*, p. 27.

36   J[ane] Roberts, *Hymnau newyddion, ar destynau efengylaidd* (Caernarfon: Peter Evans, n.d. [c.1820?]), p. 32.

37   Ibid., p. 27.

38   *Gwaith Ann Griffiths*, pp. 27, 43, 30.

39   Saunders Lewis, *Meistri'r Canrifoedd: Ysgrifau ar Hanes Llenyddiaeth Gymraeg*, ed. R. Geraint Gruffydd (Caerdydd: Gwasg Prifysgol Cymru, 1973), p. 312; see also E. Wyn James, 'Ann Griffiths: Y cefndir barddol', *Llên Cymru*, 23 (2000), 147–71.

40   R. M. Jones, *Llên Cymru a Chrefydd: Diben y Llenor* (Abertawe: Christopher Davies, 1977), pp. 474 and 476. See also, for a further analysis of the Calvinist doctrine in Ann Griffiths' poetry, E. Wyn James, 'Ann Griffiths', in E. Wyn James (ed.), *Cwmwl o Dystion* (Swansea: Christopher Davies, 1977), pp. 99–113.

41   Carneddog, 'Emynyddes anghofiedig', *Cymru*, 30 (1906), 219.

42   Ibid., 220.

43 Thomas Levi, 'Margaret Thomas yr emynyddes', *Y Traethodydd*, 59 (1904), 340.

44 J. E. D. (Rhuddwawr) [John Evan Davies], *Martha Llwyd Llanpumsaint* (Dolgellau: E. W. Evans, Swyddfa'r 'Cymro', n.d. [1925]), p. 50.

45 Ibid., p. 56.

46 Elizabeth Davies, *Dwy Gan: Cymhorth i hunan-adnabyddiaeth; Golwg ar sefyllfa Cristianogrwydd, o amser Crist hyd yn bresennol* (Aberystwyth: Samuel Williams, 1813), p. 3.

47 Alice Edwards, *Ychydig bennillion er annogaeth i Sïon i ymddiried yn ei Duw mewn blinfyd a chaledi* (Bala: J. Davies, n.d. [1812]), 2; anthologized in Charnell-White (ed.), *Beirdd Ceridwen*, p. 337.

48 Jane Hughes, 'Cân ar niwed pechodau'r oes', quoted in Meredydd Evans, '"Ryw gythraul o'i go yn canu so doh"', in *Merêd: Detholiad o ysgrifau Dr. Meredydd Evans*, ed. Ann Ffrancon and Geraint H. Jenkins (Llandysul: Gwasg Gomer, 1994), p. 216.

49 [O. M. Edwards], 'Rhwng Dwy Erthygl', *Cymru*, 46 (1914), 124.

50 *Gwaith Ann Griffiths*, p. 36.

51 Ibid., p. 32.

52 See Geraint H. Jenkins, *The Foundations of Modern Wales: Wales 1642–1780* (Oxford and Cardiff: Clarendon Press and University of Wales Press, 1987), p. 358.

53 Lewis Morris, 'Young Mends the clothier's sermon', National Library of Wales MS 67A, 57–68; quoted in Geraint H. Jenkins, 'The new enthusiasts', in Trevor Herbert and Gareth Elwyn Jones (eds), *The Remaking of Wales in the Eighteenth Century* (Cardiff: University of Wales Press, 1988), pp. 56 and 69–70.

54 Iolo Morganwg, quoted in Geraint H. Jenkins, '"Peth erchyll iawn" oedd Methodistiaeth', *Llên Cymru*, 17 (1993), 204. For recent critical discussions of Iolo Morganwg's contribution to the development of the Romantic movement, see Geraint Jenkins (ed.), *A Rattleskull Genius: The Many Faces of Iolo Morganwg* (Cardiff: University of Wales Press, 2005), pp. 71–193; and Damian Walford Davies, *Presences that Disturb: Models of Romantic Identity in the Literature and Culture of the 1790s* (Cardiff: University of Wales Press, 2002), pp. 135–92.

55 See Jon Mee, *Romanticism, Enthusiasm and Regulation: Poetics and the Policing of Culture in the Romantic Period* (Oxford: Oxford University Press, 2003); and, for a discussion of the disparagement of Methodism within English-language culture in the later Victorian period, Valentine Cunningham, *Everywhere Spoken Against: Dissent in the Victorian Novel* (Oxford: Clarendon Press, 1975)

56 Leigh Hunt, *An Attempt to Shew the Folly and Danger of Methodism. In a series of essays first published in the . . . Examiner, and now enlarged with a preface, and . . . notes* (London: printed for the author, 1809), pp. 55–6; quoted in Mee, *Romanticism, Enthusiasm and Regulation*, pp. 268–9.

57 Hunt, *An attempt . . .* , p. 12; quoted in ibid, p. 50.

58 Maria Edgeworth, *Belinda* [1801], ed. Eiléan Ní Chuilleanáin (London: Dent, 1993), p. 285.

59 Elizabeth Isabella Spence, *Old Stories*, 2 vols (London: J. Dodsley, 1822), I,

p. 27; for a further account of this text, see Davies, 'The reputed nation of inspiration', pp. 194–5.

60 Elizabeth Mavor, *Life with the Ladies of Llangollen* (Harmondsworth: Penguin, 1984), pp. 218 and 70.

61 Mary Robinson's renown has recently been revived in the twenty-first century by a spate of biographies: Paula Byrne, *Perdita: The Life of Mary Robinson* (London: HarperCollins, 2004); Hester Davenport, *The Prince's Mistress: A Life of Mary Robinson* (Stroud: Sutton, 2004); and Sarah Gristwood, *Perdita: Royal Mistress, Writer, Romantic* (London: Bantam Press, 2005). See also *Memoirs of the late Mrs Robinson, written by herself. With some posthumous pieces* [ed. Maria Elizabeth Robinson], 4 vols (London: Richard Phillips, 1801), the first two volumes of which were republished as *Perdita: The Memoirs of Mary Robinson*, ed. M. J. Levy (London: Peter Owen, 1994); and Robert D. Bass, *The Green Dragoon: The Lives of Banastre Tarleton and Mary Robinson* ([1957] Orangeburg, SC: Sandlapper Publishing, 1973).

62 See Dearnley, *Distant Fields*, p. 172.

63 Charlotte Dacre, 'To the Shade of Mary Robinson', *Hours of Solitude. A Collection of Original Poems*, 2 vols (London: Hughes and Ridgeway, 1805), I, pp. 133 and 131; the italics are the author's.

64 Levy (ed.), *Perdita*, pp. 50, 49, 69.

65 Mary Robinson, *Walsingham; or, The Pupil of Nature*, 4 vols (London: T. N. Longman, 1797); repr. in facs. edn, with intro. by Peter Garside (London: Routledge/Thoemmes Press, 1992), II, p. 328.

66 Ibid., II, p. 317.

67 Ibid., II, p. 320.

68 Anna Maria Bennett, *Anna, or, Memoirs of a Welch Heiress: interspersed with anecdotes of a Nabob*, 4 vols ([1785] 2nd edn, London: William Lane, 1786), I, pp. 12, 13 and 15.

69 Anna Maria Bennett, *The Beggar Girl and Her Benefactors*, 7 vols (London: William Lane, 1797), I, 15.

70 J. F. Fuller, *A Curious Genealogical Medley* (London: Mitchell, Hughes & Clarke, 1913), p. 2.

71 For discussions of Bennett's work, see Isobel Grundy, '"A novel in a series of letters by a lady": Richardson and some Richardsonian novels', in Margaret Doody and Peter Sabor (eds), *Samuel Richardson: Tercentenary Essays* (Cambridge: Cambridge University Press, 1989), pp. 229–31 and 289; Dearnley, *Distant Fields*, pp. 130–57; and Rhydderch, 'Dual nationality, divided identity'.

72 [Isabella Kelly], *The Abbey of Saint Asaph*, 3 vols (London: Minerva Press, 1795), I, p. 50.

73 [Eliza Ryves], *The Hermit of Snowden [sic]: or Memoirs of Albert and Lavinia* (London: Logographic Press, 1789), pp. i–ii.

74 Mary Nicholl, *The Family of George Briton: or, The Importance of a Right Education. A Moral Tale for Young Persons* (Carmarthen: J. Evans, 1822), pp. 57, 58 and 59; the italics are the author's.

75 Susannah Gunning, *Delves: A Welch Tale*, 2 vols (London: Lackington, Allen & Co., 1796), I, p. 257.

76 Ibid., II, p. 315.

77 Anna Maria Bennett, *Ellen, Countess of Castle Howel*, 2 vols (2nd edn, Dublin: Jones, Colbert, Fitzpatrick & Milliken, 1794), I, pp. 3 and 10.

78 Ibid., I, pp. 97–8.

79 The third baronet, Sir Watkin Williams Wynn, had burnt a picture of George II in 1727, and rejected a peerage, but his son, says Colley, 'might have come from a different planet'; he belonged to London's Dilettanti Society and married English women (twice, the first having died young). The fifth baronet, knighted in 1789, also married an English woman, and changed Wynnstay from being a Welsh cultural centre to a patriotic pro-Establishment military centre. See Colley, *Britons*, pp. 160–1.

80 Bennett, *Anna*, I, p. 231.

81 Ibid., IV, p. 279.

82 See Rhydderch, 'Dual nationality, divided identity', for a more extensive analysis of Bennett's novels.

83 Colley, *Britons*, p. 370.

84 For more biographical information on Sophia Lee, see the introduction to Sophia Lee, *The Recess; or, A Tale of Other Times*, ed. April Alliston (Lexington, Kentucky: University Press of Kentucky, 2000), pp. ix–xliv.

85 Sophia Lee, 'The Clergyman's Tale: Pembroke', in Harriet and Sophia Lee, *The Canterbury Tales* ([1799] repr. London: Pandora Press, 1989), p. 5.

86 Ibid., p. 6.

87 Ibid., p. 8.

88 See Dot Jones, *Statistical Evidence relating to the Welsh Language*, p. 222.

89 Lee, 'The Clergyman's Tale', pp. 10–11.

90 Quoted in Norman Davies, *The Isles: A History* (London : Macmillan, 1999), pp. 492–3

91 . Emily Frederick Clark, *Ianthé, or the Flower of Caernarvon*, 2 vols (London: printed for the author, 1798), II, p. 70. Reared by her grandfather, Colonel Frederick, professedly the illegitimate son of Theodore, King of Corsica, Clark resorted to novel-writing to maintain herself after Colonel Frederick, described by James Boswell as 'a low-lifed being', shot himself in the porch of Westminster Abbey in 1797: see Virginia Blain, Patricia Clements and Isobel Grundy (eds), *The Feminist Companion to English Literature* (London: Batsford, 1990), p. 212.

92 [Emma Parker] Emma de Lisle, *Fitz-Edward; or, the Cambrians. A Novel. Interspersed with Pieces of Poetry*, 3 vols (London: Minerva Press, 1811), II, p. 36.

93 Ibid., I, p. 44.

94 Louisa Weston, *The Cambrian Excursion: intended to inculcate a taste for the Beauties of Nature; and to direct the attention of Young People to sources of Mental Improvement* (London: A. K. Newman, 1841), pp. 146, 13.

95 Catharine Hutton, *The Welsh Mountaineer: A Novel*, 3 vols (London: Longmans, 1817), I, p. 11.

96 Ibid., I, pp. 157–8.

97 [Olivia More], *The Welsh Cottage* (Wellington, Salop: Houlston & Son, 1820), p. 129.

98 Ibid., pp. 194 and 201.

99 Elizabeth Gunning, *The Orphans of Snowdon*, 3 vols (London: H. Lowndes, 1797; 2nd edn, London: Lane, Newman & Co., 1807), I, pp. 30–1, 33.

[100] Clark, *Ianthé*, I, pp. 34–5.

[101] Bennett, *Ellen*, I, pp. 24–5.

[102] [Elizabeth Hervey], *The History of Ned Evans*, 4 vols (London: G. C. and J. Robinson, 1796), I, pp. 145–6.

[103] Ann of Swansea, *Cambrian Pictures; or, Every one has Errors*, 3 vols (London: E. Kerby, 1810), I, pp. 135–92.

[104] Catherine Parry, *Eden Vale. A Novel*, 2 vols (London: John Stockdale, 1784), II, pp. 115–21.

[105] Cecil Price, *The English Theatre in Wales in the Eighteenth and Early Nineteenth Centuries* (Cardiff: University of Wales Press, 1948), p. 40.

[106] For further biographical information, see Ivor J. Bromham, '"Ann of Swansea" (Ann Julia Hatton: 1764–1838)', *Glamorgan Historian*, 7 (1971), 173–86; and James Henderson, 'An edition of the poems of Ann of Swansea (Ann Julia Hatton, née Kemble, 1764–1838) including unpublished material' (unpub. M.Phil. thesis, University of Glamorgan, 2005).

[107] Ann of Swansea, *Cambrian Pictures*, II, pp. 348–9.

[108] Ibid., III, pp. 33–4.

[109] Lord Bulkeley to Lord Grenville, 1 October 1806: quoted in David Hempton, *Methodism and Politics in British Society 1750–1850* (London: Hutchinson, 1984), pp. 225–6.

[110] *Rules and the Design of the Religious Societies among the Welsh Methodists*, pp. 26–7.

[111] Jane Cave, 'On the Death of Mr. Howell Harris', in *A Brief Account of the Life of Howell Harris* . . . (Trefeca: printed for the Methodists, 1791); the elegy was first published in Jane Cave, *Poems on Various Subjects, Entertaining, Elegiac, and Religious* (Winchester: printed for the author by J. Sadler, 1783), pp. 83–9.

[112] For further discussion of Jane Cave's life and work, see Catherine Brennan, *Angers, Fantasies and Ghostly Fears: Nineteenth-Century Women from Wales and English-Language Poetry* (Cardiff: University of Wales Press, 2003), pp. 23–41; and Catherine Messem, 'Irreconcilable tensions: gender, class and the Welsh question in the poetry of Jane Cave', *Welsh Writing in English: A Yearbook of Critical Essays*, 2 (1996), 1–21.

[113] Cave, 'An Ode, on the Author's Father having attained the Eighty-first Year of his Age, in August 1794', *Poems* . . . (4th edn, Bristol: N. Biggs, 1794), p. 190.

[114] Cave, *Poems* (1st edn, 1783), p. 103.

[115] Ibid., pp. 84 and 86.

[116] Ibid., p. 47; also reprinted in Gramich and Brennan, *Welsh Women's Poetry*, pp. 78–9.

[117] Cave, *Poems* (4th edn), p. 189.

[118] Cave, *Poems* (1st edn), p. 2.

[119] The poem 'A Mother Dreaming of her Son's Profile done in India Ink' reveals that the son's initials were 'W. D.' and that he was the child of her 'first love'; see Mrs E. Crebar, *Poems, Religious and Moral* (Aberystwyth: printed for the author, 1811), p. 28.

[120] Ibid., p. 4.

[121] Ibid., p. 7.

[122] Ibid., pp. 9–10.

[123] Ibid., p. 8.

124 Maria James, *Wales, and Other Poems* (New York: John S. Taylor, 1839), p. 49; the poem is also reproduced in Gramich and Brennan, *Welsh Women's Poetry*, pp. 96–8.

125 A. Potter, 'Introduction', in James, *Wales, and Other Poems*, p. 19.

126 Ibid., pp. 162–3; reprinted in Gramich and Brennan, *Welsh Women's Poetry*, pp. 100–2.

127 Ibid., p. 41.

2. Writing Ancient Britain

1 Mary Barker, *A Welsh Story*, 3 vols (London: Hookham & Carpenter, 1798), I, 106–7, 109–10.

2 Rosemary Sweet, *Antiquities: The Discovery of the Past in Eighteenth-Century Britain* (London and NY: Hambledon, 2004), pp. 71–2.

3 See Prys Morgan, 'From a death to a view: the hunt for the Welsh past in the Romantic period', in Eric Hobsbawm and Terence Ranger (eds), *The Invention of Tradition* (Cambridge: Cambridge University Press, 1983), pp. 43–100; and Gwyn Alf Williams, 'Romanticism in Wales', in R. Porter and M. Teich (eds), *Romanticism in National Context* (Cambridge: Cambridge University Press, 1988), pp. 9–36.

4 Evan Evans [Ieuan Prydydd Hir], *Some Specimens of the Poetry of the Antient Welsh Bards. Translated into English* . . . (London: R. and J. Dodsley, 1764).

5 Anne Penny, 'An Elegy on Neest', *Poems* ([1771]; new edn with added poems, London: printed for the author, 1780), p. 15.

6 Anne Penny, *An Invocation to the Genius of Britain* (London: printed for the author, 1778), p. 5.

7 Ibid., pp. 10 and 11; Penny misquotes Shakespeare, *Richard II*, II. i. 46, in which England is described as 'This precious stone set in the silver sea'.

8 [Anne Bannerman], *Tales of Superstition and Chivalry* (London: Vernor & Hood, 1802), pp. 125–39.

9 [Mary] Darwall, *Poems on Several Occasions*, 2 vols (Walsall: F. Milward, 1794), II, pp. 163–4.

10 Lucy Aikin, 'Cambria: an Ode', *Epistles on Women, exemplifying their Character and Condition in Various Ages and Nations. With Miscellaneous Poems* (London: J. Johnson, 1810), p. 101.

11 Janetta Philipps, *Poems* (Oxford: privately printed by Collingwood and Co., 1811), p. 38.

12 For discussions of Ann of Swansea's poetry see Moira Dearnley, 'Condemn'd to wither on a foreign strand', *New Welsh Review*, 41, XI/i (1998), 56–9; Catherine Brennan, *Angers, Fantasies and Ghostly Fears; Nineteenth-Century Women from Wales and English-Language Poetry* (Cardiff: University of Wales Press, 2003), pp. 42–62; and James Henderson, 'An edition of the poems of Ann of Swansea (Ann Julia Hatton, née Kemble, 1764–1838) including unpublished material' (unpub. M.Phil. thesis, University of Glamorgan, 2005).

13 Mary Robinson, 'Llwhen and Gwyneth . . . From Mr. John Williams's prose translation of a lately discovered Welsh Poem, preserved in the Collections of Arthur Price, Esq. It is supposed to have been written by Tateisin in Ben

Batriddd, A.D. 534', *The Poetical Works of the late Mrs Mary Robinson: including many pieces never before published*, 3 vols (London: Richard Phillips, 1805), II, p. 22.
14 Ibid., pp. 22, 23, 27, 29.
15 See John Henderson, 'Lines addressed to Mrs. Robinson . . . On reading a little Welsh Ballad written by Mrs. Robinson entitled "Lewin and Gynniethe" [*sic*]', quoted in ibid., I, p. xlvii.
16 Philipps, *Poems*, p. 13.
17 Ibid., pp. 39–48.
18 Jane Williams, *The Literary Women of England* (London: Saunders, Otley, & Co., 1861), p. 394.
19 Felicia Hemans, *Poems of Felicia Hemans* (Edinburgh and London: Blackwood, 1852), p. 152.
20 For further material on Hemans and her popularity, see the introduction to Susan Wolfson (ed.), *Felicia Hemans: Selected Poems, Letters, Reception Materials* (Princeton and Oxford: Princeton University Press, 2000), pp. xvii–xxi.
21 See, for example, Hemans, 'The Hall of Cynddylan', *Poems*, p. 147, a free translation of verses from the anonymous ninth-century Welsh-language poem, 'Stafell Cynddylan'.
22 Ibid., p. 247; the italicized last line is a translated quotation from the Welsh Eisteddfod prayer – '*Yng ngwyneb haul ac yn llygaid goleuni*'.
23 Tricia Lootens, 'Hemans and home: Victorianism, feminine "internal enemies", and the domestication of national identity', in Angela Leighton (ed.), *Victorian Women Poets: A Critical Reader* (Oxford: Blackwell, 1996), p. 2.
24 Hemans, 'The Homes of England', *Poems*, p. 412.
25 Ibid., p. 246.
26 Ibid., pp. 63, 65.
27 *Edinburgh Monthly Review*, 2 (1819), repr. in Hemans, *Poems*, p. 66.
28 Ibid., p. 152.
29 'The Name of England', ibid., p. 567.
30 For further material on Hemans and national identities, see Brennan, *Angers, Fantasies and Ghostly Fears*, pp. 76–86; and William D. Brewer, 'Felicia Hemans, Byronic cosmopolitanism and the ancient Welsh bards', in Gerard Carruthers and Alan Rawes, *English Romanticism and the Celtic World* (Cambridge: Cambridge University Press, 2003), pp. 167–81. Brewer argues that the apparent contradictions in Hemans's position are the result of her cosmopolitan respect for patriotism, wherever it was manifested.
31 Janet W. Wilkinson, *Sketches and Legends amid the Mountains of North Wales: in verse* (London: T. & W. Boone, 1840), pp. 2–8.
32 A. E. Marshall, 'Preface', *Odds and Ends* (London: William Pickering, 1853), p. vi.
33 Ibid., p. 4.
34 Lady Marshall, 'Appendix: Note A', *A Prince of Wales Long Ago: A Bardic Legend of the Twelfth Century* (London and Chester: Whittaker and Co., and Prichard, Roberts and Co., 1855), pp. 3–5.
35 Ibid., p. 5.
36 Ibid., p. 5.

37 [William Owen Pughe], 'Preface', *Cambrian Register*, 1 (1795; actually publ. 1796), v.

38 Ibid., 3 (1818), 500–2.

39 Hester Lynch Piozzi, *Autobiography, Letters and Literary Remains of Mrs. Piozzi (Thrale)*, ed. A. Hayward, 2 vols (2nd edn, London: Longman, 1861), p. 6.

40 Piozzi, 'The Streatham Portraits', ibid., p. 173.

41 Hester Lynch Piozzi, *Retrospection: or A Review of the most striking and important events, characters and situations, and their consequences, which the last eighteen hundred years have presented to the view of mankind*, 2 vols (London: John Stockdale, 1801), I, p. 371 and II. p. 482.

42 Ibid., II, p. 511.

43 See a 1792 journal entry in which she bemoans the fact that Williams 'is on the Point of sacrificing her Reputation to her Spirit of Politics' through visiting France in the company of the married John Hurford Stone *Thraliana: The Diary of Hester Lynch Thrale (Later Mrs Piozzi) 1776–1809*, ed. Katherine C. Balderston, 2 vols (Oxford: Clarendon Press, 1942), II, p. 849. Later, in her *Retrospection*, she laments the French revolutionaries' treatment of 'Helen Williams, once so lovely and beloved, among her own friends, which for theirs, she quitted' (*Retrospection*, II, p. 510).

44 See Geraint H. Jenkins, 'The Unitarian firebrand, the Cambrian society and the Eisteddfod', in Geraint H. Jenkins (ed.), *A Rattleskull Genius: The Many Faces of Iolo Morganwg* (Cardiff: University of Wales Press, 2005), pp. 269–92.

45 For further information on Eos y Bele, see Mari Ellis, 'Rhai o Hen Bersoniaid Llengar Maldwyn', in Gwynn ap Gwilym and Richard H. Lewis (eds), *Bro'r Eisteddfod: Cyflwyniad i Faldwyn a'i Chyffiniau* (Llandybïe: Gwasg Christopher Davies, 1981), pp. 93–5. I am also indebted to E. Wyn James and to Huw Walters for their assistance in tracing the history of Elizabeth Jenkins.

46 See Mari Ellis, 'Angharad Llwyd, 1780–1866', *Taliesin*, 53 (1985), 20–1.

47 Mari Ellis, 'Teulu Darowen', *Journal of the Historical Society of the Church in Wales*, 4/1 (1954), 77.

48 Ellis, 'Angharad Llwyd', 21.

49 For further biographical information on Angharad Llwyd, see Mari Ellis, 'Angharad Llwyd, 1780–1866', *Taliesin*, 52 and 53 (1985), 10–43 and 20–31.

50 Sir John Wynn, *The History of the Gwydir Family . . . now re-edited by a Native of the Principality: to which is added An Original Work, containing Memoirs of celebrated and distinguished Contemporary Welshmen, Bishops, &c. by the same author*, ed. Angharad Llwyd (Rhuthun: Taliesin Press, 1827), p. iii.

51 Angharad Llwyd, *A History of the Island of Mona, or Anglesey: Including an Account of its Natural Productions, Druidical Antiquities, Lives of Eminent Men, the Customs of the Court of the Ancient Welsh Princes, &c.: Being the Prize Essay to which was Adjudged the First Premium at the Royal Beaumaris Eisteddfod, held in the month of August, 1832* (Rhuthun and London: R. Jones & Longman, 1833).

52 See, for example, ibid., p. 33.

53 Ibid., p. 59.

54 Ibid., p. 113.

55 Ibid., p. 116.
56 Ibid., p. 62.
57 Ibid., p. 3.
58 'A Lady of the Principality', *Stories from the History of Wales: Interspersed with Various Information and Amusement for Young Persons* (Shrewsbury: John Eddowes, 1833), 158.
59 For biographical information on 'A Lady of the Principality', see 'Letter from Captain Basil Hall to the Publisher', in *Tales about Wales, with a Catechism of Welsh History* (2nd edn, Edinburgh: Robert Cadell, 1837), p. x.
60 Ibid., pp. 107–8.
61 'A Lady of the Principality', *Stories from the History of Wales*, p. 59.
62 Ibid., pp. 154–5.
63 Catherine Sinclair, *Hill and Valley, or Wales and the Welsh* ([1838]; 2nd edn, Edinburgh: William Whyte, 1839).
64 Ibid., pp. 123, 233 and 321.
65 Ibid., pp. 201, 167–8.
66 Ibid., p. 188.
67 [Augusta Waddington Hall] Gwenynen Gwent, *The Advantages resulting from the Preservation of the Welsh Language and National Costumes of Wales* (London: Longman, 1836), pp. 3–4.
68 For further English-language biographical material on Lady Llanover and her circle, see Maxwell Fraser, 'Lady Llanover and Lady Charlotte Guest', *Anglo-Welsh Review*, 13 (1963), 36–43, and her 'Lady Llanover and her circle', *Transactions of the Honourable Society of Cymmrodorion* (1968), 170–96. Welsh-language studies include Mair Elvet Thomas, *Afiaith yng Ngwent: Hanes Cymdeithas Cymreigyddion y Fenni 1833–1854* (Caerdydd: Gwasg Prifysgol Cymru, 1978), and Prys Morgan, *Gwenynen Gwent* (Casnewydd: Pwyllgor Llên Eisteddfod Genedlaethol Casnewydd, 1988).
69 See Siân Rhiannon Williams, 'Llwydlas, Gwenynen Gwent a dadeni diwylliannol y bedwaredd ganrif ar bymtheg', in *Cof Cenedl: Ysgrifau ar Hanes Cymru XV*, ed. Geraint H. Jenkins (Llandysul: Gwasg Gomer, 2000), p. 109.
70 Ibid., p. 100.
71 See Maxwell Fraser, 'Jane Williams (Ysgafell) 1806–1885', *Brycheiniog: Journal of the Brecknock Society*, 7 (1961–2), 102.
72 Lady Llanover, *The First Principles of Good Cookery illustrated. And recipes communicated by the Welsh hermit of the cell of St. Gover, with various remarks on many things past and present (London: Richard Bentley, 1867; facs. edn Tregaron: Brefi Press, 1991)*, pp. 256–8.
73 Ibid., pp. 261 and 263.
74 [Hall], The *Advantages resulting from the Preservation of the Welsh Language*, p. 8.
75 [John Jones] Jac Glan-y-Gors, *Seren tan Gwmmwl a Toriad y Dydd* (rpr., Liverpool: Hugh Evans, 1923).
76 For further material on Augusta Hall's invention of the 'traditional' Welsh costume, see Morgan, 'From a death to a view', pp. 80–1.
77 [Hall], *The Advantages resulting from the Preservation of the Welsh Language*, p. 10; here, as elsewhere in these quotations, the italics are Lady Llanover's own.

78 [Melesina] Bowen, *Ystradffin: A Descriptive Poem, with an Appendix containing, Historical and Explanatory Notes* (London and Llandovery: Longman, Orme, Brown, Green & Longmans, and W. Rees, 1839), p. 172.

79 For further biographical information on Maria Jane Williams, see Allan James, 'Maria Jane Williams' in Hywel Teifi Edwards (ed.), *Nedd a Dulais* (Llandysul: Gwasg Gomer, 1994), pp. 95–130.

80 Lady Hall to Taliesin ap Iolo; quoted in Maria Jane Williams, *Ancient National Airs of Gwent and Morganwg*, ed. Daniel Huws ([1844] [Aberystwyth]: Cymdeithas Alawon Gwerin Cymru, 1988), p. xxx; the text italicizes.

81 Williams, 'Llwydlas, Gwenynen Gwent a dadeni diwylliannol y bedwaredd ganrif ar bymtheg', p. 114.

82 See the excellent biography by Revel Guest and Angela V. John, *Lady Charlotte: A Biography of the Nineteenth Century* (London: Weidenfeld and Nicolson, 1989), pp. 118–19

83 Belinda Humfrey, 'Prelude to the twentieth century', in M. Wynn Thomas (ed.), *Welsh Writing in English* (Cardiff: University of Wales Press, 2003), p. 39.

84 Quoted in Guest and John, *Lady Charlotte*, p. 86.

85 Ibid., pp. 31 and 33.

86 [Guest, Lady Charlotte Elizabeth Bertie (later Schreiber)] *Lady Charlotte Guest, Extracts from her Journals 1833–52*, ed. Earl of Bessborough (London: John Murray, 1950), pp. 65 and 115–16.

87 Chris Williams, 'Wales' '"Unionist Nationalist": Sir Thomas Phillips (1801–67)', *Llafur*, 8/4 (2003), 7–17.

3. Becoming National

1 See, for example, Ieuan Gwynedd Jones, '1848 ac 1868: Brad y Llyfrau Gleision a gwleidyddiaeth Cymru', in Prys Morgan (ed.), *Brad y Llyfrau Gleision: Ysgrifau ar Hanes Cymru* (Llandysul: Gwasg Gomer, 1991), p. 67: 'Am y tro cyntaf yn y ganrif roedd pobl Cymru *fel Cymry* yn gorfod pwyso a mesur beth oedd eu cenedligrwydd mewn ffordd boenus ond hynod effeithiol' ('For the first time in the century the Welsh *as the Welsh* had to weigh and measure what their nationality was in a painful but very effective way.') The text italicizes.

2 *Report of the Commission of Inquiry into the State of Education in Wales . . . In Three Parts. Part I, Carmarthen, Glamorgan and Pembroke. Part II, Brecknock, Cardigan, Radnor and Monmouth. Part III, North Wales* (London, 1847), II, p. 56.

3 Ibid., p. 60.

4 Ibid., III, pp. 67–8.

5 See Martine Segalen, *Love and Power in the Peasant Family*, trans. Sarah Matthews (Oxford: Blackwell, 1983), p. 20.

6 Hansard, 3rd series, LXXXIV, 10 March 1846; quoted in Ieuan Gwynedd Jones, *Mid-Victorian Wales: The Observers and the Observed* (Cardiff: University of Wales Press, 1992), p. 123.

7 *Report*, II, p. 57.

8   Gwyneth Tyson Roberts, *The Language of the Blue Books: The Perfect Instrument of Empire* (Cardiff: University of Wales Press, 1998), p. 58.

9   [Jane Williams, Ysgafell] *Artegall; or Remarks on the Reports of the Commissioners of Inquiry into the State of Education in Wales* (London: Longman and Co., 1848), p. 4. The title of the piece conveyed its fighting spirit from the outset: Artegall, the hero of Edmund Spenser's *The Faerie Queene* (1590–6), is portrayed in the fifth canto of the poem as a valiant fighter for Justice.

10   Ibid., pp. 26–7.

11   Ibid., p. 20.

12   Ibid., p. 29.

13   Ibid., p. 27; the text italicizes.

14   See Deidre Beddoe, 'Williams, Jane', *Oxford Dictionary of National Biography*, ed. H. C. G. Matthew and Brian Harrison (Oxford: Oxford University Press, 2004).

15   Jane Williams, Ysgafell, *A History of Wales: Derived from Authentic Sources* (London: Longmans, Green & Co., 1869). For an assessment of Jane Williams as a historian, see Neil Evans, 'Finding a new story: The search for a usable past in Wales, 1869–1930', *Transactions of the Honourable Society of Cymmrodorion*, 10 (2004), 146–9.

16   [Jane Williams, Ysgafell], *The Literary Remains of the Reverend Thomas Price, Carnhuanawc, with a memory of his life*, 2 vols (Llandovery: William Rees, 1854–5).

17   Jane Williams, *Miscellaneous Poems* (Brecknock: Priscilla Hughes, 1824), p. 37.

18   Jane Williams, Ysgafell (ed.), *The Autobiography of Elizabeth Davis, A Balaclava Nurse*, 2 vols (London: Hurst & Blackett, 1857; new edn, ed. Deirdre Beddoe, Dinas Powys: Honno Press, 1987). For further material on the representation of gender in this text, see my 'Conversions and inversions: body language in nineteenth-century Welsh women's writings', in Karen Atkinson, Sarah Oerton and Gill Plain (eds), *Feminisms on Edge: Politics, Discourses and National Identities* (Cardiff: Cardiff Academic Press, 2000), pp. 170–1.

19   Williams, *Autobiography of Elizabeth Davis*, pp. xxxiii, xxx.

20   See Evan Jones [Ieuan Gwynedd], 'A vindication of the educational and moral condition of Wales . . .' (1848), in Brinley Rees (ed.), *Ieuan Gwynedd: Detholiad o'i Ryddiaith* (Caerdydd: Gwasg Prifysgol Cymru, 1957), pp. 87–91.

21   Gwenllïan Gwent, 'Anerchiad i Gymruesau Cymru', *Y Gymraes*, 1 (1850), 11.

22   See Siân Rhiannon Williams, 'The true "Cymraes": images of women in nineteenth-century periodicals', in Angela V. John (ed.), *Our Mothers' Land: Chapters in Welsh Women's History 1830–1939* (Cardiff: University of Wales Press, 1991), p. 73.

23   Ibid., p. 8.

24   Ibid., p. 9.

25   Ibid., p. 10.

26   [Ieuan Gwynedd], 'Saisaddoliaeth', *Y Gymraes*, 1 (1850), 75 and 76.

27   But cf. Michael D. Jones, 'Ymfudo a threfedigaeth Gymreig', *Y Cronicl* (1850): 'rhaid i'r Saeson gyfnewid yn eu hymddygiadau trahaus at drigolion India, y Cymry, a'r Gwyddelod' ('the English must change their aggressive

behaviour towards the inhabitants of India, the Welsh and the Irish'); quoted in E. Pan Jones, *Oes a Gwaith y Prif Athraw y Parch. Michael Daniel Jones* (Bala: H. Evans, 1903), p. 63.

28   Ieuan Gwynedd, 'Anerchion. – Y Gymdeithas Heddwch', *Y Gymraes*, 2 (1851), 204.

29   [Ieuan Gwynedd], 'Anerchiad', ibid., 1 (1850), 6; the text's italics.

30   See Judges 5: 7: 'The inhabitants of the villages ceased, they ceased in Israel, until that I Deborah arose, that I arose a mother in Israel'; and see H. V. Morton, *Women of the Bible* (London: Methuen, 1940), p. 73: 'Deborah is the first great woman nationalist'.

31   [Ieuan Gwynedd], 'Anerchiad', 6.

32   'Brodor', 'Cyflwr cymdeithasol a moesol merched swydd Aberteifi', ibid., 333.

33   Ieuan Ceredig, 'At ferched ieuainc Cymru', ibid., 143–4.

34   Frantz Fanon, *Black Skin, White Masks*, trans. Charles Lam Markmann ([1952] London: Pluto Press, 1986), pp. 192 and 194.

35   Partha Chatterjee, *Nationalist Thought and the Colonial World: A Derivative Discourse* (London: Zed Books, 1986), p. 30.

36   [Ieuan Gwynedd], 'Anerchiad', 4.

37   'Merched Cymru', *Y Traethodydd*, 1 (1845), 72–3.

38   Ibid., 11 (1855), 120 and 119.

39   Coventry Patmore, 'The Angel in the House', *The Poems of Coventry Patmore*, ed. Frederick Page (London: Oxford University Press, 1949), 71, 202, 89, 83, 90.

40   See Peter N. Stearns, 'Working-class women in Britain, 1890–1914', in Martha Vicinus (ed.), *Suffer and Be Still: Women in the Victorian Age* (London: Methuen, 1980), p. 113.

41   Thomas Jones, *Fy Chwaer; sef, Cofiant am Miss Margaret Jones, Cefn y Gader, Wyddgrug* (Wyddgrug: Hugh Jones, 1844), pp. 70–1.

42   Ibid., p. 91.

43   Ibid., p. 28.

44   Ibid., p. 94.

45   Ibid., pp. 161 and 162–3.

46   Ibid., p. 172.

47   Roger Edwards, 'Rhagymadrodd', ibid., p. vi.

48   Lewis Edwards, 'Rhagdraeth', in J. W. Jones and J. Edmunds (eds), *Yr Athrawes o Ddifrif: sef, Lloffion o Hanes Bywyd a Marwolaeth Mrs. Edmunds, Bangor, yn nghyda Detholiad o'i Hysgrifeniadau* (Caernarfon: G. Parry, 1859), p. xiv.

49   Ibid., p. 55.

50   Ibid., p. 56.

51   Ibid., p. 76.

52   Ibid., p. 62.

53   Ibid., pp. 36–7.

54   Ibid., p. 57.

55   Elen Egryn, 'Anerchiad i Ferched Cymru', *Y Gymraes*, 1 (1850), 55; the poem was also reprinted in the first number of the second *Gymraes*, ed. Ceridwen Peris, 1 (1896), 7.

56   [Ieuan Gwynedd], 'Y llyfrgell', *Y Gymraes*, 1 (1850), 224.

57   'Rhaglith y Golygydd', *Telyn Egryn: neu Gyfansoddiadau Awenyddol Miss*

Ellin Evans (Elen Egryn), o Lanegryn, ed. W. Rees (Dolgellau: Evan Jones, 1850; facs. edn, ed. Kathryn Hughes and Ceridwen Lloyd-Morgan, Dinas Powys: Honno, 1998), p. iii.

58 Ibid., p. 7.

59 See, for further information on Elen Egryn, William Davies, *Hanes Plwyf Llanegryn* (Liverpool: Hugh Evans, 1948), pp. 193–6; Ceridwen Lloyd-Morgan, 'Elin a'i Thelyn: Carreg Filltir yn hanes llenyddiaeth y ferch', *Barn*, 314 (1989), 17–19; Kathryn Hughes and Ceridwen Lloyd-Morgan, 'Rhagymadrodd', in Elen Egryn, *Telyn Egryn* (Dinas Powys: Honno, 1998), pp. x–xxviii.

60 Cf., for example, the poetry of Marged Dafydd (*c* 1700–85?) in Cathryn A. Charnell-White (ed.), *Beirdd Ceridwen: Blodeugerdd Barddas o Ganu Menywod hyd tua 1800* (Abertawe : Cyhoeddiadau Barddas, 2005), 171–201.

61 *Telyn Egryn*, pp. 23–4.

62 [Margaret Charlotte Jones], *Glimpses . . . Mr & Mrs Jones of Pantglas* (London: privately printed for the author, 1862), p. 19.

63 See ibid., p. 40; for further biographical information on Margaret Jones, see also [Marie Eleanor Davies-Evans] (ed.), *My Dear Mrs. Jones: The Letters of the First Duke of Wellington to Mrs Jones of Pantglas* (London: The Rodale Press, 1954).

64 [Margaret Charlotte Jones] Mrs Jones, of Pantglas, 'The Welsh Living', in *Scattered Leaves; or, Twilight Trifles* (London: Routledge, 1853), p. 18.

65 Ibid., pp. 22–3.

66 Ibid., p. 181.

67 Ibid., p. 129.

68 Ibid., pp. 50–1.

69 Ibid., pp. 222 and 221.

70 Lilia Ames, *The Welsh Valley: A Tale* (London: James Nisbet, 1859), p. 50.

71 Amy Lane, *Sketches of Wales and the Welsh* (London and Bristol: Hamilton, Adams & Co. and Hugh C. Evans, 1847), p. 36.

72 See Daniel Sanjiv Roberts, 'Not "Forsworn with pink ribbons": Hannah More, Thomas De Quincey, and the literature of power', *Romanticism on the Net*, 25 (February 2002), 9. Many of Hannah More's tracts were translated into Welsh and proved widely popular; see, for example, the numerous editions of the Welsh translation of her *Village Politics* (1792), *Rheolau llywodraeth yn y llan . . .*, trans. Edward Barnes (Croesoswallt: W. Edwards, 1796). Her maxims were also quoted approvingly, in English, in such works as Jones, *Fy Chwaer* (p. 19).

73 Eleanor Griffiths, *World Worship* (London: James Nisbet & Co., 1853), p. 101.

74 Ibid., p. 369.

75 Ibid., p. 69

76 Ibid., p. 277.

77 Ibid, p. 281.

78 Ibid., p. 264.

79 Ibid., p. 189.

80 See, for example, the fate of the 1904 religious revival's converts in Allen Raine, *Queen of the Rushes* ([1906] new edn, ed. Katie Gramich, Dinas Powys: Honno, 1998).

4. Rebels and Reactionaries

1   Edward D. Said, *Orientalism* ([1978] Harmondsworth: Penguin, 1985), p. 190.

2   Elizabeth Gaskell, 'The Well of Pen-morfa', *Household Words* (1850), repr. in *Four Short Stories* (London: Pandora Press, 1983), p. 78.

3   Elizabeth Gaskell, 'The Doom of the Griffiths', *Harper's Magazine* (1858), repr. in *The Manchester Marriage and Other Stories* (Gloucester: Alan Sutton, 1985), p. 65.

4   Matthew Arnold, *On the Study of Celtic Literature* ([1867] London: Dent, 1910), p. 86.

5   [Ellen Wood] Mrs Henry Wood, *A Life's Secret* ([1867] 9th edn, London: Richard Bentley, 1882), pp. 20–1.

6   Ibid., pp. 47–8.

7   Ibid., pp. 343, 347.

8   Ibid., p. 356.

9   For further biographical details, see Marilyn Wood, *Rhoda Broughton: Profile of a Novelist* (Stamford: Paul Watkins, 1993).

10   Rhoda Broughton, *Not Wisely But Too Well* ([1867] Pocket Classics edn, Stroud: Alan Sutton, 1993), p. 6.

11   Ibid., pp. 14, 94, 76.

12   Rhoda Broughton, *Red as a Rose is She* ([1870] 2nd edn, 2 vols Liepzig: Bernhard Tauchnitz, 1870), I, pp. 13, 14, 42.

13   Ibid., I, p. 7.

14   Alfred Tennyson, 'Hail Briton!', ll. 18–20, *The Poems of Tennyson*, ed. Christopher Ricks (London: Longman, 1987); quoted in Matthew Reynolds, *The Realms of Verse 1830–1870: English Poetry in a Time of Nation-Building* (Oxford: Oxford University Press, 2001), p. 216.

15   Arnold, *On the Study of Celtic Literature*, p. 20.

16   See, in particular, Reynolds, *The Realms of Verse*.

17   Margaret Roberts's birthplace is given in Virginia Blain *et al.* (eds), *The Feminist Companion to Literature in English* (London: Batsford, 1990), p. 910, as 'Honyngs'; the transcribers of the census records give it as 'Stangons' in 1851, as 'Llanyns' in 1871, and as 'Llansing' in 1881. None of these places exist: clearly, the Welsh place-name has baffled these English transcribers. In the handwritten entry of the 1871 Census, when Margaret Roberts was living with her mother in Torquay, her birthplace is fairly clearly given as Llanynys, a village which does exist, close to Rhuthun in Denbighshire.

18   [Margaret Roberts], *Mademoiselle Mori: A Tale of Modern Rome*, 2 vols ([1860] Leipzig: Bernhard Tauchnitz, 1862), II, p. 100.

19   Ibid., I, pp. 203–4, and II, p. 17.

20   Gillian Avery, 'Introduction', in Margaret Roberts, *Stéphanie's Children* ([1896] London: Gollancz, 1969), p. 7.

21   Roberts, *Mademoiselle Mori*, II, p. 34.

22   Diana Wallace, *The Woman's Historical Novel: British Women Writers, 1900–2000* (London: Palgrave, 2005), p. 2.

23   Edmund Mortimer, the uncle of his namesake Edmund Mortimer, the fifth Earl of March, married Glyndŵr's daughter Catrin and defected to his side,

after having been captured and held hostage by him; see R. R. Davies, *The Revolt of Glyn Dŵr* (Oxford: Oxford University Press, 1995), pp. 179–80.

24 See ibid., p. 176.

25 See Brigitte Anton, 'Hardy, Elizabeth', *Oxford Dictionary of National Biography*. I am grateful to Geraint Evans for drawing my attention to Hardy's novel.

26 [Elizabeth Hardy], *Owen Glendower; or, The Prince in Wales*, 2 vols (London: Richard Bentley, 1849), I, p. 173.

27 Ibid., II, p. 300.

28 Alice Somerton, *Ida: or, The Last Struggles of the Welsh for Independence* (London and Cambridge: Whittaker and J. Hall & Son, 1858), p. 410.

29 Ibid., pp. 288–9.

30 Ibid., p. 296.

31 Ibid., p. 104.

32 Ibid., pp. 398–9.

33 Ibid., p. 329.

34 M.[Matilda] Betham-Edwards, *Holidays among the Mountains: or Scenes and Stories of Wales* (London: Griffith & Farran, 1860), p. 43.

35 Ibid., p. 62.

36 See R. Wallis Evans, 'Prophetic poetry', in *A Guide to Welsh Literature 1282–c.1550*, ed. A. O. H. Jarman and Gwyn Rees Hughes, rev. Dafydd Johnston (Cardiff: University of Wales Press, 1997), pp. 256–74; and Glanmor Williams, 'Y Mab Darogan: national hero or confidence trickster?', *Planet*, 52 (1985), 106–10.

37 [Emma Robinson], *Owen Tudor: An Historical Romance* ([1849] London: G. Routledge, 1857), p. 25.

38 Ibid., p. 212.

39 Frances Georgiana Herbert, *A Legend of Pembroke Castle, and Other Tales*, 2 vols (London: Richard Bentley, 1853), II, pp. 73–4.

40 Ibid., I, p. 212.

41 Spooner was much lauded as engineer of the narrow-gauge railway from Blaenau Ffestiniog to Porthmadog: see 'James Spooner, 1789–1856', in *Y Bywgraffiadur Cymreig hyd 1940* (Llundain: Anrhydeddus Gymdeithas y Cymmrodorion, 1953), pp. 864–5.

42 Louisa Spooner's decision to try her hand at writing fiction may have been influenced by acquaintance with Samuel Holland's niece, Elizabeth Gaskell, who frequently visited Holland at his home in Plas Penrhyn, Porthmadog. See Winifred Gérin, *Elizabeth Gaskell: A Biography* (Oxford: Clarendon Press, 1976), pp. 49–50, 90.

43 L.M.S. [Louisa Matilda Spooner], *Gladys of Harlech; or, The Sacrifice. A Romance of Welsh History*, 3 vols (London: Charles J. Skeet, 1858), III, p. 111.

44 Ibid., p. 60.

45 Ibid., p. 66.

46 Ibid., p. 54.

47 Ibid., p. 229.

48 Ibid., p. 309.

49 Ibid., pp. 315–16.

50 See, for further discussion of these issues, Dafydd Glyn Jones, *Agoriad yr Oes: Erthyglau ar Lên, Hanes a Gwleidyddiaeth Cymru* (Talybont: Y Lolfa, 2001).

51   L. M. S. [Louisa Matilda Spooner], *Country Landlords*, 3 vols (London: T. C. Newby, 1860), II, pp. 198–9.
52   'Angharad' is in Welsh a woman's name, not a town's.
53   L. M. S., *Country Landlords*, ii, 289–90.
54   Ibid., p. 295.
55   Ibid., pp. 320–1.
56   For further biographical information, see '"Sadie": in memory of an esteemed contributor', *Good Words* (1868), 379–83; E. H. Plumptre, 'Memoir', in Sarah Williams (Sadie), *Twilight Hours: A Legacy of Verse* (London: Strahan & Co, 1868), pp. vii–xxxiii; and, for further critical discussion, see Catherine Brennan, 'Death and identity in the poetry of Sarah Williams', in *Angers, Fantasies and Ghostly Fears: Nineteenth-Century Women from Wales and English-Language Poetry* (Cardiff: University of Wales Press, 2003), pp. 111–42.
57   Williams, *Twilight Hours* p. 37.
58   Ibid., p. 47.
59   Ibid., p. 58.
60   Ibid., p. 56.
61   Ibid., p. 41.
62   Ibid., pp. 31–2.
63   See Angela Leighton and Margaret Reynolds (eds), *Victorian Women Poets: An Anthology* (London: Blackwell, 1995), p. 342; and Katie Gramich and Catherine Brennan (eds), *Welsh Women's Poetry 1460–2001: An Anthology* (Dinas Powys: Honno Press, 2003), pp. 113–16. For discussions of Pfeiffer's poetry, see Kathleen Hickok, 'Why is this woman still missing? Emily Pfeiffer, Victorian poet', in Isabel Armstrong and Virginia Blain, (eds), *Women's Poetry, Late Romantic to Late Victorian: Gender and Genre 1830–1900* (Basingstoke: Macmillan, 1999), pp. 373–89; and Brennan, 'Emily Jane Pfeiffer and the dilemma of progress', in *Angers, Fantasies and Ghostly Fears*, 143–69.
64   Quoted in 'Works of Emily Pfeiffer', in Emily Pfeiffer, *Under the Aspens: Lyrical and Dramatic* (London: Kegan Paul, Trench & Co., 1882), pp. 6 and 5.
65   Emily Pfeiffer, *Glân-Alarch: His Silence and Song* (London: Henry S. King & Co., 1877), p. 37.
66   Ibid., pp. 255–6.
67   Ibid., pp. 47–8.
68   Pfeiffer, 'The Wynnes of Wynhavod: A Drama of Modern Life', *Under the Aspens*, pp. 133–311.
69   William Davies [Gwilym Teilo], *Llandeilo-Vawr and its Neighbourhood* (Llandeilo: D. W. & G. Jones, 1858), p. 46. For further biographical and critical material on Anne Beale, see also Moira Dearnley, '"I came hither, a stranger": a view of Wales in the novels of Anne Beale', *New Welsh Review*, 1/4 (1989), 27–32.
70   Anne Beale, *The Vale of the Towey; or, Sketches in South Wales* (1844); 2nd edn, *Traits and Stories of the Welsh Peasantry* (London: George Routledge & Co, 1849), pp. 20–1.
71   Ibid., p. 25.
72   Ibid, pp. 43 and 143.

73   Ibid., p. 150.
74   Ibid., p. 262.
75   Anne Beale, *Seven Years for Rachel, or, Welsh Pictures Sketched from Life* (London: Religious Tract Society, n.d. [1886]), p. 17.
76   Ibid., p. 136.
77   See Marie Trevelyan, 'Welsh smugglers and wreckers', *Glimpses of Welsh Life and Character* (London: John Hogg, n.d. [1893]), pp. 312–17.
78   Williams, 'The Coast Guard's Story', *Twilight Hours*, p. 102.
79   [Frances Parthenope] Lady Verney, *The Llanaly Reefs* (London: Smith, Elder & Co., 1873), p. 321.
80   Anne Beale, *The Pennant Family* (3 vols; London: Hurst & Blackett, 1876; 1 vol. edn, London: Hodder & Stoughton, n.d.), p. 149.
81   Ibid., p. 19.
82   For an account of the Rebecca riots, see David Williams, *The Rebecca Riots: A Study in Agrarian Discontent* (Cardiff: University of Wales Press, 1955), or David J. V. Jones, *Rebecca's Children: A Study of Rural Society, Crime and Protest* (Oxford: Clarendon Press, 1989).
83   Anne Beale, *Rose Mervyn, of Whitelake*, reprinted as *Rose Mervyn: A Tale of the Rebecca Riots* ([1879] London and Sydney: Griffith, Farran, Okeden & Welsh, n.d. [1889]), pp. 14–15.
84   Ibid., p. 374.
85   Elizabeth Amy Dillwyn, *The Rebecca Rioter: A Story of Killay Life* ([1880] rpr., Dinas Powys: Honno, 2001), p. 65.
86   Ibid., p. 174.
87   For further information on Amy Dillwyn's unusual career, see David Painting, *Amy Dillwyn* (Cardiff: University of Wales Press, 1987), and Katie Gramich, 'Introduction', Amy Dillwyn, *The Rebecca Rioter* (Dinas Powys: Honno, 2001), pp. v–xxii.
88   Quoted in Painting, *Amy Dillwyn*, pp. 71–2.
89   [E. A. Dillwyn], *Chloe Arguelle*, 2 vols (London: Tinsley Bros., 1881), II, p. 224.
90   E. A. Dillwyn, *A Burglary: or, Unconscious Influence*, 3 vols (London: Tinsley Bros., 1883), I, p. 8.
91   Ibid., pp. 62–3.
92   Painting, *Amy Dillwyn*, p. 102.

5. Developing Women's Welsh-language Print Culture

1   [O. M. Edwards] 'At ohebwyr', *Cymru*, 12 (1896), 196.
2   Ellen Hughes, 'Yng nghymdeithas Cranogwen', *Y Gymraes*, 27 (1923), 134.
3   See Jane Aaron, *Pur fel y Dur: Y Gymraes yn Llên Menywod y Bedwaredd Ganrif ar Bymtheg* (Caerdydd: Gwasg Prifysgol Cymru, 1998), pp. 159–60 and 201–5, for further material on the authorial careers of Anne Rees and Mary Oliver Jones.
4   [Cranogwen], 'Y traethodau', *Y Frythones*, 1 (1879), 67.
5   Cranogwen, 'Miss Ellen Hughes, Llanengan', *Y Gymraes*, 4 (1900), 7.
6   J. Evans-Owen, 'Mrs John Peter 1833–1889', ibid., 1 (1896), 21; see also Anna Ionawr, 'Eliza Peter', *Y Frythones*, 11 (1889), 197–203.

7   [Eliza Peter], 'Diwylliad y rhyw fenywaidd', *Y Beirniad*, 5 (1863), 159.
8   Ibid., 162.
9   Eliza Peter, 'Iechyd a phrydferthwch', *Y Frythones*, 1 (1879), 24 and 26.
10 'Cwestiynau ac Atebion', ibid., 7 (1885), 98.
11 Catrin Stevens, *Arferion Caru* (Gwasg Gomer: Llandysul, 1977), p. 67.
12 'Cwestiynau ac Atebion', *Y Frythones*, 2 (1880), 130.
13 Ibid., 2 (1880), 226.
14 Ibid., 3 (1881), 323.
15 Ibid., 290.
16 D. G. Jones, *Cofiant Cranogwen* (Caernarfon: Argraffdy'r Methodistiaid Calfinaidd, n.d. [1932]), p. 164.
17 Cranogwen, *Caniadau Cranogwen* (Dolgellau: R. O. Rees, n.d. [1870]), pp. 74–6; this poem is reprinted, with a translation by Katie Gramich, in Katie Gramich and Catherine Brennan (eds), *Welsh Women's Poetry 1460–2001: An Anthology* (Dinas Powys: Honno Press, 2003), pp. 128–33.
18 [Cranogwen], 'Dalen o'n dyddlyfr yn y flwyddyn 1870', *Y Frythones*, 5 (1883), 190.
19 See D. G. Jones, *Cofiant Cranogwen*, p. 102; and Gerallt Jones, *Cranogwen: Portread Newydd* (Llandysul: Gwasg Gomer, 1981), pp. 35, 46 and 49.
20 Henry Havelock Ellis, *Studies in the Psychology of Sex: Vol. I. Sexual Inversion* (London: Wilson & Macmillan, 1897). See also Richard von Krafft-Ebing, *Psychopathia Sexualis* [1882], trans. C. G. Chaddock (Philadelphia and London: F. A. Davies & Co., 1892).
21 See Lillian Faderman, *Surpassing the Love of Men: Romantic Friendship and Love between Women from the Renaissance to the Present* (London: Junction Books, n.d. [1981]), pp. 147–230, for further information on the popularity of 'romantic friendships' between women during the nineteenth century.
22 For a contemporary appreciation of the series, see, for example, Ellen Hughes, 'Yng nghymdeithas Cranogwen', *Y Gymraes*, 27 (1923), 35.
23 [Cranogwen], 'Esther Judith', *Y Frythones*, 2 (1880), 330, 332. The series 'Esther Judith' was published anonymously, but it is evident from its content and style that Cranogwen was its author.
24 Ibid., 3 (1881), 81.
25 Ibid., 145.
26 Ibid., 145–6.
27 Nantlais, 'Cranogwen'; quoted in Jones, *Cofiant Cranogwen*, p. 162.
28 Ceridwen Lloyd Morgan, 'From temperance to suffrage?' in Angela V. John (ed.), *Our Mothers' Land: Chapters in Welsh Women's History 1830 1939* (Cardiff: University of Wales Press, 1991), pp. 138 and 144.
29 Anna Ionawr, 'Gyfran y merched yn ffurfiad cymeriad genedl y Cymry', *Y Frythones*, 11 (1889), 346.
30 Buddug [Catherine Jane Prichard], 'Na chaffed Hudoles fyw', *Y Gymraes*, 4 (1900), 78.
31 Mair Eifion [Mary Davies], *Blodeu Eifion: sef Gwaith Barddonol Mair Eifion, Porthmadog* (Pwllheli: Richard Jones, n.d. [1882]), pp. 35–6.
32 Ibid., p. 17.
33 For a description of this Mission, see Ruth [Annie Catherine Prichard], 'Myfanwy Meirion a "Chenhadaeth Pont Gobaith", Llundain', *Y Gymraes*, 3 (1899), 97–101.

34 Margaret Jones (Myfanwy Meirion), '"Bridge of Hope Mission" Dwyreinbarth Llundain', *Y Frythones*, 7 (1885), 110.

35 Myfanwy Meirion, '"A Ddarlleno Ystyried"', *Y Gymraes*, 6 (1902), 76; and *Caniadau Myfanwy Meirion* (Liverpool: printed for the author, 1930), p. 41.

36 [Annie Catherine Prichard], *Adroddiad a Gweithrediadau Deunawfed Cynghor Blynyddol Undeb Dirwestol Merched Gogledd Cymru* (Denbigh: Gee & Son, 1910), p. 42.

37 See, for example, 'Treio effaith y gown gorau', *Y Gymraes*, 1 (1897), 73–6, and 'Lle gwell Betsi Evans', ibid., 7 (1903), 88–90.

38 Ruth [Annie Catherine Prichard], 'Y can' cymaint', ibid., 3 (1899), 72–3.

39 Ibid., 74.

40 For further information on the life and work of Buddug, see R. Môn Williams, 'Buddug', *Cymru*, 39 (1909), 221–4; Mair Ogwen [Mary Griffith], *Chwiorydd Enwog y Cyfundeb* (Caernarfon: Llyfrfa'r Methodistiaid Calfinaidd, n.d. [1925]), pp. 79–82; and Iorwen Myfanwy Jones, 'Merched llên Cymru o 1850 i 1914' (unpub. MA thesis, University of Wales, Bangor 1935), pp. 114–17.

41 [O. M. Edwards], 'Llyfrau a llenorion', *Cymru*, 30 (1906), 195.

42 Buddug [Catherine Jane Prichard], 'Yr Eneth a'r Gasgen', *Y Gymraes*, 8 (1904), 10.

43 *Caniadau Buddug. Wedi eu casglu a'u dethol gan ei phriod* (Caernarfon: Swyddfa 'Cymru', 1911), pp. 31–2; for a reproduction of this poem with a translation by Katie Gramich, see also Gramich and Brennan, *Welsh Women's Poetry*, pp. 144–7.

44 Ceridwen Peris [Alice Gray Jones], 'Allegori – Blodau Pleser', *Y Frythones*, 1 (1879), 208–9; for a more detailed analysis of this tale, see Jane Aaron, 'Darllen yn groes i'r drefn', in John Rowlands (ed.), *Sglefrio ar Eiriau* (Llandysul: Gwasg Gomer, 1992), pp. 76–8.

45 Ceridwen Peris, 'Y Fun a'r Faner Wen', *Y Traethodydd*, 48 (1893), 428.

46 For further information on the contents of this periodical see Ceridwen Lloyd Morgan, 'Anturiaethau'r Gymraes', *Y Casglwr*, 16 (1982), 11; and Siân Rhiannon Williams, 'Y Frythones: portread cyfnodolion merched y bedwaredd ganrif ar bymtheg o Gymraes yr oes', *Llafur*, 4 (1984), 43–54.

47 [Alice Gray Jones], *Caniadau Ceridwen Peris* (Caernarfon: Llyfrfa'r Methodistiaid Calfinaidd, n.d. [1934]), p. 65.

48 Ceridwen Peris, 'Un o'n gweithwyr', *Y Gymraes*, 11 (1907), 81.

49 Ann Evans, *Llythyr Ann Evans . . .* (Bala: R. Saunderson, 1818). For a more detailed account of Ann Evans's letter see my article 'Slaughter and salvation: Welsh missionary activity and British imperialism', in Charlotte Williams, Neil Evans and Paul O'Leary (eds), *A Tolerant Nation? Exploring Ethnic Diversity in Wales* (Cardiff: University of Wales Press, 2003), pp. 35–48.

50 G. Penar Griffith, *Hanes Bywgraffiadol o Genadon Cymreig i Wledydd Paganaidd* (Cardiff: published by the author, 1897), pp. 133–40.

51 Cathryn A. Charnell-White, *Beirdd Ceridwen: Blodeugerdd Barddas o Ganu Menywod hyd tua 1800* (Swansea: Cyhoeddiadau Barddas, 2005), pp. 344 and 346.

52 Ibid., pp. 354–5.

53 In 1890, for example, in the year of the Calvinist Methodist Missionary

Society's Jubilee, Welsh Methodist chapels collected the sum of £37,326 15s. 5d. for the cause. See John Hughes Morris, *Hanes Cenhadaeth Dramor y Methodistiaid Calfinaidd Cymreig, hyd diwedd y flwyddyn 1904* (Caernarfon: Llyfrfa'r Cyfundeb, 1907), p. 259.

54 For further discussion of Welsh missionary activity, see Aled Jones, 'Meddylier am India': tair taith y genhadeth Gymreig yn Sylhet, 1887–1947', *Transactions of the Honourable Society of Cymmrodorion* (1997), pp. 84–110; and his 'The other internationalist? Missionary activity and Welsh Nonconformist perceptions of the world in the nineteenth and twentieth centuries', in Williams, Evans and O'Leary (eds), *A Tolerant Nation?*, pp. 49–60.

55 Sara Maria Saunders, *Llon a Lleddf* (Holywell: P. M. Evans a'i Fab, 1897), pp. 77, 56, 71.

56 Cranogwen, 'Mrs Evans, Llanwrtyd', *Y Gymraes*, 5 (1901), 149.

57 See E. E. Bhoi, Llanwrtyd, 'Babu Dulal', ibid., 1 (1897), 163.

58 Emma Roberts, *Notes of an Overland Journey through France and Egypt to Bombay . . . with a memoir* (London: W. H. Allen, 1841), p. 10.

59 Ibid., pp. 134–5.

60 Earl Grey, quoted in Peter Marshall (ed.), *The Cambridge Illustrated History of the British Empire* (Cambridge: Cambridge University Press, 1996), p. 30.

61 Margaret Jones, *Morocco, a'r Hyn a Welais Yno* (Wrexham: Hughes & Son, 1883), p. 133.

62 [Cranogwen], 'Y flwyddyn 1884', *Y Frythones*, 7 (1885), 6.

63 Ellen Hughes, 'Y Nadolig', *Y Gymraes*, 3 (1899), 178.

64 For details of Ellen Hughes's career, see Morris, *Hanes Cenhadaeth Dramor y Methodistiaid Calfinaidd Cymreig*, p. 274.

65 Ellen Hughes, *Hanes Hom Ray, a'r Canlyniadau* (Dolgellau: E. W. Evans, n.d.), p. 1.

66 Ibid., p. 4.

67 See [Cranogwen], 'Dyfodol merched Cymru', *Y Frythones*, 9 (1887), 202.

68 See [Anon.], 'Mrs John Roberts, Khasia', *Y Gymraes*, 1 (1897), 225–7.

69 [Anon.], 'Mrs J. M. Saunders, Penarth', ibid., 98.

70 Mrs Owen, Sherlock St., Liverpool, 'Miss Annie Williams, Shillong', ibid., 194.

71 Elizabeth Williams, 'Sylhet: gwaith ymysg y merched', *Y Drysorfa*, 60 (1890), 319.

72 Elizabeth Ann Roberts, 'Sylhet', ibid., 72 (1902), 570–1.

73 Morris, *Hanes Cenhadaeth Dramor y Methodistiaid Calfinaidd Cymreig*, p. 312.

74 Roberts, 'Sylhet', 571.

6. Writing Young Wales

1 See William George, *Cymru Fydd: Hanes y Mudiad Cenedlaethol Cyntaf* (Lerpwl: Gwasg y Brython, 1945), p. 19.

2 See Dewi Rowland Hughes, *Cymru Fydd* (Caerdydd: Gwasg Prifysgol Cymru, 2006), pp. 1–67, for the fullest account to date of the founding and history of the movement.

3 George, *Cymru Fydd*, pp. 15, 23–32.

4   See Kenneth O. Morgan, *Rebirth of a Nation: Wales 1880–1980* (Oxford and Cardiff: Clarendon Press and University of Wales Press, 1981), p. 50.

5   George, *Cymru Fydd*, p. 42; Morgan, *Rebirth of a Nation*, p. 118.

6   Nora Philipps and Elsbeth Philipps, 'Progress of women in Wales', *Young Wales*, 2 (1896), 67. For further material on the relation between the Women's Liberal Association and Cymru Fydd, see Ursula Masson, '"Hand in hand with women, forward we will go": Welsh nationalism and feminism in the 1890s', *Women's History Review*, 12 (2003), 357–86.

7   W. Llewelyn Williams, 'O Fôn i Fynwy', *Young Wales*, 1 (1895), 22.

8   But see Ursula Masson (ed.), *Women's Rights and Womanly Duties: The Aberdare Women's Liberal Association 1891–1910* (Cardiff: South Wales Record Society, 2005), p. 10, for the suggestion that 'the journal over time developed a more conservative vision of the role of women in relation to national aspirations'.

9   Philipps and Philipps, 'Progress of women in Wales', *Young Wales*, 2 (1896), 66.

10 Gwyneth Vaughan, 'Women and their questions', ibid., 3 (1897), 19–20.

11 T. Athol Joyce and N. W. Thomas (eds), *Women of All Nations: A Record of their Characteristics, Habits, Manners, Customs, and Influence* (London: Cassell, 1909), p. 756.

12 W. Gareth Evans, 'Addysgu mwy na hanner y genedl': yr ymgyrch i hyrwyddo addysg y ferch yng Nghymru', in Geraint H. Jenkins (ed.), *Cof Cenedl IV: Ysgrifau ar Hanes Cymru* (Llandysul: Gwasg Gomer, 1989), pp. 99 and 105.

13 For further information on Frances Hoggan, see W. Gareth Evans, *Education and Female Emancipation: The Welsh Experience 1847–1914* (Cardiff: University of Wales Press, 1990), pp. 100–4, 112–16, 125–9.

14 Frances Hoggan, *Education for Girls in Wales* (London: Women's Printing Society, n.d. [1882]), p. 31.

15 See Evans, *Education and Female Emancipation*, p. 150.

16 For further information on Elizabeth Hughes's career, see W. Gareth Evans, 'Un o ferched Britannia: gyrfa yr addysgwraig Elizabeth P. Hughes', in Geraint T. Jenkins (ed.), *Cof Cenedl XVI: Ysgrifau ar Hanes Cymru* (Llandysul: Gwasg Gomer, 2001), pp. 95–122.

17 Lord Aberdare, 'Adjudications: The higher education of girls in Wales, with practical suggestions as to the best means of promoting it', *Transactions of the Liverpool National Eisteddfod 1884* (Liverpool: Isaac Foulkes, 1885), p. 38.

18 Elizabeth Phillips Hughes, 'The higher education of girls in Wales', *Transactions of the Liverpool National Eisteddfod 1884* (Liverpool: Isaac Foulkes, 1885), p. 57.

19 Elizabeth Phillips Hughes, 'A national education for Wales', *Young Wales*, 1, (1895), 105.

20 Elizabeth Phillips Hughes, 'The Welsh University: its message to the women of Wales', ibid., 2 (1896), 149.

21 See Evans, *Education and Female Emancipation*, pp. 111–76; and see also, for further material on advances in Welsh women's education during this period, Deirdre Beddoe, *Out of the Shadows: A History of Women in Twentieth-Century Wales* (Cardiff: University of Wales Press, 2000), pp. 27–8. Isambard Owen was Dean of St George's Medical Hospital in London and a

pillar of the Cymmrodorion Society, which also adopted the cause of improving Welsh women's education.

22 See L. J. Williams and Dot Jones, 'Women at work in nineteenth-century Wales', *Llafur*, 3/3 (1982), 30.

23 See Ceridwen Lloyd-Morgan, 'From temperance to suffrage?', in Angela V. John (ed.), *Our Mothers' Land: Chapters in Welsh Women's History 1830–1939* (Cardiff: University of Wales Press, 1991), pp. 152–3.

24 Cranogwen, 'Dyrchafiad merched', *Y Frythones*, 8 (1886), 236.

25 'Dadl. – Y merched a'r bleidlais', *Y Gymraes*, 4 (1900), 183–6.

26 Ellen Hughes, 'Merched a chynrychiolaeth', ibid., 14 (1910), 148.

27 For further information on the life and work of Ellen Hughes, see Cranogwen, 'Miss Ellen Hughes, Llanengan', ibid., 4 (1900), 5–8; Iorwen Myfanwy Jones, 'Merched llên Cymru o 1850 i 1914' (unpub. M.Phil. thesis, University of Wales, Bangor, 1935), pp. 212–23; and Ceridwen Lloyd-Morgan, 'From temperance to suffrage?', p. 154.

28 Ellen Hughes, 'Y Ddynes Newydd', *Y Gymraes*, 1 (1896), 28–9.

29 Ellen Hughes, Llanengan, *Murmur y Gragen: sef Detholion o Gyfansoddiadau Barddonol a Rhyddiaethol* (Dolgellau: Swyddfa'r 'Goleuad', 1907), pp. 37–40 and 87–114.

30 Ellen Hughes, 'Angylion yr aelwyd' (1899), ibid., pp. 39–40.

31 Reviews of *Fraternity*, in *The Scotsman*, 18 June 1888; and *The Literary World*, 20 July 1888.

32 [Mabel Holland Grave], *From Heart to Heart: A Book of Verses* by the Author of *Fraternity* (London: Kegan Paul, 1892), p. 8.

33 [Mabel Holland Grave], *Fraternity: A Romance*, 2 vols (London: Macmillan, 1888), II, pp. 56 and 51.

34 See Geraint H. Jenkins (ed.), *A Rattleskull Genius: The Many Faces of Iolo Morganwg* (Cardiff: University of Wales Press, 2005), pp. 90–2 and elsewhere, for details of Iolo Morganwg's invention of the 'Gorsedd'.

35 [Grave], *Fraternity*, II, pp. 44, 45, 46.

36 Ibid., I, p. 15.

37 Ibid., II, p. 66.

38 Ibid., I, p. 217.

39 Ibid., II, p. 263.

40 See Kenneth O. Morgan, *Rebirth of a Nation: Wales 1880–1980* (Oxford and Cardiff: Clarendon Press and University of Wales Press, 1981), p. 12.

41 Lady Watkin Williams, *Even Such Is Life: A Story of To-day*, 3 vols (London: Chapman & Hall, 1888), I, pp. 209–10.

42 Ibid., I, pp. 135–6.

43 Ibid., III, p. 95.

44 Ibid., I, p. 213.

45 Gwyneth Vaughan, *The Christian Commonwealth*, 8 February 1900.

46 Gwyneth Vaughan, 'Women and their questions', *Young Wales*, 3 (1897), 20.

47 Gwyneth Vaughan, *Plant y Gorthrwm* (Cardiff: Educational Publishing, 1908), pp. 86–7.

48 Ibid., p. 26.

49 Gwyneth Vaughan, *O Gorlannau y Defaid* (Caerfyrddin: W. Spurrell & Son, 1905), p. 164.

50 Gwyneth Vaughan, 'Troad y Rhod', *Y Brython*, 1 April 1909.

51 Ibid., 25 March 1909.
52 Ibid., 15 April 1909.
53 Thomas Parry, 'Gwyneth Vaughan', *Cylchgrawn Cymdeithas Hanes a Chofnodion Sir Feirionnydd*, 3 (1979), 233–4, 235.
54 For further information on Mallt Williams, see Marion Löffler, 'A romantic nationalist', *Planet*, 121 (1997), 58–66.
55 Y Ddau Wynne, *One of the Royal Celts* (London: Spencer Blackett & Hallam, 1889), p. 395.
56 Ibid., p. 188.
57 Löffler, 'A romantic nationalist', 60.
58 Y Ddau Wynne, *A Maid of Cymru: A Patriotic Romance* (London and Carmarthen: Simpkin, Marshal & Co., and Spurrell & Son, n.d. [1901]), p. 185.
59 Eluned Morgan to William George, 1 September 1905, in W. R. P. George (ed.), *'Gyfaill Hoff . . .': Detholiad o Lythyrau Eluned Morgan* (Llandysul: Gwasg Gomer, 1972), p. 110.
60 Eluned Morgan to D. R. Daniel, 30 June 1893, ibid., p. 35.
61 See Marged Lloyd Jones, *Nel Fach y Bwcs* (Llandysul: Gwasg Gomer, 1992), p. 11, for an account of how Eluned Morgan gained her name.
62 Robert Owen Jones, 'The Welsh language in Patagonia', Geraint H. Jenkins (ed.), *Language and Community in the Nineteenth Century* (Cardiff: University of Wales Press, 1998), p. 298.
63 Eluned Morgan, *Dringo'r Andes* (Y Fenni: Y Brodyr Owen, 1904), p. 40; see also, new edn, *Dringo'r Andes & Gwymon y Môr*, ed. Ceridwen Lloyd-Morgan and Kathryn Hughes (Dinas Powys: Gwasg Honno, 2001).
64 Ibid., p. 49.
65 Michael D. Jones, *Y Cenhadwr Americanaidd*, January 1849, 12; quoted in R. Bryn Williams, *Y Wladfa* (Cardiff: University of Wales Press, 1962), p. 20.
66 Eluned Morgan to William George, 17 November 1901, in George (ed.), *'Gyfaill Hoff . . .'*, p. 74.
67 Quoted in R. Bryn Williams, *Eluned Morgan: Bywgraffiad a Detholiad* (Llandysul: Y Clwb Llyfrau Cymreig, 1948), p. 11.
68 Ellen Hughes, 'Ymadawiad y Frenhines', *Y Gymraes*, 5 (1901), 56.
69 [Catherine Jane Prichard], 'Can y Jiwbili, 1887', *Caniadau Buddug: wedi eu casglu a'u dethol gan ei phriod* (Caernarfon: Swyddfa'r 'Cymru', 1911), p. 29.
70 C. E. Phillimore, 'Jubilee Ode', trans. R. A. Williams, 'Buddugoliaeth Buddug' (Oswestry: *Oswestry and Borders County Advertizer*, 1897), pp. 6–7.
71 Ruth, 'Victoria ein Brenhines', *Y Gymraes*, 1 (1897), 131.
72 Mair Hydref, *Autumn Leaves*, 4th edn (Wrecsam: Hughes a'i Fab, 1889), pp. 64–5.
73 Anna Walter Thomas, 'Monody on the Death of Albert Victor Christian Edward, Duke of Clarence and Avondale', *Cofnodion a Chyfansoddiadau Eisteddfod Genedlaethol 1892 (Rhyl)* (Oswestry: printed for the Eisteddfod, 1895), p. 149.
74 For further information on Anna Walter Thomas see W. Glynn Williams, *Memoir of Mrs Anna Walter Thomas (Morfudd Eryri)* (Holywell: W. Williams, n.d. [1922]); and Brennan, *Angers, Fantasies and Ghostly Fears*, pp. 170–99.

75 Marie Trevelyan, *Britain's Greatness Foretold: The Story of Boadicea, the British Warrior Queen* (London: John Hogg, 1900), pp. ix and xii.

76 R. Palmer Parry, 'Winnie Parry a'i gwaith', *Taliesin*, 46 (1983), 26.

77 See Winnie Parry, *Sioned* (Caernarfon: Cwmni y Cyhoeddwyr Cymreig, Swyddfa *Cymru*, n.d. [1906]); for further biographical and critical material on Winnie Parry see also Margaret Lloyd Jones's introduction to a new edition of *Sioned* (Dinas Powys: Honno, 1988), pp. xi–xvi.

78 For further biographical information, see Sally Roberts Jones, *Allen Raine*, Writers of Wales series (Cardiff: University of Wales Press, 1979).

79 Allen Raine, *By Berwen Banks* (London: Hutchinson & Co., 1899), p. 28.

80 For a further account of *Queen of the Rushes*, see Katie Gramich, 'Introduction', in Allen Raine, *Queen of the Rushes* (Dinas Powys: Honno Press, 1998), pp. 1–23.

81 Violet Jacob, *The Sheep-Stealers* (London: Heinemann, 1902), p. 7.

82 Ibid., p. 15

83 For further information on the career of Sara Maria Saunders, see Ruth, 'S.M.S.' *Y Gymraes*, 9 (1905), 33–4, and Jones, 'Merched Llên Cymru o 1850 i 1914', pp. 227–33.

84 S. M. Saunders, *Y Diwygiad ym Mhentre Alun, gydag ysgrifau ereill* (Wrecsam: Hughes a'i Fab, 1907), p. 15.

85 Ibid., p. 307.

86 Ibid., p. 2.

87 Ibid., p. 307.

88 See Sara Maria Saunders, 'Nancy on the Warpath', in Jane Aaron (ed.), *A View across the Valley: Short Stories by Women from Wales c.1850–1950* (Dinas Powys: Honno, 1999), pp. 27–36.

89 S. M. S. [Sara Maria Saunders], 'Welsh Rural Sketches V. A Wolf in Sheep's Clothing', *Young Wales*, 3 (1897), 247.

Epilogue

1 Sarah Richards, 'The Eve of the Twentieth Century', *Memories of Home* (Bridgend: Wesley Williams, 1903), p. 114.

2 Ibid., p. 115.

3 See Siwan M. Rosser, *Y Ferch ym Myd y Faled: Delweddau o'r Ferch ym Maledi'r Ddeunawfed Ganrif* (Cardiff: University of Wales Press, 2005), p. 4.

4 See, for example, Elizabeth Davies, Neath, *Lines on the Departure of an Ancient, Worthy, and Benevolent Welsh family from Dyffryn House, near Neath, It is to be hoped for a short period* (Neath: M. Whittington, n.d. [1850]).

5 Elizabeth Davies, Neath, *Lines on the Passing of the South Wales Railway Bill in the House of Lords. Dedicated to I. K. Brunel, Esq.* (Neath: Mary Whittington, n.d.).

6 Elizabeth Davies, Neath, *Verses to the Ivorites for their Great Love of the Welsh Language* (Neath: Mary Whittington, n.d. [1850]).

7 Dorothy Jones (Dora Eifion), *Gemau yr Awen; sef, Cyfansoddiadau Barddonol* (Bethesda: printed for the author, n.d. [c.1870]), p. 30. I am grateful to Huw Walters for drawing my attention to Dora Eifion's volume.

8   Ibid., p. 51.
9   Henry Richard, *Letters on the Social and Political Condition of Wales* (London: Jackson, Walford and Hodder, 1867), p. 80; quoted in Dewi Rowland Hughes, *Cymru Fydd*, (Caerdydd: Gwasg Prifysgol Cymru, 2006), p. 6.
10   See the tables given in Hughes, *Cymru Fydd*, pp. 69–71, 87–8.

Selected Bibliography

Primary sources

Aikin, Lucy, 'Cambria: an Ode', *Epistles on Women, exemplifying their Character and Condition in Various Ages and Nations. With Miscellaneous Poems* (London: J. Johnson, 1810).

Ames, Lilia, *The Welsh Valley: A Tale* (London: James Nisbet, 1859).

Austen, Jane, 'A Tour through Wales – in a Letter from a young Lady' [1790–2], *Catharine and Other Writings*, ed. Margaret Anne Doody and Douglas Murray (Oxford: Oxford University Press, 1993).

[Bannerman, Anne], Tales of Superstition and Chivalry (London: Vernor & Hood, 1802).

Barker, Mary, *A Welsh Story*, 3 vols (London: Hookham & Carpenter, 1798).

Beale, Anne, *The Vale of the Towey; or, Sketches in South Wales* (London: Longman, Brown, Green & Longman, 1844; new edn, *Traits and Stories of the Welsh Peasantry*, London: George Routledge & Co., 1849; abridged edn, *Seven Years for Rachel, or, Welsh Pictures Sketched from Life*, London: Religious Trust Society, n.d. [1886]).

——, *The Pennant Family*, 3 vols (London: Hurst & Blackett, 1876).

——, *Rose Mervyn, of Whitelake*, 3 vols (London: Hurst & Blackett, 1879; new edn, 1 vol., *Rose Mervyn: A Tale of the Rebecca Riots*, London: Griffith, Farran, Okeden & Welsh, n.d. [1889]).

Bennett, Anna Maria, *Anna: or Memoirs of a Welch Heiress: interspersed with anecdotes of a Nabob*, 4 vols (London: William Lane, 1785; 2nd edn, London: William Lane, 1786).

——, *Ellen, Countess of Castle Howel*, 4 vols (London: 1794; 2nd edn, 2 vols, Dublin: Jones, Colbert, Fitzpatrick & Milliken, 1794).

——, *The Beggar Girl and her Benefactors*, 7 vols (London: William Lane, 1797).

Betham-Edwards, Matilda Barbara, *Holidays among the Mountains: or Scenes and Stories of Wales* (London: Griffith & Farran, 1860).

Bevan, Mary, *Ymadawiad y Cenadau. Can, a gyfansoddwyd gan Mr. Bevan, y Cenadwr, ar ei fynediad o Brydain i Madagascar; Hefyd rhai penillion gan Mrs. Bevan, ar yr un achlysur* (Carmathen: J. Evans,

1818; repr. in Cathryn A. Charnell-White (ed.), *Beirdd Ceridwen: Blodeugerdd Barddas o Ganu Menywod hyd tua 1800*, Swansea: Cyhoeddiadau Barddas, 2005, pp. 354–6).

Bowen, Melesina, *Ystradffin: A Descriptive Poem, with an Appendix containing Historical and Explanatory Notes* (London and Llandovery: Longman, Orme, Brown, Green & Longmans and W. Rees, 1839).

Broughton, Rhoda, *Not Wisely But Too Well*, 3 vols (London: Tinsley Brothers, 1867; new edn, Stroud: Alan Sutton, 1993).

——, *Red as a Rose is She*, 3 vols (London: Richard Bentley & Son, 1870; 2nd edn, 2 vols, Leipzig: Bernhard Tauchnitz, 1870).

[Campbell, Eliza Constantia] 'A Lady of the Principality', *The History of Wales: containing some interesting facts concerning the existence of a Welsh tribe among the aborigines of America. Arranged as a Catechism for young persons* (Shrewsbury: John Eddowes, 1833).

——, *Stories from the History of Wales: Interspersed with Various Information and Amusement for Young Persons* (Shrewsbury: John Eddowes, 1833).

——, *Tales about Wales, with a Catechism of Welsh History*, ed. Captain Basil Hall (Edinburgh: Robert Cadell; London: Whittaker & Co., 1837) (2nd edn of two preceding works combined).

Cave, Jane, *Poems on Various Subjects, Entertaining, Elegiac, and Religious* (Winchester: printed for the author, 1783; 2nd edn, Bristol: printed for the author, 1786; 3rd edn, Shrewsbury: printed for the author, 1789; 4th edn, Bristol: N. Biggs, 1794).

——, 'On the Death of Mr. Howell Harris', in *A Brief Account of the Life of Howell Harris, Extracted from Papers written by himself* (Trefeca: printed for the Methodists, 1791).

Clark, Emily Frederick, *Ianthé, or the Flower of Caernarvon*, 2 vols (London: printed for the author, 1798).

Crebar, Elizabeth, *Poems, Religious and Moral* (Aberystwyth: printed for the author, 1811).

Darwall [Mary], *Poems on Several Occasions*, 2 vols (Walsall: F. Milward, 1794).

Davies, Catherine, *Eleven Years' Residence in the Family of Murat, King of Naples* (London: How & Parsons, 1841).

Davies, Elizabeth, *Dwy Gan: Cymhorth i hunan-adnabyddiaeth; Golwg ar sefyllfa Cristianogrwydd, o amser Crist hyd yn bresennol* (Aberystwyth: Samuel Williams, 1813).

Davies, Elizabeth, *Verses to the Ivorites for their Great Love of the Welsh Language* (Neath: Mary Whittington [1850]).

——, *Lines on the departure of an ancient, worthy and benevolent Welsh family from Dyffryn House, near Neath, It is to be hoped for a short period* (Neath: Mary Whittington n.d. [1850]).

——, *Lines on the Passing of the South Wales Railway Bill in the House of Lords. Dedicated to I. K. Brunel, Esq.* (Neath: Mary Whittington, n.d.).

[Davies, Mary] Mair Eifion, *Blodau Eifion: sef Gwaith Barddonol Mair Eifion, Porthmadog*, ed. Gwilym Eryri (Pwllheli: Richard Jones, n.d. [1882]).

Dillwyn, Elizabeth Amy, *The Rebecca Rioter: A Story of Killay Life*, 2 vols (London: Macmillan, 1880).

——, *Chloe Arguelle*, 2 vols (London: Tinsley Bros, 1881).

——, *A Burglary: or, Unconscious Influence*, 3 vols (London: Tinsley Bros., 1883).

Edward, Jane (later Jane Ellis), *Ychydig hymnau, a gyfansoddwyd ar amrywiol achosion* (Bala: R. Saunderson, 1816; 3rd edn, Jane Ellis, *Casgliad o Hymnau, Carolau a Marwnadau a gyfansoddwyd ar amrywiol achosion*, Wyddgrug: H. & O. Jones, 1840).

Edwards, Alice, *Ychydig bennillion er anogaeth i Sïon i ymddiried yn ei Duw mewn blinfyd a chaledi* (Bala: J. Davies, n.d. [1812]; repr. in Cathryn A. Charnell-White (ed.), *Beirdd Ceridwen: Blodeugerdd Barddas o Ganu Menywod hyd tua 1800*, Swansea: Cyhoeddiadau Barddas, 2005, pp. 337–42).

Evans, Ann, *Llythyr Ann Evans . . . yn cynnwys hanes ei thaith o'r Penrhyn Gobaith Da i Bethelsdorp, yn Neheudir Affrica* (Bala: R. Saunderson, 1818).

[Evans, Elin] Elen Egryn, *Telyn Egryn: neu Gyfansoddiadau Awenyddol Miss Ellin Evans (Elen Egryn), o Lanegryn*, ed. W[illiam] Rees (Dolgellau: Evan Jones, 1850; facs. new edn, ed. Kathryn Hughes and Ceridwen Lloyd-Morgan, Dinas Powys: Honno, 1998).

——, 'Anerchiad i ferched Cymru', *Y Gymraes*, 1 (1850), 55; and *Y Gymraes*, 1 (1896), 7.

Gaskell, Elizabeth, 'The Well of Pen-morfa', *Household Words* (1850), repr. in *Four Short Stories* (London: Pandora Press, 1983).

——, 'The Doom of the Griffiths', Harper's Magazine (1858), repr. in *The Manchester Marriage and Other Stories* (Gloucester: Alan Sutton, 1985).

Griffiths, Ann, *Casgliad o Hymnau gan mwyaf heb erioed eu hargraffu o'r blaen*, ed. Thomas Charles (Bala: R. Saunderson, 1806).

——, *Gwaith Ann Griffiths,* ed. O. M. Edwards (Llanuwchllyn: Ab Owen, 1905).

Griffiths, Eleanor, *World Worship* (London: James Nisbet & Co., 1853).

[Grave, Mabel Holland], *Fraternity: A Romance*, 2 vols (London: Macmillan, 1888).

——, *From Heart to Heart: A Book of Verses* (London: Kegan Paul, 1892).

——, *Some Welsh Children* (London: Elkin Mathews, 1898; 2nd edn, 1920).

Guest, Lady Charlotte Elizabeth Bertie (later Schreiber), *The Mabinogion: from the Llyfr Coch o Hergest, and other ancient Welsh manuscripts, with an English translation and notes*, 3 vols (1838–45; London and Llandovery: W. Rees, 1849).

——, *Lady Charlotte Guest, Extracts from her journals 1833–52*, ed. Earl of Bessborough (London: John Murray, 1950).

Gunning, Elizabeth (later Plunkett), *The Orphans of Snowdon*, 3 vols (London: H. Lowndes, 1797; 2nd edn, London: Lane, Newman & Co., 1807).

Gunning, Susannah (née Minife), *Delves; A Welch tale*, 2 vols (London: Lackington, Allen & Co., 1796).

Hall, Augusta Waddington, Lady Llanover (Gwenynen Gwent), *The Advantages resulting from the Preservation of the Welsh Language and National Costumes of Wales* (London: Longman, 1836).

——, (Gwenllïan Gwent), 'Anerchiad i Gymruesau Cymru', *Y Gymraes*, 1 (1850), 8–11.

——, *The First Principles of Good Cookery illustrated. And recipes communicated by the Welsh hermit of the cell of St. Gover, with various remarks on many things past and present* (London: Richard Bentley, 1867; facs, new edn, Tregaron: Brefi Press, 1991).

Hardy, Elizabeth, *Owen Glendower, or, the Prince in Wales*, 2 vols (London: Richard Bentley, 1849).

[Hatton, Ann Julia] Ann of Swansea, *Poems on Miscellaneous Subjects* (London: Millan & Rae, 1783).

——, *Cambrian Pictures; or, Every one has Errors*, 3 vols (London: E. Kerby, 1810).

——, *Poetic Trifles* (Waterford: printed for the authoress, 1811).

Hemans, Felicia Dorothea, *A Selection of Welsh Melodies, with symphonies and accompaniments by John Parry and characteristic words by Mrs Hemans*, 3 vols (London: J. Power, 1822–9).

——, *Poems of Felicia Hemans* (Edinburgh and London: Blackwood, 1852).

Herbert, Frances Georgiana, *A Legend of Pembroke Castle, and Other Tales*, 2 vols (London: Richard Bentley, 1853).

[Hervey, Elizabeth], *The History of Ned Evans* (London: G. C. & J. Robinson, 1796).

Hoggan, Frances Elizabeth (née Morgan), *Education for Girls in Wales* (London: Women's Printing Society, n.d. [1882]).

[Hughes, Annie Harriet] Gwyneth Vaughan, 'Women and their questions', *Young Wales*, 3 (1897), 19–20.

——, 'Gweledigaeth y Babell Wâg', *Cymru*, 22 (1902), 24–8.

——, 'Bryn Ardudwy a'i Bobl', *Yr Haul* (1903–5), monthly.

——, *O Gorlannau y Defaid* (Caerfyrddin: W. Spurrell a'i Fab, 1905; first pub. *Y Cymro*, 1903–4, weekly).

——, 'Breuddwyd nos Nadolig', *Cymru*, 29 (1905), 245–8.

——, *Plant y Gorthrwm* (Cardiff: Educational Publishing Co., 1908).

——, 'Troad y Rhod', *Y Brython* (Feb.–Dec. 1909), weekly.

Hughes, Elizabeth Phillips, 'The higher education of girls in Wales', *Transactions of the Liverpool National Eisteddfod 1884* (Liverpool: Isaac Foulkes, 1885), pp. 40–62.

——, *The Education of Welsh Women* (London: W. Speaight, 1887).

——, 'A national education for Wales', *Young Wales*, 1 (1895), 102–5.

——, 'The Welsh University: its message to the women of Wales', *Young Wales*, 2 (1896), 148–9.

Hughes, Ellen, *Sibrwd yr Awel; sef cyfansoddiadau barddonol* (Pwllheli: R. Owen, n.d. [1887]).

——, 'Merch – ei hawliau a'i hiawnderau', *Cyfaill yr Aelwyd a'r Frythones*, (1892), 251–4.

——, 'Y Ddynes Newydd', *Y Gymraes*, 1 (1896–7), 28–9.

——, *Murmur y Gragen: sef Detholion o Gyfansoddiadau Barddonol a Rhyddiaethol* (Dolgellau: Swyddfa'r 'Goleuad', 1907).

——, 'Merched a Chynrychiolaeth', *Y Gymraes*, 14 (1910), 147–8.

——, 'Yng Nghymdeithas Cranogwen', *Y Gymraes*, 27–9 (1923–5), monthly.

Hughes, Ellen, *Hanes Hom Ray, a'r Canlyniadau* (Dolgellau: E. W. Evans, n.d.).

Hughes, Jane (Debora Maldwyn), *Buddugoliaeth y credadun trwy ffydd ar ei elynion* (Aberystwyth: J. Cox, n.d.).

——, *Telyn y Cristion yn anialwch y byd, yn canu ar daith ei bererindod o'r Aipht i'r Ganaan ysprydol* (Caernarfon: H. Humphreys, 1877).

——, *Can o waith Jane Hughes, Pontrobert, mewn myfyrdod ar Ddiwedd y flwyddyn 1876, a dechreu y flwyddyn 1877* (Caernarfon: H. Humphreys, 1877).

——, *Yr Ephra Lawn o Ymborth Ysprydol i bererinion Seion* (Caernarfon: H. Humphreys, 1877).

Humphreys-Jones, J., 'Beirdd anadnabyddus Cymru: VI. Anna Roberts', *Cymru*, 2 (1892), 63–4.

Hutton, Catharine, *The Welsh Mountaineer: A Novel*, 3 vols (London: Longmans, 1817).

Jacob, Violet, *The Sheep-Stealers* (London: Heinemann, 1902).

James, Maria, *Wales, and Other Poems* (New York: John S. Taylor, 1839).

[Jones, Alice Gray] Ceridwen Peris, 'Allegori – Blodau Pleser', *Y Frythones*, 1 (1879), 208–9.

——, 'Y Fun a'r Faner Wen', *Y Traethodydd*, 48 (1893), 426–31.

——, *Caniadau Ceridwen Peris* (Caernarfon: Llyfrfa'r Methodistiaid Calfinaidd, n.d. [1934]).

Jones, Catherine, *Marwnad er Coffadwriaeth am Mrs Barbara Vaughan, o Gaerffili* (Merthyr Tudful: W. Williams, 1808; repr. in Cathryn A. Charnell-White (ed.), *Beirdd Ceridwen: Blodeugerdd Barddas o Ganu Menywod hyd tua 1800*, Swansea: Cyhoeddiadau Barddas, 2005, pp. 315–19).

[Jones, Dorothy] Dora Eifion, Gemau yr Awen; sef, Cyfansoddiadau barddonol (Bethesda: printed for the author, n.d. [c1870]).

Jones, J. W. and J. Edmunds, *Yr Athrawes o Ddifrif: sef, Lloffion o Hanes Bywyd a Marwolaeth Mrs. Edmunds, Bangor, yn nghyda Detholiad o'i Hysgrifeniadau* (Caernarfon: G. Parry, 1859).

Jones, Margaret Charlotte, *Scattered Leaves; or, Twilight Trifles* (London: Routledge, 1853).

——, *Glimpses . . . Mr & Mrs Jones of Pantglas* (London: privately printed, 1862).

[Jones, Margaret] 'Y Gymraes o Ganaan', *Llythyrau Cymraes o Wlad Canaan* (Liverpool: Swyddfa'r Cymreig, 1869).

——, *Morocco, a'r Hyn a Welais Yno* (Wrecsam: Hughes a'i Fab, 1883).

[Jones, Margaret] Myfanwy Meirion, '"Bridge of Hope Mission" Dywrein-barth Llundain', *Y Frythones*, 7 (1885), 109–11.

——, 'Gwyliwch yr hudwr', *Y Gymraes*, 5 (1901), 84–5.

——, '"A ddarlleno ystyried"', *Y Gymraes*, 6 (1902), 76.

——, *Caniadau Myfanwy Meirion* (Lerpwl: printed for the author, 1930).

Jones, Mary Oliver, 'Claudia, neu, Gwnawn ein Dyledswydd a daw pob peth yn dda', *Y Frythones*, 2 (April–Sept. 1880), monthly.

Jones, Thomas, *Fy Chwaer; sef, Cofiant am Miss Margaret Jones, Cefn y Gader, Wyddgrug* (Wyddgrug: Hugh Jones, 1844).

[Kelly, Isabella] *The Abbey of Saint Asaph*, 3 vols (London: Minerva Press, 1795).

Lane, Amy, *Sketches of Wales and the Welsh* (London and Bristol: Hamilton, Adams, & Co. and Hugh C. Evans, 1847).

Lee, Sophia, 'The Clergyman's Tale: Pembroke', in Harriet and Sophia Lee, *The Canterbury Tales*, III ([1799] repr. London: Pandora Press, 1989).

Llwyd, Angharad, ed. Sir John Wynn, *The History of the Gwydir Family . . . now re-edited by a Native of the Principality: to which is added An Original Work, containing Memoirs of celebrated and distinguished Contemporary Welshmen, Bishops, &c.* by the same author (Ruthun: Taliesin Press, 1827).

——, *A History of the Island of Mona, or Anglesey: Including an Account of its Natural Productions, Druidical Antiquities, Lives of Eminent Men, the Customs of the Court of the Ancient Welsh Princes, &c.: Being the Prize Essay to which was Adjudged the First Premium at the Royal Beaumaris Eisteddfod, held in the month of August, 1832* (Ruthun and London: R. Jones & Longman, 1833).

Marshall, Augusta Eliza, *Odds and Ends* (London: William Pickering, 1853).

——, *A Prince of Wales Long Ago: A Bardic Legend of the Twelfth Century* (London and Chester: Whittaker & Co., and Prichard, Roberts & Co., 1855; repr. Kessinger, 2005).

[More, Olivia], *The Welsh Cottage* (Wellington, Salop: Houlston & Son, 1820).

Morgan, Eluned, *Dringo'r Andes* (Y Fenni: Y Brodyr Owen, 1904; new edn, *Dringo'r Andes a Gwymon y Môr*, ed. Ceridwen Lloyd-Morgan and Katherine Hughes, Dinas Powys: Honno, 2001).

——, W. R. P. George (ed.), *'Gyfaill Hoff . . .': Detholiad o Lythyrau Eluned Morgan* (Llandysul: Gwasg Gomer, 1972).

——, Dafydd Ifans (ed.), *Tyred Drosodd: Gohebiaeth Eluned Morgan a Nantlais* (Pen-y-bont ar Ogwr: Gwasg Efengylaidd Cymru, 1977).

Nicholl, Mary, *The Family of George Briton: or, The Importance of a Right Education. A Moral Tale for Young Persons* (Carmarthen: J. Evans, 1822).

Owen, Mary, *Hymnau ar Amryw Destunau* (Caernarfon: P. Evans, 1839; 2nd edn, Llanelli: Rees & Tomos, 1840).

Owain, O. Llew, *Cofiant Mrs Fanny Jones, Gweddw y Diweddar Barch J. Jones, Talysarn* (Machynlleth and Caernarfon: Cwmni y Cyhoeddwyr Cymreig, 1907).

Parker, Emma ('Emma de Lisle'), *Fitz-Edward; or The Cambrians. A Novel. Interspersed with Pieces of Poetry*, 3 vols (London: Minerva, 1811).

Parry, Catherine, *Eden Vale: A Novel*, 2 vols (London: John Stockdale, 1784).

Parry, Winnie, *Sioned* (Caernarfon: Cwmni y Cyhoeddwyr Cymreig, Swyddfa Cymru, n.d. [1906]; new edn, Dinas Powys: Honno, 1988; 1st pub. *Cymru*, vii–xi (1894–6), monthly).

Penny, Anne, *Poems with a Dramatic Entertainment* (London: printed for the author, [1771]), 2nd edn, with new material, *Poems* (London: printed for the author, 1780).

——, *An Invocation to the Genius of Britain* (London: printed for the author, 1778).

Peter, Eliza, 'Diwylliad y rhyw fenywaidd', *Y Beirniad*, 5 (1863), 152–62.

——, 'Iechyd a phrydferthwch', *Y Frythones*, 1 (1879), 24–6.

——, 'Hanfodion iechyd', *Y Frythones*, 1 (1879), 175–7, 210–11 and 334–6.

Pfeiffer, Emily Jane, *Gerard's Monument and other poems* (London: 1873; 2nd edn, London: Kegan Paul & Co., 1878).

——, *Glân-Alarch: His Silence and Song* (London: Henry S. King & Co., 1877).

——, *The Wynnes of Wynhavod: a drama of modern life*, in *Under the Aspens: Lyrical and Dramatic* (London: Kegan Paul, Trench & Co., 1882).

Phillimore, C. E., 'Jubilee Ode', trans. R. A. Williams, 'Buddugoliaeth Buddug' (Oswestry: *Oswestry and Borders County Advertizer*, 1897).

Philipps, Janetta, *Poems* (Oxford: privately printed by Collingwood and Co., 1811).

Philipps, Nora and Elsbeth Philipps, 'Progress of women in Wales', *Young Wales*, ii (1896), 66–7.

Piozzi, Hester Lynch, *Retrospection: or A Review of the most striking and important events, characters and situations, and their consequences, which the last eighteen hundred years have presented to the view of mankind*, 2 vols (London: John Stockdale, 1801).

——, *Autobiography, Letters and Literary Remains of Mrs. Piozzi* (Thrale), ed. A. Hayward, 2 vols (2nd edn, London: Longman, 1861).

——, *Thraliana: The Diary of Mrs. Hester Lynch Thrale* (Later Mrs. Piozzi) 1776–1809, ed. Katherine C. Balderston, 2 vols (Oxford: Clarendon Press, 1942).

——, *Dr Johnson & Mrs Thrale's Tour in North Wales 1774*, ed. Adrian Bristow (Wrexham: Bridge Books, 1995).

[Prichard, Annie Catherine] Ruth, 'Cranogwen', *Y Gymraes*, 1 (1896–7), 3–5.

——, 'Treio effaith y gown gorau', *Y Gymraes*, 1 (1896–7), 73–6.

——, 'Y can' cymaint', *Y Gymraes*, 3 (1899), 72–5.

——, 'Myfanwy Meirion a "Chenhadaeth Pont Gobaith", Llundain', *Y Gymraes*, 3 (1899), 97–101.

——, 'Lle gwell Betsi Evans', *Y Gymraes*, 7 (1903), 88–90.

——, *Troedigaeth Mrs. Evans yr Hafod* (Caernarfon: G. Evans, n.d.).

——, *Bore Oes: Hanes Undeb Dirwestol Merched Gogledd Cymru* (Dinbych: Gee a'i Fab, 1910).

[Prichard, Catherine Jane] Buddug, 'Paham yn arbenig y dylai merched bleidio dirwest', *Y Frythones*, 2 (1880), 369–71.

——, 'Na chaffed hudoles fyw', *Y Gymraes*, 4 (1900), 78–9.

——, 'Yr eneth a'r gasgen', *Y Gymraes*, 8 (1904), 10.

——, *Arholydd Dirwestol* (Dinbych: Gee a'i Fab, 1905).

——, *Caniadau Buddug: wedi eu casglu a'u dethol gan ei phriod* (Caernarfon: Swyddfa 'Cymru', 1911).

[Puclieu, Emma Mary] Marie Trevelyan, *Glimpses of Welsh Life and Character* (London: John Hogg, n.d. [1893]).

——, *From Snowdon to the Sea: Stirring Stories of North and South Wales* (London: John Hogg, 1895).

——, *Britain's Greatness Foretold: The Story of Boadicea, the British Warrior Queen* (London: John Hogg, 1900).

——, *Folk-lore and Folk-stories of Wales* (London: Elliot Stock, 1909).

[Puddicombe, Anne Adaliza Beynon] Allen Raine, *A Welsh Singer* (London: Hutchinson & Co., 1897).

——, *By Berwen Banks* (London: Hutchinson & Co., 1899).

——, *Queen of the Rushes: A Tale of the Welsh Revival* (London: Hutchinson & Co., 1906; new edn, ed. Katie Gramich, Dinas Powys: Honno, 1998).

——, *Where Billows Roll; a tale of the Welsh coast* (London: Hutchinson & Co., 1909).

Rees, Anne, 'Pa un o'r ddau ryw a ddangosodd fwyaf o gariad at yr Arglwydd Iesu Grist?', *Y Frythones*, 1 (1879), 160–1.

——, 'Eveleen Davies, neu, Gwnaf, am mai felly y dymunai fy mam', *Y Frythones*, 2–3 (1880–1), monthly.

[Rees, Sarah Jane] Cranogwen, *Caniadau Cranogwen* (Dolgellau: R. O. Rees, n.d. [1870]).

——, 'Cwestiynau ac atebion', *Y Frythones*, 2–11 (1880–9), monthly.

——, 'Esther Judith', *Y Frythones*, 2–3 (Oct. 1880–July 1881), monthly.

——, 'Hunan-goffa', *Y Frythones*, 5–6 (1883–4), monthly.

——, 'Dalen o'n Dyddlyfr yn y flwyddyn 1870', *Y Frythones* (1883), monthly.

——, 'Dyrchafiad merched', *Y Frythones*, 8 (1886), 235–7.

——, 'Dyfodol merched Cymru', *Y Frythones*, 9 (1889), 199–202.

——, 'Miss Ellen Hughes, Llanengan', *Y Gymraes*, 4 (1900), 5–8.

Report of the Commission of Inquiry into the State of Education in Wales ... In Three Parts. Part I, Carmarthen, Glamorgan and Pembroke. Part II, Brecknock, Cardigan, Radnor and Monmouth. Part III, North Wales (London, 1847).

Richards, Sarah, *Memories of Home* (Bridgend: Wesley Williams, 1903).

Roberts, Emma, *Notes of an Overland Journey through France and Egypt to Bombay ... with a memoir* (London: W. H. Allen, 1841).

Roberts, Elizabeth A., 'Sylhet', *Y Drysorfa*, 72 (1902), 570–2.

Roberts, Jane, *Hymnau newyddion, ar Destynau Efengylaidd* (Caernarfon: Peter Evans, n.d. [c1820]).

——, *Porth y Deml: sef Hymnau Efengylaidd* (Caernarfon: Peter Evans, 1834).

Roberts, Margaret Eliza, *Mademoiselle Mori: A Tale of Modern Rome*, 2 vols (London: John W. Parker and Son, 1860).

——, *Stephanie's Children* (London: National Society's Depository, 1896; repr., ed. Gillian Avery, London: Victor Gollancz, 1969).

Roberts, Sidney Margaret, *The Revival in the Khasia Hills* (Newport, Mon.: printed for the author, 1907).

Robinson, Emma, *Owen Tudor: An Historical Romance* ([1849] London: G. Routledge, 1857).

Robinson, Mary (Perdita), *Poems* (London: 1775; rev. edn, London: T. Silsbury & Son, 1795).

——, *Walsingham; or, The Pupil of Nature*, 4 vols (London: T. N. Longman, 1797; new edn, ed. Peter Garside, London: Routledge/ Thoemmes Press, 1992).

——, *A Letter to the Women of England, on the Injustice of Mental Subordination* (London: T. N. Longman and O. Rees, 1799; published under the pseudonym Anne Frances Randall).

——, *Memoirs of the late Mrs Robinson, written by herself. With some posthumous pieces* [ed. Maria Elizabeth Robinson], 4 vols (London: Richard Phillips, 1801; first 2 vols repr. as *Perdita: The Memoirs of Mary Robinson*, ed. M. J. Levy, London: Peter Owen, 1994).

——, *The Poetical Works of the late Mrs Mary Robinson: including many pieces never before published*, 3 vols (London: Richard Phillips, 1805).

[Ryves, Eliza], *The Hermit of Snowden [sic]: or Memoirs of Albert and Lavinia* (London: Logographic Press, 1789).

[Saunders, Sara Maria] S.M.S., 'Welsh Rural Sketches', *Young Wales*, 2–5 (1896–9), occasionally.

——, *Llon a Lleddf* (Treffynnon: P. M. Evans a'i Fab, 1897).

——, 'Women's place in fiction', *Young Wales*, 3 (1897), 230–1.

——, 'Storïau o ddydd-lyfr Martha Jones', *Y Gymraes*, 7–8 (1903–4), monthly.

——, *Y Diwygiad ym Mhentre Alun, gydag ysgrifau ereill* (Wrecsam: Hughes a'i Fab, 1907).

——, 'An open letter to the young women of Wales', in T. Stephens (ed.), *Wales: Today and To-morrow* (Cardiff: Western Mail, 1907), pp. 148–9.

——, *Llithiau o Bentre Alun* (Wrecsam: Hughes a'i Fab, 1908).

——, *A Bird's Eye View of our Foreign Fields* (Caernarfon: Calvinist Methodist Book Agency, 1919).

Seward, Anna, *Llangollen Vale, with other Poems* (London: G. Sael, 1796).

Sinclair, Catherine, *Hill and Valley, or Hours in England and Wales* (Edinburgh: William Whyte, 1838); 2nd edn, Hill and Valley, or Wales and the Welsh (Edinburgh: William Whyte, 1839).

Somerton, Alice, *Ida: or, The Last Struggles of the Welsh for Independence* (London and Cambridge: Whittaker and J. Hall & Son, 1858).

Spence, Elizabeth Isabella, *Old Stories*, 2 vols (London: J. Dodsley, 1822).

[Spooner, Louisa Matilda] L.M.S., *Gladys of Harlech; or, The Sacrifice. A Romance of Welsh History*, 3 vols (London: Charles J. Skeet, 1858).

——, *Country Landlords*, 3 vols (London: T. C. Newby, 1860).

——, *The Welsh Heiress: A novel*, 2 vols (London: T. Cautley Newby, 1868).

Thomas, Anna Walter (Morfudd Eryri), 'Llandaff', *Transactions of the Royal National Eisteddfod of Wales held at Cardiff . . . in 1883*, ed. David Tudor Evans (Caerdydd: printed for the Eisteddfod, 1884), 65–88.

——, 'Monody on the Death of Albert Victor Christian Edward, Duke of Clarence and Avondale', *Cofnodion a Chyfansoddiadau Eisteddfod Genedlaethol 1892* (Rhyl) (Oswestry: printed for the Eisteddfod, 1895), pp. 147–51.

[Vaughan, Annie] Anna Ionawr, 'Eliza Peter', *Y Frythones*, 11 (1889), 197–203.

——, 'Gyfran y merched yn ffurfiad cymeriad genedl y Cymry', *Y Frythones*, 11 (1889), 346.

Verney, Frances Parthenope, Lady (née Nightingale), *The Llanaly Reefs* (London: Smith, Elder & Co., 1873).

Weston, Louisa, *The Cambrian Excursion: intended to inculcate a taste for the Beauties of Nature; and to direct the attention of Young People to sources of Mental Improvement* (London: A. K. Newman, 1841).

Wilkinson, Janet W., *Sketches and Legends amid the Mountains of North Wales: in verse* (London: T. & W. Boone, 1840).

Williams, Elizabeth, 'Sylhet', *Y Drysorfa*, 60 (1890), 318–20; 61 (1891), 78–9, 38–9, 159; 319–20; 60 (1902), 319.

Williams, Elizabeth Watkin, Lady, *Even Such Is Life: A Story of To-day*, 3 vols (London: Chapman & Hall, 1888).

Williams, Jane (Ysgafell), *Miscellaneous Poems* (Brecon: Priscilla Hughes, 1824).

——, *Artegall; or Remarks on the Reports of the Commissioners of Inquiry into the State of Education in Wales* (London: Longman and Co., 1848).

——, *The Literary Remains of the Reverend Thomas Price, Carnhuanawc, with a memory of his life*, 2 vols (Llandovery: William Rees, 1854–5).

——, *The Autobiography of Elizabeth Davis: A Balaclava Nurse*, 2 vols (London: Hurst & Blackett, 1857; new edn, ed. Deirdre Beddoe, Dinas Powys: Honno Press, 1987).

——, *The Literary Women of England* (London: Saunders, Otley, & Co., 1861).

——, *A History of Wales: Derived from Authentic Sources* (London: Longmans, Green & Co., 1869).

[Williams, Alis Mallt and Gwenffreda] Y Ddau Wynne, *One of the Royal Celts* (London: Spencer Blackett & Hallam, 1889).

——, 'Patriotism and the Women of Cymru', *Young Wales*, 4 (1898), 115.

——, *A Maid of Cymru: A Patriotic Romance* (London and Carmarthen: Simpkin, Marshal & Co., and Spurrell & Son, n.d. [1901]; pub. *Young Wales*, vi–vii, 1900–1, monthly).

——, 'Madame Gwyneth Vaughan', *Young Wales*, 7 (1901), 188.

——, 'Welshwomen's mission in the twentieth century', in T. Stephens (ed.), *Wales: Today and To-morrow* (Cardiff: *Western Mail*, 1907), 142–7.

Williams, Maria Jane (Llinos), *Ancient National Airs of Gwent and Morganwg* (Llandovery: William Rees, 1844; facs. edn, ed. D. Huws [Aberystwyth]: Cymdeithas Alawon Gwerin Cymru, 1988).

[Williams, Mary Jane] Mair Hydref, *Autumn Leaves* (Rhyl: J. Morris, n. d. [1879]; 2nd edn, Treffynnon: P. M. Evans & Son, 1881; 3rd edn, Liverpool: Baskerville Printing Co., 1883; 4th edn, Wrecsam: Hughes a'i Fab, 1889).

Williams, Sarah (Sadie), *Twilight Hours: A Legacy of Verse* (London: Strahan & Co., 1868).

Wood [Ellen], Mrs Henry, *A Life's Secret* (2 vols, 1867; 9th edn, 1 vol., London: Richard Bentley, 1882).

Secondary sources

Aaron, Jane, 'Darllen yn groes i'r drefn', in John Rowlands (ed.), *Sglefrio ar Eiriau* (Llandysul: Gwasg Gomer, 1992), pp. 63–83.

——, 'Seduction and betrayal: Wales in women's fiction, 1785–1810', *Women's Writing*, 1 (1994), 65–76.

——, 'The way above the world: religion and gender in Welsh and Anglo-Welsh women's writing 1780–1830', in Carol Shiner Wilson and Joel Hafner (eds), *Re-Visioning Romanticism: British Women Writers, 1776–1837* (Philadelphia: University of Pennsylvania Press, 1994), pp. 111–27.

——, 'The hoydens of wild Wales: representations of Welsh women in Victorian and Edwardian fiction', *Welsh Writing in English: A Yearbook of Critical Essays*, 1 (1995), 23–39.

——, *Pur fel y Dur: Y Gymraes yn Llên Menywod y Bedwaredd Ganrif ar Bymtheg* (Caerdydd: Gwasg Prifysgol Cymru, 1998).

——, 'Conversions and inversions: body language in nineteenth-century Welsh women's writings', in Karen Atkinson, Sarah Oerton and Gill Plain (eds), *Feminisms on Edge: Politics, Discourses and National Identities* (Cardiff: Cardiff Academic Press, 2000), pp. 161–71.

——, '"Saxon, think not all is won": Felicia Hemans and the making of Britons', *Cardiff Corvey: Reading the Romantic Text*, 4 (May 2000), *http://www.cf.ac.uk./corvey/articles/cco4_n01.html*

——, 'Slaughter and salvation: Welsh missionary activity and British imperialism', in Charlotte Williams, Neil Evans and Paul O'Leary (eds), *A Tolerant Nation? Exploring Ethnic Diversity in Wales* (Cardiff: University of Wales Press, 2003), pp. 35–48.

Allchin, A. M., *Ann Griffiths*, Writers of Wales series (Cardiff: University of Wales Press, 1976).

Anderson, Benedict, *Imagined Communities: Reflections on the Origin and Spread of Nationalism* (London: Verso, 1983 [rev. edn, 1991]).

[Anon.] '"Sadie": In memory of an esteemed contributor', *Good Words* (June 1868), 379–83.

Armstrong, Isabel and Virginia Blain (eds), *Women's Poetry, Late Romantic to Late Victorian: Gender and Genre 1830–1900* (Basingstoke: Macmillan, 1999).

Selected Bibliography

Arnold, Matthew, *On the Study of Celtic Literature and Other Essays* ([1867] London: Dent, 1910).

Ashcroft, Bill, Gareth Griffiths and Helen Tiffin, *The Post-Colonial Studies Reader* (London: Routledge, 1995).

Barnes, David Russell, *People of Seion: Patterns of Nonconformity in Cardiganshire and Carmarthenshire in the Century preceding the Religious Census of 1851* (Llandysul: Gwasg Gomer, 1995).

Bass, Robert D., *The Green Dragoon: The Lives of Banastre Tarleton and Mary Robinson* ([1957] Orangeburg, SC: Sandlapper Publishing, 1973).

Beddoe, Deirdre, 'Images of Welsh women', in Tony Curtis (ed.), *Wales: The Imagined Nation* (Bridgend: Poetry Wales Press, 1986), pp. 225–38.

——, *Out of the Shadows: A History of Women in Twentieth-Century Wales* (Cardiff: University of Wales Press, 2000).

Bhabha, Homi K., *The Location of Culture* (London: Routledge, 1994).

——, (ed.), *Nation and Narration* (London: Routledge, 1990).

Blakey, Dorothy, *The Minerva Press, 1790–1820* (Oxford: Oxford University Press, 1935).

Blom, Ida, Karen Hagemann and Catherine Hall (eds), *Gendered Nations: Nationalisms and Gender Order in the Long Nineteenth Century* (Oxford: Berg, 2000).

Bohata, Kirsti, *Postcolonialism Revisited* (Cardiff: University of Wales Press, 2004).

——, 'En-gendering a new Wales: female allegories, Home Rule and imperialism 1893–1910', in Alyce von Rothkirch and Daniel Williams (eds), *Beyond the Difference: Welsh Literature in Comparative Contexts* (Cardiff: University of Wales Press, 2004), pp. 57–70.

Brennan, Catherine, *Angers, Fantasies and Ghostly Fears: Nineteenth-Century Women from Wales and English-Language Poetry* (Cardiff: University of Wales Press, 2003).

[——], Messem, Catherine, 'Irreconcilable tensions: gender, class and the Welsh question in the poetry of Jane Cave', *Welsh Writing in English: A Yearbook of Critical Essays*, 2 (1996), 1–21.

Bromham, Ivor J., '"Ann of Swansea" (Ann Julia Hatton: 1764–1838)', *Glamorgan Historian*, 7 (1971), 173–86.

Byrne, Paula, *Perdita: The Life of Mary Robinson* (London: HarperCollins, 2004).

Carruthers, Gerard, and Alan Rawes (eds), *English Romanticism and the Celtic World* (Cambridge: Cambridge University Press, 2003).

Charnell-White, Cathryn A., 'Marwnadau Pantycelyn a pharagonau o'r rhyw deg', *Tu Chwith*, 6 (1996), 131–41.

——, 'Galaru a gwaddoli ym marwnadau Williams Pantycelyn', *Llên Cymru*, 26 (2003), 40–62.

——, *Beirdd Ceridwen: Blodeugerdd Barddas o Ganu Menywod hyd tua 1800* (Swansea: Cyhoeddiadau Barddas, 2005).

Chatterjee, Partha, *The Nation and its Fragments: Colonial and Postcolonial Histories* (Princeton, NJ: Princeton University Press, 1993).

233

Colley, Linda, *Britons: Forging the Nation 1707–1837* (New Haven and London: Yale University Press, 1992).

Conran, Anthony, 'The lack of the feminine', *New Welsh Review*, 5/1 [17] (1992), 28–31.

Cunningham, Valentine, *Everywhere Spoken Against: Dissent in the Victorian Novel* (Oxford: Clarendon Press, 1975).

Davies, Andrew, 'The reputed nation of inspiration: representations of Wales in fiction from the Romantic period, 1780–1830' (unpub. Ph.D. thesis, Cardiff University, 2001).

Davies, Damian Walford, *Presences that Disturb: Models of Romantic Identity in the Literature and Culture of the 1790s* (Cardiff: University of Wales Press, 2002).

Davies, E. T., *Religion in the Industrial Revolution in South Wales* (Cardiff: University of Wales Press, 1965).

[Davies, John Evan], J. E. D. (Rhuddwawr) *Martha Llwyd Llanpumsaint* (Dolgellau: E. W. Evans, Swyddfa'r 'Cymru', n.d. [1925]).

Davies, Leith, *Acts of Union: Scotland and the Literary Negotiation of the British Nation, 1707–1830* (Stanford, CA: Stanford University Press, 1998).

Davies, Norman, *The Isles: A History* (London: Macmillan, 1999).

Davies, Russell, *Secret Sins: Sex, Violence and Society in Carmarthenshire 1870–1920* (Cardiff: University of Wales Press, 1996).

——, *Hope and Heartbreak: A Social History of Wales and the Welsh, 1776–1871* (Cardiff: University of Wales Press, 2005).

Dearnley, Moira, *Distant Fields: Eighteenth-Century Fictions of Wales* (Cardiff: University of Wales Press, 2001).

——, '"I came hither, a stranger": a view of Wales in the novels of Anne Beale', *New Welsh Review*, 1/4 (1989), 27–32.

——, '"Condemn'd to wither on a foreign strand": Ann of Swansea's manuscript poems', *New Welsh Review*, 41 (1998), 56–8.

Edwards, Hywel Teifi, *Codi'r Hen Wlad yn ei Hôl* (Llandysul: Gwasg Gomer, 1989).

Elfed, 'Mrs. Mary Owen', *Ceninen Gŵyl Dewi* (1903), pp. 17–20.

Ellis, Mari, 'Angharad Llwyd, 1780–1866', *Taliesin*, 52 and 53 (1985), 10–43 and 20–31.

——, 'Rhai o hen bersoniaid llengar Maldwyn', in Gwynn ap Gwilym and Richard H. Lewis (eds), *Bro'r Eisteddfod: Cyflwyniad i Faldwyn a'i Chyffiniau* (Llandybïe: Gwasg Christopher Davies, 1981), pp. 93–5.

——, 'Teulu Darowen', *Journal of the Historical Society of the Church in Wales*, 3 and 4 (1953 and 1954), 120–39 and 58–88.

Evans, Meredydd, 'Ryw gythraul o'i go yn canu so doh', *Journal of the Welsh Folk-Song Society*, 5 (1971), 124–34.

Evans, Neil, 'Finding a new story: The search for a usable past in Wales, 1869–1930', *Transactions of the Honourable Society of Cymmrodorion*, 10 (2004), 144–63.

Evans, W. Gareth, *Education and Female Emancipation: The Welsh Experience, 1847–1914* (Cardiff: University of Wales Press, 1990).

——, 'Un o ferched Britannia: gyrfa yr addysgwraig Elizabeth P. Hughes', in Geraint T. Jenkins (ed.), *Cof Cenedl XVI: Ysgrifau ar Hanes Cymru* (Llandysul: Gwasg Gomer, 2001), pp. 95–122.

Faderman, Lillian, *Surpassing the Love of Men: Romantic Friendship and Love between Women from the Renaissance to the Present* (London: Junction Books, n.d. [1981]).

Fanon, Frantz, *The Wretched of the Earth* [1961], trans. C. Farrington (London: MacGibbon & Kee, 1965; new edn, NY: Grove Press, 1991).

——, *Black Skin, White Masks* [1952], trans. C. L. Markmann (London: Pluto Press, 1986).

Fraser, Maxwell, 'Lady Llanover and Lady Charlotte Guest', *Anglo-Welsh Review*, 13 [31] (1963), 36–43.

——, 'Lady Llanover and her circle', *Transactions of the Honourable Society of Cymmrodorion* (1968), 170–96.

——, 'Jane Williams (Ysgafell) 1806–1885', *Brycheiniog (Journal of the Brecknock Society)*, 7 (1961–2), 95–114.

Fuller, J. F., *A Curious Genealogical Medley* (London: Mitchell, Hughes & Clarke, 1913).

Gellner, Ernest, *Nation and Nationalism* (Oxford: Blackwell, 1983).

George, William, *Cymru Fydd: Hanes y Mudiad Cenedlaethol Cyntaf* (Liverpool: Gwasg y Brython, 1945).

Gérin, Winifred, *Elizabeth Gaskell: A Biography* (Oxford: Clarendon Press, 1976).

Gibson, John, *The Emancipation of Women*, ed. W. Gareth Edwards (1891; Llandysul: Gwasg Gomer, 1992).

Gramich, Katie, and Catherine Brennan (eds), *Welsh Women's Poetry 1460–2001: An Anthology* (Dinas Powys: Honno Press, 2003).

Griffith, G. Penar, *Hanes Bywgraffiadol o Genadon Cymreig i Wledydd Paganaidd* (Cardiff: pub. by the author, 1897).

[Griffith, Richard] Carneddog, 'Emynyddes anghofiedig', *Cymru*, 30 (1906), 217–20.

Griffiths, W. A., *Hanes Emynwyr Cymru* (Caernarfon: Swyddfa'r 'Geninen', n.d. [1892]).

Gristwood, Sarah, *Perdita: Royal Mistress, Writer, Romantic* (London: Bantam Press, 2005).

Grundy, Isobel, '"A novel in a series of letters by a lady": Richardson and some Richardsonian novels', in Margaret Doody and Peter Sabor (eds), *Samuel Richardson: Tercentenary Essays* (Cambridge: Cambridge University Press, 1989), pp. 229–31.

Guest, Revel and Angela V. John, *Lady Charlotte: A Biography of the Nineteenth Century* (London: Weidenfeld and Nicolson, 1989).

Hall, Catherine, *White, Male and Middle Class: Explorations in Feminism and History* (London: Polity Press, 1992).

——, (ed.), *Cultures of Empire: Colonizers in Britain and the Empire in the Nineteenth and Twentieth Centuries* (Manchester: Manchester University Press, 2000).

Harris, John, 'Queen of the rushes: Allen Raine and her public', *Planet*, 97 (1993), 64–72.

Hechter, Michael, *Internal Colonialism: The Celtic Fringe in British National Development* ([1975] new edn, New Brunswick, NJ: Transaction Publishers, 1999).

Hempton, David, *Methodism and Politics in British Society 1750–1850* (London: Hutchinson, 1984).

Henderson, James, 'An edition of the poems of Ann of Swansea (Ann Julia Hatton, née Kemble, 1764–1838) including unpublished material', unpub. M.Phil. thesis, University of Glamorgan, 2006).

Hickok, Kathleen, 'Why is this woman still missing? Emily Pfeiffer, Victorian poet', in Isabel Armstrong and Virginia Blain (eds), *Women's Poetry, Late Romantic to Late Victorian: Gender and Genre 1830–1900* (Basingstoke: Macmillan, 1999), pp. 373– 89.

Hill, Bridget, *Women, Work, and Sexual Politics in Eighteenth-Century England* (Oxford: Basil Blackwell, 1989).

Hobsbawm, E. J., *Nations and Nationalism since 1780: Programme, Myth, Reality* (Cambridge: Cambridge University Press, 1990).

—— and Terence Ranger (eds), *The Invention of Tradition* (Cambridge: Cambridge University Press, 1983).

Hughes, Dewi Rowland, *Cymru Fydd* (Caerdydd: Gwasg Prifysgol Cymru, 2006).

Hughes, John, *Methodistiaeth Cymru: sef Hanes Blaenorol a Gwedd Bresenol y Methodistiaid Calfinaidd yng Nghymru; o ddechreuad y cyfundeb hyd y flwyddyn 1850* (Wrexham: Hughes & Son, 1851).

Humfrey, Belinda, 'Prelude to the twentieth century', M. Wynn Thomas (ed.), *Welsh Writing in English* (Cardiff: University of Wales Press, 2003), 7–46.

Humphreys-Jones, J., 'Beirdd Anadnabyddus Cymru: VI. Anna Roberts', *Cymru*, 2 (1892), 63–4.

Ifans, Dafydd, 'Syniadau crefyddol Eluned Morgan', *Y Traethodydd*, 128 (1973), 274– 85.

Irigaray, Luce, *Speculum of the Other Woman*, trans. Gillian C. Gill (Ithaca, NY: Cornell University Press, 1974).

James, Allan, 'Maria Jane Williams', in Hywel Teifi Edwards (ed.), *Nedd a Dulais* (Llandysul: Gwasg Gomer, 1994), pp. 95–130.

James, E. Wyn, 'Ann Griffiths', in E. Wyn James (ed.), *Cwmwl o Dystion* (Swansea: Christopher Davies, 1977), 99–113.

——, 'Ann Griffiths: y cefndir barddol', *Llên Cymru*, 23 (2000), 147–71.

Jarvis, Branwen, 'Mary Owen yr emynyddes', *Y Traethodydd*, 143 (1988), 45–53.

Jenkins, Geraint H., *The Foundations of Modern Wales: Wales 1642–1780* (Oxford and Cardiff: Clarendon Press and University of Wales Press, 1987).

——, 'The new enthusiasts', in Trevor Herbert and Gareth Elwyn Jones (eds), *The Remaking of Wales in the Eighteenth Century* (Cardiff: University of Wales Press, 1988), pp. 43–75.

——, '"Peth erchyll iawn" oedd Methodistiaeth', *Llên Cymru*, 17 (1993), 195–204.

——, (ed.), *Language and Community in the Nineteenth Century* (Cardiff: University of Wales Press, 1998).

——, (ed.), *The Welsh Language and its Social Domains 1801–1911* (Cardiff: University of Wales Press, 2000).

——, (ed.) *A Rattleskull Genius: The Many Faces of Iolo Morganwg* (Cardiff: University of Wales Press, 2005).

Jenkins, Philip, *The Making of a Ruling Class: The Glamorgan Gentry 1640–1790* (Cambridge: Cambridge University Press, 1983).

Jenkins, R. T., *Hanes Cymru yn y Bedwaredd Ganrif ar Bymtheg: Y Gyfrol Gyntaf (1789–1843)* (Caerdydd: Gwasg Prifysgol Cymru, 1933).

John, Angela V. (ed.), *Our Mothers' Land: Chapters in Welsh Women's History 1830–1939* (Cardiff: University of Wales Press, 1991).

Jones, Aled Gruffydd, '"Meddylier am India": tair taith y genhadeth Gymreig yn Sylhet, 1887–1947', *Transactions of the Honourable Society of Cymmrodorion* (1997), 84–110.

——, 'The other internationalism? Missionary activity and Welsh Nonconformist perceptions of the world in the nineteenth and twentieth centuries', in Charlotte Williams, Neil Evans and Paul O'Leary (eds), *A Tolerant Nation? Exploring Ethnic Diversity in Wales* (Cardiff: University of Wales Press, 2003), 49–60.

Jones, D. G., *Cofiant Cranogwen* (Caernarfon: Argraffdy'r Methodistiaid Calfinaidd, n.d. [1932]).

Jones, Dot, *Statistical Evidence relating to the Welsh Language 1801–1911* (Cardiff: University of Wales Press, 1998).

Jones, E. Pan, *Oes a Gwaith y Prif Athraw y Parch. Michael Daniel Jones* (Bala: H. Evans, 1903).

Jones, Emrys (ed.), *The Welsh in London 1500–2000* (Cardiff: Honourable Society of Cymmrodorion, 2001).

Jones, Gerallt, *Cranogwen: Portread Newydd* (Llandysul: Gwasg Gomer, 1981).

Jones, Ieuan Gwynedd, *Explorations and Explanations: Essays in the Social History of Victorian Wales* (Llandysul: Gwasg Gomer, 1981).

——, *Mid-Victorian Wales: The Observers and the Observed* (Cardiff: University of Wales Press, 1992).

Jones, Iorwen Myfanwy, 'Merched llên Cymru o 1850 i 1914' (unpub. MA thesis, University of Wales, Bangor, 1935).

Jones, R. M., *Llên Cymru a Chrefydd: Diben y Llenor* (Abertawe: Christopher Davies, 1977).

Jones, R. Tudur, 'The evangelical revival in Wales: a study in spirituality', in *An Introduction to Celtic Christianity*, ed. James P. Mackey (Edinburgh: T. & T. Clark, 1989), pp. 237–67.

——, 'Daearu'r angylion: sylwadau ar ferched mewn llenyddiaeth, 1860–1900', in J. E. Caerwyn Williams (ed.), *Ysgrifau Beirniadol XI* (Dinbych: Gwasg Gee, 1979), pp. 194–212.

Jones, Rosemary, '"Separate spheres"? Women, language and respectability in Victorian Wales', in Geraint H. Jenkins (ed.), *The Welsh Language and its Social Domains 1801–1911* (Cardiff: University of Wales Press, 2000), pp. 177–214.

Jones, Sally Roberts, *Allen Raine*, Writers of Wales series (Cardiff: University of Wales Press, 1979).

Jones, T. M., *Llenyddiaeth fy Ngwlad: sef hanes y newyddiadur a'r cylchgrawn Cymreig yn Nghymru, America, ac Awstralia yn nghyd a'u dylanwad ar fywyd cenedl y Cymry* (Treffynnon: P. M. Evans, 1893).

Knight, Stephen, *A Hundred Years of Fiction: Writing Wales in English* (Cardiff: University of Wales Press, 2004).

Leighton, Angela, *Victorian Women Poets: Writing against the Heart* (London: Harvester Wheatsheaf, 1992).

Levi, Thomas, 'Margaret Thomas yr emynyddes', *Y Traethodydd*, 59 (1904), 338–43.

Lewis, Saunders, *Williams Pantycelyn* ([1927] Caerdydd: Gwasg Prifysgol Cymru, 1991).

——, *Meistri'r Canrifoedd: Ysgrifau ar Hanes Llenyddiaeth Gymraeg*, ed. R. Geraint Gruffydd (Caerdydd: Gwasg Prifysgol Cymru, 1973).

Lloyd-Morgan, Ceridwen, 'A local institution: day-to-day life of the Ladies of Llangollen', *Planet*, 91 (1992), 28–35.

——, 'From temperance to suffrage?', in Angela V. John (ed.), *Our Mothers' Land: Chapters in Welsh Women's History 1830–1939* (Cardiff: University of Wales Press, 1991), pp. 135–58.

Löffler, Marion, 'A romantic nationalist', *Planet*, 121 (1997), 58–66.

Lootens, Tricia, 'Hemans and home: Victorianism, feminine "internal enemies", and the domestication of national identity', in Angela Leighton (ed.), *Victorian Women Poets: A Critical Reader* (Oxford: Blackwell, 1996), pp. 1–23.

McGann, Jerome J., 'Literary history, Romanticism, and Felicia Hemans', in Carol Shiner Wilson and Joel Hafner (eds), *Re-visioning Romanticism: British Women Writers 1776–1837* (Philadelphia: University of Pennsylvania Press, 1994), pp. 210–27.

Makdisi, Saree, *Romantic Imperialism: Universal Empire and the Culture of Modernity*, Cambridge Studies in Romanticism 27 (Cambridge: Cambridge University Press, 1998).

Masson, Ursula, '"Hand in hand with women, forward we will go": Welsh nationalism and feminism in the 1890s', *Women's History Review*, 12 (2003), 357–86.

——, (ed.), *Women's Rights and Womanly Duties: The Aberdare Women's Liberal Association 1891–1910* (Cardiff: South Wales Record Society, 2005).

Mavor, Elizabeth, *The Ladies of Llangollen: A Study in Romantic Friendship* (London: Michael Joseph, 1971).

——, *Life with the Ladies of Llangollen* (Harmondsworth: Penguin, 1984).

Mayer, Tamar (ed.), *Gender Ironies of Nationalism: Sexing the Nation* (London: Routledge, 2000).

Mee, Jon, *Romanticism, Enthusiasm and Regulation: Poetics and the Policing of Culture in the Romantic Period* (Oxford: Oxford University Press, 2003).

Mellor, Anne K. (ed.), *Romanticism and Feminism* (Bloomington: Indiana University Press, 1988).

——, *Mothers of the Nation: Women's Political Writing in England, 1780–1830* (Bloomington and Indianapolis: Indiana University Press, 2000).

Morgan, Derec Llwyd, *Pobl Pantycelyn* (Llandysul: Gwasg Gomer, 1986).

——, *The Great Awakening in Wales*, trans. Dyfnallt Morgan (London: Epworth Press, 1988).

Morgan, Kenneth O., *Rebirth of a Nation: Wales 1880–1980* (Oxford and Cardiff: Clarendon Press and University of Wales Press, 1981).

——, *Wales in British Politics 1868–1922* (Cardiff: University of Wales Press, 1963).

Morgan, Prys (ed.), *Brad y Llyfrau Gleision: Ysgrifau ar Hanes Cymru* (Llandysul: Gwasg Gomer, 1991).

——, 'From a death to a view: the hunt for the Welsh past in the Romantic period', in Eric Hobsbawm and Terence Ranger (eds), *The Invention of Tradition* (Cambridge: Cambridge University Press, 1983), pp. 43–100.

Morris, John Hughes, *Hanes Cenhadaeth Dramor y Methodistiaid Calfinaidd Cymreig, hyd diwedd y flwyddyn 1904* (Caernarfon: Llyfrfa'r Cyfundeb, 1907).

Owain, O. Llew, *Cofiant Mrs Fanny Jones, Gweddw y Diweddar Barch J. Jones, Talysarn* (Machynlleth a Chaernarfon: Cwmni y Cyhoeddwyr Cymreig, 1907).

Painting, David, *Amy Dillwyn* (Cardiff: University of Wales Press, 1987).

Parry, R. Palmer, 'Winnie Parry a'i gwaith', *Taliesin*, 46 (1983), 10–41.

Parry, Thomas, 'Gwyneth Vaughan', *Cylchgrawn Cymdeithas Hanes a Chofnodion Sir Feirionnydd*, 3 (1979), 225–36.

Pennant, Thomas, *A Tour in Wales*, 2 vols (London: Henry Hughes, 1778–81).

Pittock, Murray G. H., *Celtic Identity and the British Image* (Manchester and NY: Manchester University Press, 1999).

Pope, Robert (ed.), *Religion and National Identity: Wales and Scotland c.1700–2000* (Cardiff: University of Wales Press, 2001).

Price, Cecil, *The English Theatre in Wales in the Eighteenth and Early Nineteenth Centuries* (Cardiff: University of Wales Press, 1948).

Rees, Brinley (ed.), *Ieuan Gwynedd: Detholiad o'i Ryddiaith* (Caerdydd: Gwasg Prifysgol Cymru, 1957).

Rees, J. Seymour, 'Mary Owen, yr emynyddes', *Y Llenor*, 24 (1945), 68–75.

Reynolds, Matthew, *The Realms of Verse 1830–1870: English Poetry in a Time of Nation-Building* (Oxford: Oxford University Press, 2001).

Rhydderch, Francesca, 'Dual nationality, divided identity: ambivalent narratives of Britishness in the Welsh novels of Anna Maria Bennett', *Welsh Writing in English: A Yearbook of Critical Essays*, 3 (1997), 1–17.

Roberts, Gwyneth Tyson, *The Language of the Blue Books: The Perfect Instrument of Empire* (Cardiff: University of Wales Press, 1998).

Rosser, Siwan M., *Y Ferch ym Myd y Faled: Delweddau o'r Ferch ym Maledi'r Ddeunawfed Ganrif* (Cardiff: University of Wales Press, 2005).

Said, Edward W., *Orientalism* (Harmondsworth: Penguin, 1978).

Shaw, Jane, and Alan Kreider (eds), *Culture and the Nonconformist Tradition* (Cardiff: University of Wales Press, 1999).

Semmel, Bernard, *The Methodist Revolution* (London: Heinemann, 1974).

Shattock, Joanne, *Women and Literature in Britain 1800–1900* (Cambridge: Cambridge University Press, 2000).

Spivak, Gayatri Chakravorty, 'Three women's texts and a critique of imperialism', in Catherine Belsey and Jane Moore (eds), *The Feminist Reader: Essays in Gender and the Politics of Literary Criticism* (Basingstoke and London: Macmillan, 1989), pp. 175–96.

Stevens, Catrin, *Arferion Caru* (Gwasg Gomer: Llandysul, 1977).

Sweet, Rosemary, *Antiquities: The Discovery of the Past in Eighteenth-Century Britain* (London and NY: Hambledon, 2004).

Thomas, M. Wynn (ed.), *Welsh Writing in English* (Cardiff: University of Wales Press, 2003).

Trinder, Peter W., *Mrs Hemans* (Cardiff: University of Wales Press, 1984).

Trumpener, Katie, *Bardic Nationalism: The Romantic Novel and the British Empire* (Princeton, NJ: Princeton University Press, 1997).

Wallace, Diana, *The Woman's Historical Novel: British Women Writers, 1900–2000* (London: Palgrave, 2005).

White, Eryn M., '"Y Byd, y Cnawd a'r Cythraul": disgyblaeth a threfn seaiadau Methodistaidd de-orllewin Cymru 1737–1750', *Cof Cenedl*, 8 (1993), 69– 102.

——, *Praidd Bach y Bugail Mawr: Seiadau Methodistaidd De-Orllewin Cymru* (Llandysul: Gwasg Gomer, 1995).

——, '"Myrdd o wragedd": merched a'r diwygiad Methodistaidd'. *Llên Cymru*, 20 (1997), 62–74.

——, 'Women in the early Methodist societies in Wales', *Journal of Welsh Religious History*, 7 (1999), 95–108.

Williams, Chris, 'Wales' "Unionist Nationalist": Sir Thomas Phillips (1801–67)', *Llafur*, 8/4 (2003), 7–17.

Williams, Euronia Lucretia, 'Lost in the shadows: Welsh women poets writing in English, c.1840–1970' (unpub. Ph.D. thesis, University of Wales, Bangor, 2006).

Williams, Gwyn A., 'Romanticism in Wales', in Roy Porter and Mikuláš Teich (eds), *Romanticism in National Context* (Cambridge: Cambridge University Press, 1988), pp. 9–36.

Williams, L. J. and Dot Jones, 'Women at work in nineteenth-century Wales', *Llafur*, 3/3 (1982).

Williams, R. Bryn, *Eluned Morgan: Bywgraffiad a Detholiad* (Llandysul: Y Clwb Llyfrau Cymreig, 1948).

Williams, Raymond, *Who Speaks for Wales? Nation, Culture, Identity*, ed. Daniel Williams (Cardiff: University of Wales Press, 2003).

Williams, Siân Rhiannon, 'The true "Cymraes": images of women in women's nineteenth-century Welsh periodicals', in Angela V. John (ed.), *Our Mothers' Land: Chapters in Welsh Women's History 1830–1939* (Cardiff: University of Wales Press, 1991), pp. 69–91.

——, 'Llwydlas, Gwenynen Gwent a dadeni diwylliannol y bedwaredd ganrif ar bymtheg', *Cof Cenedl: Ysgrifau ar Hanes Cymru XV*, ed. Geraint H. Jenkins (Llandysul: Gwasg Gomer, 2000), pp. 99–128.

Williams, W. Samlet, 'Pegi Shenkin, Trelalas', *Y Gymraes*, 8 (1904), 155.

Williams, William Glynn, *Memoir of Mrs Anna Walter Thomas (Morfudd Eryri)* (Holywell: W. Williams & Son, n.d. [1922]).

Wolfson, Susan J. (ed.), *Felicia Hemans: Selected Poems, Letters, Reception Materials* (Princeton and Oxford: Princeton University Press, 2000).

Wood, Marilyn, *Rhoda Broughton: Profile of a Novelist* (Stamford: Paul Watkins, 1993).

Yuval-Davies, Nira and Floya Anthias (eds), *Woman-Nation-State* (London: Macmillan, 1989).

Index